Hamilton Mack Laing:
Hunter-Naturalist

Hamilton Mack Laing:

1985

Sono Nis Press

VICTORIA, BRITISH COLUMBIA

Hunter-Naturalist

RICHARD MACKIE

Canadian Cataloguing in Publication Data

Mackie, Richard, 1957-
   Hamilton Mack Laing, hunter naturalist

  Bibliography: p. 215

  ISBN 0-919203-74-4

  1. Laing, Hamilton M. (Hamilton Mack),
1883-1982. 2. Naturalists — Canada —
Biography. 3. Hunters — Canada — Biography.
I. Title.

QH31.L34M33 1985   574'.092'4   C85-091412-4

This book has been published with the assistance
of the Canada Council Block Grant Program.

Published by
SONO NIS PRESS
1745 Blanshard Street
Victoria, British Columbia

Designed at Morriss Printing by Bev Leech

Printed and bound in Canada by
MORRISS PRINTING COMPANY LTD.
Victoria, British Columbia

Acknowledgements

I would like to thank the Town of Comox and Alderman Alice Bullen for allowing me the opportunity to write this biography.

I interviewed the following friends and relatives of Hamilton Mack Laing: Alice Bullen, Ian McTaggart Cowan, James and Elizabeth Curtis, Yorke Edwards, Elsie Eiriksson, Charles and Muriel Guiguet, Harold Hosford, Mack Tripney and Mary Laing, Neville and Myrtle Mayers, Kay Pollock, Eileen and Clare Robertson, Alan and Suzanne Stewart, and James and Elizabeth Stubbs. I am indebted to them for their help and interest.

The following people provided valuable assistance on a multitude of subjects: Deborah Bassinger, Elizabeth Blight, Kathy Bridge, Allan C. Brooks, M. Ralph Browning, the Cook family of Salt Spring Island, Jack Cranmer-Byng, Anne Crayston, Helen Dale, D. Barry Dickson, Lois Dickson, Nora Doherty, Michel Gosselin, Phyllis Hallett, Valerie Hatten, Harry G. Heiss, A. Earl Henderson, Alice Laing, Ed Laing, Nellie Pearl Lawrence, Bev Leech, Elizabeth Lloyd, Mike McNall, Ian MacPherson, Eva Major-Marothy, Julia Matthews, Mervyn Mitchell, Sue Mitchell, Kate Munson, Henri Ouellet, the staff of the Provincial Archives of British Columbia, Lois Robson, D. Alan Sampson, Lyman Smith, Ron Smith, John Tayliss, Ann Yates, and Dorothy Yeoman.

Alexander Mackie, George Mackie and Rachel Mackie helped reproduce and assemble the photographs. April McIlhagga and Brenda Davies typed the manuscript. Elizabeth Curtis, James Curtis, George Mackie and Gillian Mackie read and provided critical comments on various drafts of the manuscript.

R.M.

Contents

Foreword

EVERY DAY I THANK THE LORD AND BROOKS
I CAME TO COMOX.

— *Hamilton Laing to Percy Taverner*
April 24, 1923[1]

On the morning of June 28, 1922, the Canadian Pacific Steamer *Charmer* entered Comox Harbour on Vancouver Island on its regular run to the communities of the North Island. It tied up at the wharf at the foot of Port Augusta Avenue and off the ship stepped a powerfully built thirty-nine-year-old man with piercing grey eyes and a closely trimmed military moustache. He was the Canadian naturalist Hamilton Mack Laing.

Mack was accompanied by two other naturalists: D. Alan Sampson, a summer student from Saskatchewan, and Percy Algernon Taverner, the Chief Ornithologist at the National Museum, Ottawa. Together, they helped unload their gear from the *Charmer*: crates, tents, hip waders, powdered alum for curing animal skins, plant presses, "Nipper" brand mouse traps and, most important, rifles and shotguns were taken up the wharf to the Elk Hotel.[2]

The naturalists had just completed an eight-week investigation of the birds of the Southern Okanagan for the National Museum in co-operation with the bird painter Allan Brooks. Mack had been captivated by the Okanagan and had made firm plans to settle there. Before he could do so, however, he had to complete the season's work at Comox. Gradually it dawned on him that Comox, and not the Okanagan, would become his home: as an ornithologist he

9

would have, at Comox, the greatest possible opportunity to study the rich bird life of the coast of British Columbia.

At the Elk Hotel they were met by Ronald Macdonald Stewart or "Martukoo," the Comox naturalist, hunter, bird collector and local game warden. Stewart had received a letter from his old hunting friend Brooks warning him of their arrival. After a couple of hours of enthusiastic planning and conversation, the naturalists retired to their rooms at the hotel where Mack got out his diary and described his arrival.

Two bald eagles, one very adult and the other juvenile circling over bay when we arrived at Comox. Four blue herons cross bay. Several crows. The note of the north-west crow is not a real "caw!" like the eastern bird, but a petulant harsh "caa!". Cliff swallows and north-west violet greens noted in front of hotel. Two or three goldfinches, one song sparrow in song, one cedar wax wing. A raft of birds one hundred strong like ducks noted in bay on calm water. . . . In evening a dark-backed gull with black wing tips seen in near distance.[3]

Not a word given of conversation, places visited, or people met — only birds. Yet that summer and winter Mack was a man full of confidence. Over the preceding few years his personal life and his career had blossomed. He had brought his work to the notice of the Canadian ornithological community, he had broken into the cozy world of museum work, and his natural history articles were selling as fast as he could write them. Months earlier he had met and become fast friends with Brooks, whose work he had admired for twenty years. It was Brooks, the greatest bird painter Canada has produced, who had directed Taverner's field party to collect the rich bird life of Comox harbour.

Mack's personal life had never seemed better. Two months earlier he had become engaged to his Portland, Oregon, sweetheart, Ethel Hart. The two rarely saw each other, owing to the nature of Mack's work, but Comox seemed to offer the perfect opportunity of a new life. Within weeks of his arrival he decided to settle down and build a house for Ethel. He was embarking on what he would later call "Life's Best Adventure": the inter-war years at Comox when his personal happiness and professional accomplishments reached their peak.

But Mack Laing's life did not begin at Comox. His first thirty-nine formative years were spent elsewhere, and he had already had successful careers as a school principal in Manitoba, as an instructor in the Royal Flying Corps, and as a "motorcycle naturalist," a job description of his own invention.

Today, Mack Laing's early life is largely forgotten. There are only a few people who remember him from his pre-Comox days. Many more can remember his years at Comox and his work as a collector for the National Museum. Yet he will be remembered largely for his writing which reached its peak at Comox between 1922 and 1940.

Two themes are persistent in both his life and his writing: a love of nature and a love of hunting. To the modern reader these two passions may seem entirely incompatible, but to Mack Laing, hunting was a perfectly valid part of nature study. Like several of his naturalist contemporaries, Mack was brought up in a frontier farming environment where hunting was both necessary and acceptable. The attitudes bred in him as a boy were to stay with him during his long and remarkable life.

I

Background and Early Memories
1883-1888

FOR THE STORY OF THE OUT-OF-DOORS IS LIKE NO STORY
RETWEEN THE COVERS OF A BOOK. THE FORMER HAS NO END
OR BEGINNING. THE STORY OF THE NATURALIST IS BOUNDED
ONLY BY HIS LIMITS OF PERCEPTION AND THE SPAN OF
HIS YEARS.

— Hamilton Laing
Comox, British Columbia, 1922[1]

David Hamilton Mack Laing came from a family of early Ontario and Manitoba Scots-Irish pioneers. His mother, Rachel Melvina Mack, was born in Hensall, Huron County, Ontario, in 1852 to Irish-born David Mack (1817-1895) and Rachel Hamilton (1823-1909). David and Rachel Mack had emigrated from Ireland in the 1840's to the newly settled district of Hensall where they brought up their large family of eleven children. Two of their daughters — Mary and Rachel — would in time marry two young Scottish immigrants, Thomas and William Laing, and move to Manitoba to repeat their parents' pioneering experience.

On his father's side, Mack Laing was descended from what he termed Scottish "land-owning stock." His grandparents were Thomas Laing of Muirhead Farm and Janet Oswald Mains of Myothill Farm, who raised a family of at least five children at the village of Denny, Stirlingshire, Scotland. One child was Mack's father, William Oswald Laing, who was born at Denny in 1841. An excellent pupil, William started teaching while still in his early teens; and in the Scottish census of 1861 — just prior to emigrating to Canada — he is listed as a "Pupil Teacher" at Denny. Another son was John, who migrated to Canada in the 1850's and established a farm at Huron County, Hay Township, Ontario. A third son, Thomas, visited Canada and the United States in the late 1850's.

In about 1860 disaster struck: The boys' mother Janet and their sister Jean died. Their father had died previously. In 1861 the surviving children held an estate sale at Denny and "sold everything off" that had belonged to their parents' household.[2]

The three remaining Laing children, Thomas, William and Isabella (Bella) left for Canada in 1861, perhaps lured by the prospect of good and cheap land. They landed in Montreal in August 1861. Thomas and Bella moved on immediately to brother John's farm in Ontario but William, after staying for a time in Montreal improving his knowledge of French, went to work for his cousin Mr. Oswald on his farm near Montreal. Here, his nephew David Laing related, he learned to plough: "with an old team of Mares 25 and 29 years old and seemed to be proud he could plough a straight furrow even if he had never worked on a farm before."[3]

But William's stay on his cousin's farm was short-lived. In 1862, still aged only twenty, he joined Thomas and Bella at John's farm in Ontario. The Laing family stayed here until 1870 helping John clear his fifty acres of dense bush. Mack later recalled the difficulties his father and uncles encountered clearing land when farms were being hacked out of the hardwood bush: "Here, William learned how to use an axe, to hew with the broad axe to the chalk line, to cut a corner for a log house, sugar making, roof making, rifle shooting and other things of the pioneer life that were to help him later."[4] It was while farming at Huron County that the young Scottish immigrants met the thirteen-member Irish-Canadian family of David and Rachel Mack. In the mid-1860's Thomas Laing married Mary Mack, and William struck up a friendship with another Mack daughter, Rachel Melvina, which would result in their marriage in 1874. Bella Laing learned how to make bread and butter from old Mrs. Mack, the female head of the Mack household.

In 1870 John Laing mortgaged his farm and gave Thomas, William and Bella $1,000 each. Bella stayed in Ontario where she married a man named Patterson, but Thomas, Mary, their baby girl, and William left for Manitoba in the spring of 1870, carrying their $2,000 worth of gold coins in their money belts. There being no road between Ontario and Manitoba, they were forced to take a southerly railway route through the United States. In 1951, Mack recalled that the Manitoba Act had just set up the Red River region as a new province, and that "the call of the West was then strong for young men."[5]

St. Cloud, Minnesota, was the nearest rail point to the Canadian prairies and it was here that the Laings unloaded their team of horses and farming equipment. They also brought an American wagon to carry their goods the four hundred miles north to Manitoba. They had originally intended to go as far west as the Edmonton district but, while crossing the border into Manitoba, they were stopped by border guards on account of the "disturbances" at Red River caused by Louis Riel and his Métis followers. After a four-week wait at Pembina, William dodged the border patrols and, armed with his rifle, revolver and knapsack, he scouted ahead on foot the seventy miles from Pembina to Fort Garry (Winnipeg). Travelling only by night, William encountered three armed men on horseback who turned out to be Riel and two of his aides "beating a hasty retreat south across the American border."[6] When William arrived at Fort Garry he was directed to Colonel Wolseley, the leader of the military expedition sent to impose order at Red River. Wolseley had just arrived, and William found him down at the Red River washing the mud from his boots. He chided Laing for not taking a shot at Riel and his aides.

Soon after his arrival at Fort Garry, William met two settlers, James Finnigan and a Mr. Ramsey, who had taken up land at the settlement of St. Anne on the Seine River, some twenty-five miles south of Fort Garry. They advised William not to make for Edmonton that winter, but to settle at St. Anne where there was a good supply of hay in addition to plenty of wood for use as fuel and building materials. Acting on their advice, William took up River Lot Number One at St. Anne des Chênes. Only a few chains wide by a mile long, this lot was characteristic of the type found in the Red River area. By early September 1870 (when Thomas, Mary and their "bairn" finally arrived from Pembina) William had built a shack, a stable and had cut a winter's supply of feed for the horses. The brothers, however, did not take kindly to the "long narrow French survey farms" on the Seine River so they moved, in 1872, a few miles south to a recently surveyed area later known as Clearsprings.

In their first winter at the new settlement they lived in very primitive conditions "in a tent walled with logs and banked with sod." But they were not the only settlers at Clearsprings: a year or two before, Mary's brother John Mack and his wife Benthie had left Ontario and settled in the new district, becoming the first to do so.[7]

Seventy years later Mack described the ideal homestead discovered by his family:

Advocates of mixed farming, the springs, Coulee with its abundant wild hay, the poplar "bluffs" offered shelter and fuel, the rich loamy soil, and real timber — cedar, spruce, jack pine, and tamarack nearby to eastward all seemed to hold out what they were looking for — This first house . . . wore a roof of thatch, from material abundant in the meadow.[8]

The brothers gradually cleared and cultivated the wild prairie of the Clearsprings district. In 1872 William wrote to his brother-in-law James Mack enthusing over the quality of the Manitoba soil at the expense of that in Ontario: "You think Jim that your lowland is rich, but it is nothing compared to the land here. To give you an idea how rich, and how uniformly rich the land is, you may look over a field of wheat, and every part of it is alike, you can't say one part is richer than another."[9]

Despite the excellent soil, life for the Laings was difficult and the prairie winters colder than anything they had encountered in Ontario. In their early years at Clearsprings misfortune struck when the thatched roof of their house caught fire. They had to tear off the entire roof to save the walls from burning, and begin again. The several families were isolated and concerned with survival in the wilderness. Mack's cousin David Laing reflected in 1951 that "back in the early times we were all poor together, and endeavoured to help each other all we could."[10] The families survived, and William's dour form of Scottish humour appears occasionally in his letters back to Ontario. In 1873, for example, he wrote home to say that:

A stove is a necessity in Manitoba. You can't keep a house warm without one. A chimney, and the bigger the worse, creates such a draft that one's back will be freezing while his face will be burning, so that you have to turn yourself before the fire to enjoy it properly. The only plan (and for which I intend to take out a patent) is to suspend yourself from a beam by a chair or rope with a swivel to prevent accidents by winding up too close, and then at a proper distance from the fire get some one to give you a whirl, so as to keep you turning slowly round. This is the only way (I think) to get the full benefit of the fireplace. Don't breathe a whisper of this beautiful contrivance, or some fellow may steal the patent. They have many a contrivance to economise fuel but this is economising heat, is it not? A little nonsense now and then, is relished by the wisest men, and I have said enough on that point.[11]

In 1874 William returned to Hensall and married Mary's younger sister Rachel Mack, then aged twenty-two. This time, the newlywed couple travelled to Manitoba by an overland route across Canadian soil, but first they had to cross the Great Lakes by boat. They left Goderich, Ontario, in a big thunderstorm and after a harrowing voyage landed safely at Port Arthur. Of all the passengers on board only Rachel Laing was not seasick. From Port Arthur they took the Dawson Road to Red River in company with several other immigrant families. Rachel was one of the first women to travel over the makeshift military trail that took them over lakes, portages, corduroy, swamps and rough roads. At Clearsprings, Rachel and William joined John and Benthie Mack and Thomas and Mary Laing. These three couples and their children were joined in 1876 by another Mack sister, Jane, who had married John Langille. These four families — Mack, Laing and Langille — together with the Alexander McCaskill and Jamieson families were largely responsible for settling Clearsprings.

Indeed, William Laing named the settlement after the three springs on his farm, and eventually "Clearsprings" was applied to the entire district. The Manitoba Directory for the years 1877-78 gives a brief description of Clearsprings, located in: "Township 7, Range VI, East. This settlement was started in 1872, and comprises only one-fourth of the Township, the rest being part of the Mennonite Reserves. The land is rich and well cultivated. The nearest post office in Ste. Anne. Mail once a week."[12] By the late 1880's one of every four children at the Clearsprings rural school was a Laing, Mack or Langille. It was in the midst of this large, extended family network that Mack Laing spent his youth, and with which he stayed in contact for the rest of his life.

One of the disappointments of Mack's life was that in the winter of 1882-83 his parents paid a visit to the Mack family homestead in Hensall, Ontario, where he was born in February 1883. So strongly did he feel himself to be a pioneer Manitoban — brought up on the edge of the Canadian frontier — that he felt cheated out of his birthright. Later in life he lamented the surroundings of his birth and stated that he "should" have been born in Manitoba where his three elder sisters (Rachel, Jean and Ethel, who died in infancy) and his younger brother (James) were born. His only consolation was that although he was born in Ontario, he was born in the same log house his mother had been born in. Though a third generation Canadian, Mack ultimately carried his sense of being on the edge of a frontier to British Columbia, where instead of buying land in a cleared or settled area, he chose a heavily timbered piece of rain forest, which after a great deal of effort, he converted into a pro-ductive nut farm. Indeed, he carried his frontier sense — the sense that the wilderness had to be explored and understood before it could be accepted — into every aspect of his life and work.

The Clearsprings Laings were truly first generation Manitobans: Their post office address for their first year or two in Manitoba was c/o The Hudson's Bay Company, Fort Garry. Moreover, in 1870, the year William Laing arrived in Manitoba, he claimed to have witnessed "the last string of Red River carts leave on the last buf-falo hunt that chased the last buffalo herd from the Saskatchewan plains." When Mack was growing up, unploughed sections of the prairie were still littered with buffalo skulls and the "blind springs and bogs" contained buffalo bones. As a youth he formed a sizeable collection of Indian arrowheads and other artifacts that were fre-quently turned up on the newly ploughed prairie. Indians had not yet entirely abandoned their traditional rounds of hunting and gathering in favour of reservation life. This benefited William Laing as he had an Indian friend named Kawawap who called about four times a winter to collect coyote carcasses, for which the Laings had little use, in exchange for moose meat, known as "native beef."[13]

Each Laing brother originally had a quarter section (160 acres) although later they added considerably to their holdings. William and Rachel Laing ran a herd of Scottish shorthorns for beef, kept

18

a few sheep but, in later years, developed what was primarily a dairy farm. Rachel Laing made butter, cheese, soap, and other milk and beef by-products for home use and for the Winnipeg market, a thirty-six mile or three-day drive. She also made tallow candles and picked and preserved the abundant wild fruits of the Clear-springs area. It was on this dairy farm that Mack was brought up and it was in this pioneer landscape that he discovered his interest in natural history.[14]

Birds were the first and major passion of his life. His mother recalled that from his earliest days a bird "always excited him." His keen ornithological eye and attention to detail were apparent right from the start. In "Early Memories," Laing's first autobiographical sketch dating from the late 1970's, he recalled his first memories of bird life:

Another of my earliest memories . . . concerns birds — naturally. I was born a naturalist. Like poets, painters, musicians and others of that ilk naturalists are not made in college.

I was somewhere between three and four years old and walking slowly hand in hand with mother over the big bridge that midway between the two Laing homesites spanned the coulee to take care of the over-flow of spring break-up. Down in the black pool below the grade left by the scrapers in a small shallow pool was a small flock of about a dozen beautiful birds the like of which I had never seen before. . . . There was something wrong with that picture — beautiful birds wading about in that black muddy pool. The naturalist blood in me had asserted itself and I couldn't forget. I had seen that in the dozen birds about half of them were bigger than the others and also far more brightly coloured — a lot of white, some black and some pronounced pinkish tints. The smaller birds were much greyer . . . it took me a long time to work out the details of the mystery birds. . . . Then one spring day in 1905 on a Saturday, as in rubber boots I sloshed through the shallows of Whitewater Lake near Boissevain there they were again and the meeting surely gave me a tingle. Again a flock of about a dozen big and smaller, some bright and some drab — a duplicate of the flock years ago except that the new flock was in a clean, grassy location. After straining my field glasses to assure myself that they were naturally really wading birds I turned to dry land and my bicycle and broke all records home to the Frank Latimer farm where I boarded near the Caranton School. Here my ornithological bible: Chapman's Color Key to North American Birds said, of course: Wilson's Phala-ropes.[15]

Although many of Mack's earliest memories concern his first meetings with rare or unusual birds, many also revolve around his efforts at keeping his parents' farm free of the mammals, birds and insects that were in some way considered predators or pests. Several early memories concern his earliest hunting exploits. As a pre-schooler, he became proficient in the use of traps and snares, and as he grew older he graduated to rifles and shotguns in his attempt to eliminate predators and bring home food for the table. Mice, voles, squirrels, gophers, coyotes, wolves, hawks, crows, owls and the potato bug were all considered worthy of extermination. They were Mack's enemies in the struggle for life. William Laing, who was himself a keen hunter and an outdoorsman by necessity, brought up his eldest son as gamewarden of the Clearsprings farm. Mack recalled that his father was "... born with the instincts of a hunter. Long before I was allowed to use firearms I was interested in my father's shooting. He had brought to Manitoba in 1870 one of the earliest breech-loading rifles in the province. He had the eye and steady nerve of the rifleman.... He seldom missed."[16] William Laing taught his son that on the isolated prairie farm — geared towards the production of crops and the rearing of livestock — certain wild animals posed a very serious threat. Mack was trained at an early age to trap and shoot predators or pests that threatened the smooth and economical operation of family farm. He learned at an early age that some animals were "good" and some were "bad." He recalled, for example, that at Clearsprings:

Two breeds of mice were generally abundant, the short-tailed mouse, a vole, was found in numbers in the coulee grass and to the fore at haying time. The other was the white-footed mouse Peromyscus common about everywhere he was not wanted, a pest to all the buildings.... As garden warden it was my duty to battle its pests and one of these was the pocket gopher which was a very common small animal at Clearsprings.... The pocket gopher was a rodent that had gone underground like a mole but was vegetarian and lived by cutting the roots of living plants. When he got loose for a night or two among carrots, beets and peas he could raise a lot of hell. He worked by both day and night. I had a healthy grudge against this underground root eater.... However, most of my early talent as a trapper was spent controlling the ubiquitous Franklin ground squirrel. At first, when the young dairy farm was a bit primitive, before we had the advantage of the cold artesian well cooling system, we raised the cream by setting the milk pans in a row in the milk house and skimming the pans by hand with the skimmer. Twice a squirrel dug under the foundation log of the milk house and on one occasion the invader went down the row of cooling pans after the cream has risen and gave his belly an oleaginous treat on the house by sampling every pan! My mother was furious. She had very decided ideas on cleanliness and consigned that milking to the potato patch; and I doubt that she slept well till that dirty little beast had got his desserts.[17]

As Mack grew older he was given more responsibility. Mack the trapper became Mack the hunter at the age of eleven in 1894, when he was first allowed to use his father's rifle:

I began with the rifle. I think my father would have allowed me to shoot earlier but my mother objected. She was afraid of guns. I got my chance one day. Sitting on a fence post close to the west wall of the cow stable where he had a good view of the chicken yard was a big red-tailed hawk and he seemed far too interested in what he saw there. Neither father nor the hired man was available. I rushed to the house "Hawk in the henyard!" and leaned heavily on those two broods of day-old chicks turned loose that very morning. "Just let me" and I pointed at the open pantry door where the Remington was at home. "Well all right, but be careful!" In about two seconds I had that rifle down, turned my back on my gun-shy mother and made for that hawk that was still waiting for me. . . . And I missed him! And the startled predator sprang up and away giving those hoarse squeals of the red-tail as though he had a bad cold, which in my then frame of mind made me feel that he was laughing at me. How perfectly rotten I felt. How proud I would have been to be able to present to my father that chicken-robbing bird dead, victim of my first shot from his pet rifle.[18]

Mack recalled his hunting exploits with great lucidity and detail even after eighty years. The next year, in 1895, he was introduced to the shotgun by a friend of his father's in Winnipeg — a butter customer, who gave him an old single barrel muzzle loader. William Laing passed along the shotgun to his son, who remembered:

I was soon bringing game to the kitchen — which meant ruffed grouse that we called "partridge" and sharp-tailed grouse that we called "chicken" and snowshoe rabbits common in our woods. The only fly in the ointment here was that the Queen of our kitchen had established an inexorable edict that whoever brought game to the kitchen, whether fur or feathers, had to skin or pluck it, and that meant gut it too.

It was this year 1895 that new game came on the scene. The first Clearsprings prairie hare, real game that 10 lb. hare — an invader from the west — was killed in the Laing garden. It was my discovery but the hired man stole my shot which hurt a lot. But I had soon snared, trapped and shot 3 of my own which really meant something in a skillet where fresh meat during half the year was hard to come by.[19]

These examples of Mack's early efforts as hunter and game-warden are significant because they greatly coloured his view of nature in later life. Hamilton M. Laing, the writer, journalist, orchardist and naturalist, remained Hammie Laing the "official pest-warden" of his parents' farm, intent on pleasing his parents by reducing the number of predatory and undesirable animals. As a naturalist he was never able to forget his early experiences on the dairy farm and fully embrace the principles of the conservation movement. To Mack, the gamewarden-naturalist, the conservation of wildlife meant the nonsensical protection of predatory birds and mammals, who then had free rein to destroy the crops and kill all the nesting birds they desired. He did not believe that nature should be left to balance itself: rather, he believed that the balance of nature — on a household or national level — could be achieved most successfully by man in the role of gamewarden. Nature left to its own devices would invariably result in a reign of terror by crows, hawks, eagles, owls and wolves.

Mack's philosophy of natural history must be placed within the context of a farming community on the new Canadian frontier. He had, as he put it, "made war" on several predatory species at Clear-springs.[20] The young naturalist's first battleground was his parents' farm, where the destructive natural predators and pests presented a constant threat to their crops and livestock. The validity of Mack's world-view was that it stemmed from the very practical and utili-tarian truth of frontier life, where predators threatened a farm's productivity and where hunting and trapping were economically valuable activities. In these sensitive frontier conditions he developed a keen appreciation of the value of birds and mammals to the kitchen pot of the remote farm. Indeed as a ten-year-old he bartered his own mink, weasel and muskrat pelts at the Reimer general store in Steinbach in exchange for school supplies which he recalled gave him "a tiny puff of independence."[21]

But simultaneously he was learning the habits of the birds and mammals he snared, trapped and shot. In order to hunt them most effectively he had to learn their life histories. The emerging young naturalist therefore made it his business to know the life of every inch of the Clearsprings farm.[22]

II

The Student
1888-1900

I HAD A MEMORY LIKE A CHINESE LAUNDRYMAN AND
STORED IN MY HEAD ONLY THE TRUTH ABOUT THINGS.

— *Hamilton Laing, 1980*[1]

Mack's first school was the Ridgewood Rural School — a two-mile walk from his parents' farm — which he entered on May 1, 1888, at the age of five. After two years he and his older sister Jean were transferred to the Clearsprings Rural School a mile from the Laing farm, where he stayed until 1898 when he went away to high school in Winnipeg.[2]

Mack was brought up in a strict Presbyterian household where education was taken very seriously. William Laing had taught school before immigrating to Canada. Both Jennie, Mack's sister, and Jim, his younger brother, became teachers. Four of his five teachers at Clearsprings boarded at the Laing farm, as also did one Presbyterian minister. William and Rachel Laing were pillars of the local community: the first church service in Clearsprings was held in their home in 1873. In 1879, William donated the land necessary for the construction of a school, a cemetery and a church. A log schoolhouse was built upon this land in 1880 which was replaced by a more substantial structure in 1882. William Laing subsequently became secretary-treasurer of the school board and one of the first church trustees. He also held a weekly music class at his home, and provided his children with a sound musical education. In 1884 he was appointed first municipal clerk of the newly formed municipality of La Broquerie which included Clearsprings.[3]

Mack's mother, Rachel Laing, was a powerful character, well suited, by her upbringing in rural Ontario, to the life of a prairie farmer. She was responsible for the hard domestic labour on the farm: preparing the dairy products for the Winnipeg market, bringing up four children, and looking after the needs of boarding teachers and clergymen. Her neice, Mary Simpson, remembered her as:

...a splendid seamstress and in addition to the family sewing made beautiful quilts, rugs, embroidery and other needlework and took prizes in the early Fort Garry fairs. Practically everything worn in those early days was hand-made. She washed, carded and spun into yarn the wool from their own sheep and turned it into socks, and stockings, mittens, mufflers and smaller garments though no actual weaving was ever attempted.[4]

Rachel Laing was also a strict disciplinarian in matters of child-raising. In 1977 her son stated that he could still feel "a glow in my sit-downer when I recollect the change she made in it when she took down my pants." Her instrument was a leather strap known as "the taws," which Mack recalled was kept hanging on a nail "on the wall where it would be in plain sight and also handy. I could recognize that strap yet in a thousand. It was two short straps joined by a copper rivet that I think added weight and authority to it when driven by the stout R. arm of my mother, always in splendid condition from spanking butter in the big wooden tray...."[5]

Mack's reminiscences, while supposedly concerned with his years at school, more often than not relate stories of his own development as a hunter and naturalist. His transfer from Ridgewood to Clearsprings school, for example, "made little difference in my job of small pest warden of the home farm."[6] Natural history seemed to offer a world more exciting and colourful than the bleak prairie landscape. He later described Clearsprings school as:

The usual rural school of the age; not a tree or shrub or flowering plant. To lessen the loneliness, or perhaps to increase it, two back houses and a tiny woodpile were the complement of the building site. The fence with its gate helped a little. The vacant school quarter lay beyond the gate. Primitive, but a lot of good men got some schooling in such scenes where the boys had to pair off and take turns at packing a bucket of drinking water half a mile from the nearest pump.[7]

The intelligent and observant young naturalist clearly found his early school years unchallenging, and his independent cast of mind asserted itself at an early age.

Though early I was the official vermin trapper of the Laing farm I did not let it interfere with my schooling. Sometimes when I look backward through the years I feel I learned as much outside those four walls as I learned between. That was somewhat due to my bent for natural history. . . . I remember my surprise when I had to disagree with my father — silently of course. I had heard him several times maintain that coyotes, despite their yodelling in the night, never made a sound when shot or bludgeoned in a trap. Then one morning I watched him go to his coulee set to bring home a capture. When the victim saw his nemesis coming, he stood at the head of his chain facing his foe and barked threateningly till silenced by the club on his head. Fathers were not always right, I decided.[8]

Mack was not, however, completely concerned wtih natural history. He was a keen soccer player and belonged to the Clearsprings Literary Society — as did his sister Jean and his cousins David Laing, John Langille and Mary Langille. All local transportation was by foot, and he adapted a peculiar quick jogging gait early in life which he preferred to the more normal human walk. He learned this jog while a pupil at the Ridgewood school at the age of six when, before school each morning, he had to herd his uncle's and his father's cows through his uncle's woods and fields to the pasture. He explained:

. . . it was easier to put the boys to work. So it fell to my lot to take the combined herd, nearly one hundred of stock, to the pasture gate by the road on my way to school and the job of my cousins to bring home the combined herds in the evening. It was quite a smooth arrangement but I still walked two miles to school. But "walking" is scarcely the truth. I had a horror of being late for school. And that is where and when I learned to jog. I hit a good jog . . . till I was through the woods and could keep my eyes on the school and see if the soccer ball was bouncing. I walked only the last hundred yards prepared to do a sprint if necessary. There is no record of my ever being late.[9]

The school soccer team, consisting of barefooted boys and girls, was the pride of Clearsprings and the scourge of neighbouring schools. Mack believed that "Mother Nature had designed me for that forward soccer line right wing where a lot of leg work comes in handy." Their main rival was the Mennonite boys' team from nearby Steinbach which he rated very low: "Though by age and poundage they were much above us we beat them easily. They were not a team; they were a rabble with no cohesion. Each man played the game for himself."[10]

Mack the schoolboy was known as Hammie Laing — and his sisters and brother as Nellie, Jennie and Jimmy, following the Scots' habit. The Clearsprings folk maintained the Scots' pronunciation of Laing, as in "laying an egg," a cause of much confusion many years later when his relations tried to locate "Hammie Leng" in Comox. "Yes they called me Hammie," Mack recalled:

... or worse still "Ham" when I was too young to defend myself. Now ham is the west end of a pig travelling east. And I didn't like it. Ham Lang was too Chinesey. I decided that when I left home I was going to be called Mack, my second name and unless the other fellow was a hell of a lot bigger than me he wouldn't get away with any hamming.[11]

At school Mack had the benefit of some good teachers. Of his six teachers at Ridgewood and Clearsprings "only one was a female — a demure young chick from Ontario." He wrote damningly that she "made little impression," and if he remembered her name, he did not record it in his reminiscences.[12] She was followed by Mr. Doubleday, an Englishman who Mack described as "a grand mixer" with a "grand sense of humour." An Ontarian, Jim Hamilton, followed but after only a year at Clearsprings he entered medical college. Hamilton "knew what to do with music in school and did it":[13]

I missed Jim Hamilton after his year with us. He was very musical and handled the Doherty organ well and played accompaniments to father's violin. The organ was situated in the big room below my upstairs bedroom. We always called it "big room," "parlour" sounded a bit too stilted for the Laings. I was sent to bed at 9 o'clock, but there was no power on earth could prevent me lying stark awake for a couple of hours soaking up that music that came up through the floor.[14]

His fourth teacher was a character named Joe Martin, a Prince Edward Islander with a handlebar moustache, a poor teacher and the "epitome of slow motion."[15] Mack had nothing good to say about Martin, who boarded at his home. Old age did not diminish his resentment.

I don't think he ever hurried in his life and that didn't sit too well with the Laings. It took him about twice as long to do his morning mile to school as it took me to do twice the distance by having to pasture the two Laing herds on my way to school. As a teacher I just naturally rated him low. He took practically all of the classes sitting down and used the blackboard little. There wasn't a note of music in the lout and as it was on our curriculum, he turned the music lesson over to one of the senior girls, usually my sister who was present during his term of office. He never took part in the school games or showed any interest in them. In short if I'm telling the story, Martin was a frost and I was glad to hear he was not rehired.[16]

Of all his teachers at Clearsprings, Mack had the best memories of the last, George Bartlett, who shared his interest in soccer, hunting and natural history. Bartlett evidently sensed that it was worth spending time with his enthusiastic and capable pupil:

George was more than just a rural school teacher. He was a good athlete himself and put know-how into our school football. He was a good botanist and at Clearsprings was a field of wild flowers I never saw surpassed. What new flowers he found he could work out from his Botanical Key. He was not strong on birds so I swapped birds for his botany and learned a lot.[17]

Mack recalled with pleasure the field of flowers, located in the upper corner of his Uncle Tom Laing's farm, where he and Bartlett did their botanizing.

It was about thirty acres of natural prairie clear of brush and each season they mowed it for a hay crop. I never saw its equal at prairie level. The crowning flower there was the big single-flowered lily which we called the tiger lily. It opened its huge orange red chalice to the sky a little taller than the hay. The grand flower was always plentiful and it always hurt me to see the mower there. Lilies, and what lilies, falling over that cutting bar to feed cows![18]

Bartlett also supported Mack's youthful campaign against the crow which was a relative newcomer to Clearsprings. His father told him that in 1870 only a few crows had "hung around the first Kildonan Scotch settlement where the grainfields attracted them. With the development of the Clearsprings settlement and the Mennonite fields westward, the crow soon took possession of the country."[19] Following their declaration of war on the Clearsprings crows in the 1890's, Mack and Bartlett killed as many as forty in a single day.

We were both hunters in game season and out of season kept our eyes keen by keeping the crow population in bounds. We had no waterfowl to protect but a strong prairie chicken and ruffed grouse population to defend against crow predation. Now that I had grown useful on Saturdays on the farm my game wardening days did not amount to much. I always figured I was of help if I [could] use my gun on one of the black pirates and destroy their nest.[20]

His days on the farm were now drawing to a close. At Clearsprings, he had learned the economic value of game birds such as geese and grouse, as well as the constant danger presented to a farm economy by pests and predators. In exterminating predators he showed no mercy: they were inherently "bad" animals.[21] Moreover, predators posed a threat to the song birds that Mack increasingly found captivating. In hunting game birds, however, he exercised restraint, killing no more than necessary for food. He disapproved of his neighbour William Bruce, a "market hunter," who every fall went to Lake Manitoba to shoot ducks for sale on the Winnipeg market.[22] But his most pressing concern in 1898 was getting an education in order to earn a living.

In the summer of 1898 at the age of fifteen Mack followed his sister Jean from Clearsprings to Winnipeg to attend the Winnipeg Collegiate Institute, an imposing four-storey late-Victorian brick building with a mansard roof. Here, he intended to complete his schooling and qualify for teacher training, as Jean had done. The teacher training course stipulated that a candidate, after he had completed grade eight, take three years of intensive schooling known as Forms I, II and III. His adversary — at least in his eyes — throughout his stay at the collegiate was the crusty principal F. H. Schofield who ruled that the over-anxious country boy spend six qualifying months in the grade eight classroom, located in the school's dark cellar. In 1899 he graduated to Form I, where he throve under the guidance of the teacher, Miss Stewart. He admitted, "I was a bit spoiled, because like my sister before me I could sing like a nightingale — my voice hadn't changed yet!" Miss Stewart was impressed by the fact that Mack could recite McCaulay's "Lays of Ancient Rome" by the yard.[23] Near the end of Form I he and a pal named Harold somehow obtained the Form III entrance exam papers. "We were sure we could handle them," recalled Mack. They conceived a plot to leap directly from Form I to Form III: "So we went to the principal — the only stinker I met in the profession — and he refused to sign our papers and was very short about it." Luck, however, was on their side, because the despised principal Schofield promptly got sick and vice-principal Mr. A. E. Garrett took over, who obligingly signed their applications. The principal returned to find Mack, Harold and two motivated girls in Form III; there was nothing he could do to put them back in Form II.

In the difficult Form III curriculum, mathematics was the only subject that really troubled Mack. Unfortunately it was the subject taught by the irascible Mr. Schofield, who made life as difficult as possible for him. "At every exhibition of my stupidity — which was daily — his face carried the sneer that meant — 'Well, you asked for it.' " But a lucky circumstance carried Mack through:

And here is where Frank Powell enters the story. Powell and his wife were the caretakers of the block in which I ran my bach hall study home. Powell was a bricklayer by trade but — wonder of wonders — a mathematician as a hobbyist. He interested himself in my studies and when he found I was floundering in mathematics he took me under his wing and untied the knots in my disjointed course and put me back on the track. Every evening he came in and worked with me filling in what I had missed in Form II so that I hit a decent mark on the monthly exam, and if my principal wondered where I got the new brains, he said nothing about it. . . . To shorten a long story: in final exams end of June [1900] I passed. The principal's pet class mathematician failed. I won the second-hand bicycle my mother had promised me if I took the two years in one . . . I was 17 years old in knee pants till the principal advised longies when I did my experimental pupil teaching in the city.[24]

Perhaps the most valuable aspect of Mack's years in Winnipeg was the "array of able teachers" at the collegiate, who gave him a solid grounding in English Language and Literature, Physics, Physiology, Geography, History, Drawing, Painting and Music.[25] In the late nineteenth century the collegiate acted as a halfway house for young and ambitious school teachers, several of whom went on to teach at the University of Manitoba and elsewhere. One such teacher was the despised principal F. H. Schofield, whose three-volume history, *The Story of Manitoba*, was published in 1913.[26]

Another was David (Davy) Duncan, who spent the years 1895-1908 as Classical Master at the Collegiate. In 1903 Duncan published *A History of Manitoba and the Northwest Territories*.[27] Others were Miss Mckeown, who taught music; Miss B. F. Stewart (art); Miss Johnson (history); Mr. A. E. Garrett (geography), and J. C. Saul, whose "obvious love of poetry" radiated through his lessons in English Literature. Saul was co-author of *England's Story: A History for Public Schools* published in Toronto in 1903.[28] The most remarkable teacher was Agnes Laut (1871-1936), author of numerous popular and semi-popular books and articles dealing with the history and natural history of the Canadian west. Laut began writing for the outdoor magazines such as *Outing* about a decade before Mack did, and she soon abandoned teaching for a professional writing career. Mack does not mention Laut in his reminiscences; his only reference to her is steeped in the sexism of the time. In 1926 J. H. Fleming of the Royal Ontario Museum sent him one of Laut's recent books as a present. Mack replied: "Thanks for the fine book by A. C. Laut. She doesn't write like a woman. Where does she get it all? I read a lot of it tonight waiting for the grub frying."[29]

After the country life at Clearsprings Mack found the collegiate and the city a "prison."[30] His feeling of claustrophobia was lessened somewhat thanks to his mother, who kept him amply provided with home cooking by way of the Clearsprings farmers' weekly market trip to Winnipeg.[31] Moreover, he still had the weekends free to pursue his ornithological interests. His favourite haunts were the parks around Winnipeg: Birds Hill, Headingly, Elmwood Park, River Park, Norwood and Stony Mountain, where he found tree swallows, bluebirds and the purple martin which had never visited Clearsprings. "I never neglected any bird study on Saturdays and Sundays," he recalled. "On Saturdays I prowled with Mr. Powell's gun. Audubon carried a gun, why shouldn't I? Guns were verboten on Sundays, but I filled the gap by using 5 heavy-shot pellets in the pouch of my sling-shot and I collected several strange birds that way."[32] Mack did not preserve any of the birds he collected, although he was developing an increasing interest in, and a greater knowledge of, Manitoba birdlife.

My ornithology got a boost at the Collegiate about 1899. At a Christmas concert the Literary Society of the Collegiate made $100 and strangely enough — I do not know who was responsible — only it wasn't the Principal because he didn't know a hawk from a handsaw — but the $100 was spent on birds. For that price the Provincial Naturalist of Portage la Prairie [George Atkinson] gave us a case of 100 mounted birds. It stood near the entrance. It was hard for me to pass it daily without stopping.[33]

In June 1900 Mack had completed his Form III and following four months of Normal Teachers' Training in Winnipeg schools, he obtained his third-class Normal School teacher's diploma. By the end of October 1900 he had completed the first phase of his education and he was still only seventeen years old. Early in 1901 he boarded the train to Glenora, Manitoba. He was picked up at the Baldur station by Gregor Fraser with whose family he was to board for the next two years. He recalled his meeting with Fraser with a mixture of humility and pride: "If Mr. Gregor Fraser was a bit disappointed when he met the new teacher at Baldur platform he was too much of a gentleman to show it. Anyway all I lacked was a few inches and a few pounds. I had the certificate."[34]

III

The Teacher
1901-1911

WE ARE ALL SO MERCENARY AND INFERNALLY BUSY
CHASING THE GREEN BACK DOLLAR THAT WE HAVE
NO TIME FOR THE BEAUTIFUL AND WONDERFUL!

— *Hamilton Laing to Percy Taverner*
June 5, 1919[1]

Mack's first school was a one-room little red schoolhouse at Glenora, Manitoba, where he taught from 1901 until 1903. The formidable Mr. Gregor Fraser, who had met him at the railway station in January 1901, later paid him the compliment of being "a competent teacher in all the grades and an excellent disciplinarian."[2] Typically, Mack had chosen Glenora because it was situated only three miles from Rock Lake and a mile from Fisher Lake, where he had the opportunity to hunt, fish and acquaint himself with water birds which had been largely absent at both Clearsprings and Winnipeg. "There was fishing in both summer and winter — the woods were full of grouse and there was lots of deer also. Now how could I, a born hunter miss in region like that?"[3] It was here that he first started hunting Canada Geese, an obsession that would form the basis of many of his early stories. At Glenora he also learned three important skills which he would employ later in life as a field naturalist: he began a daily nature diary (1901), he began to draw his bird specimens (1903), and he learned taxidermy (1903). In 1977 he recalled these beginnings:

It was now I decided to take up taxidermy to save specimens I shot. My father had a small treatise on the art — why, I never knew — and I took possession of it and got along fine till I had half a dozen mounts on the back of the piano in the parlour when the house cat

35

that had growing kittens went beserk one night and horribly mangled my taxidermy beyond all salvage and when the specimens I sent home for safe keeping got a reception not so much better than the cat's, I saw I was on the wrong track. It was now I took to my ability to draw and establish my record of the bird by an outline drawing that showed the type (shape) and filled in the details in writing. I still have that folio of sketches of early birds that crossed my path. That is the way I kept records for some years.[4]

In 1903 Mack left Glenora to teach at Runnymead School five miles southeast of Oak Lake, where he boarded at the farm belonging to Robert Alford.[5] Evidently he found it difficult to keep his mind on the classroom: one of his former students recalled that "When Mr. Laing taught in the town he would not eat lunch. Instead he would walk north to the Assiniboine River (about $1\frac{1}{2}$ miles) to study wildlife. He said that anyone working on the sedentary job of teaching did not need to eat lunch."[6] At Oak Lake he continued his program of self-improvement by becoming, in November 1903, a member of the League of American Sportsmen, a conservationist group opposed to market hunting and in favour of the preservation of game birds.[7] And although his earnings as a schoolteacher at Runnymead were not great — he received part of his $35 monthly salary in kind — he still managed to purchase out of his "skimpy earnings" what he called his "Ornithological Bible." This was F. C. Chapman's *Color Key to North American Birds*, which he used for most of the next eighty years, even after the publication of Roger Tory Petersen's definitive field guides.[8] He also indulged his hunting instincts by taking a deer-hunting trip to the Riding Mountains of northern Manitoba.[9] Of the many friends he made at Oak Lake perhaps the most important was Mrs. Beverly Sharman, an artist who later would advise him to study at the Pratt Institute in New York. Mack met Mrs. Sharman in September 1903 when her son Eddie, one of his pupils, invited him home for the weekend at Oak Lake.[10]

The next two years, 1904 and 1905, saw Mack teaching at Caranton School, a rural school northwest of the town of Boissevain in eastern Manitoba. His principal memory was that Caranton was located on the north side of Whitewater Lake, "which at that time was one of the most famous goose-shooting grounds in [North]

36

America."[11] At Caranton he shot a rare whooping crane, a feat he greatly regretted twenty years later when the birds were close to extinction. He sent the whooping crane to taxidermist George Atkinson of Portage La Prairie, who prepared and mounted the bird for display. Mack then loaned the mounted bird to the Provincial Norman School in Winnipeg where it stood until he asked for it back in the 1920's.[12] At Caranton he boarded with the Frank Latimer family who, a great nephew recalled in 1984, "Loved to hunt and kept hounds for fox hunting. They and Laing hunted wildfowl particularly geese and ducks together.... Laing hunted with the neighbours a great deal and also with the older people."[13] Mack continued his study of taxidermy and on top of the Latimer piano stood a mounted goose, a prairie chicken and an owl.

An embarrassing incident occurred on his first day at school. He had been invited to dinner wtih a neighbour, a Mr. Laurence, whose daughter Pearl was in Mack's class. He recalled: "I was a bit discouraged when Pearl slid into her seat and her father said, 'Well Pearl, what did you learn today?' and Pearl answered the asinine question with a slight suggestion of disgust saying, 'Nothing!'"[14] Mack explained to Mr. Laurence that on his first day of classes he customarily taught only rudimentary phonetics. Another student, A. Earl Henderson, felt Mack was a "very good" teacher and "a wonderful naturalist and sportsman." Henderson recalled in 1983: "He was a very ardent hunter and a good sport. If occasion demanded, he'd regiment you during school hours even to the point of using the strap, then go out hunting geese with you. He was very good to mix with the students in sports such as baseball or football [soccer]."[15] While at Caranton, Mack took a correspondence course in story writing offered by the National Press Association of Indianapolis, Indiana, in which he obtained "the highest credit." He completed the course in January 1905, and it would later be of value in his writing career.[16]

Early in 1906, aged only twenty-three, Mack took a break from teaching and returned to Winnipeg to upgrade his teaching certificate from third-class to second-class standard. This would enable him to teach high school rather than rural school. Not a moment of his time was wasted.

1906 is a worthy year of my career as I took a holiday in the first half of the year and in the second went back to Normal School to make my certificate professional. My folks now had sold the farm at Clear-springs and bought a new home in Winnipeg [1901] so study was now a bit more pleasant than when I bached [*sic*] alone. . . . Also in 1906 I bought my first camera and became a nature photographer. It was a 4 x 5 plate glass camera. The "Kodak" with its roll film was not yet born. At the first try-out of the new weapon I went to River Park to make a study of the new born growth of the elm and I produced some weird negatives, but I had it all to learn.[17]

Though he said he took a holiday in the first half of the year, it is more probable that he spent his time learning photography and writing stories. He was staying at his parents' boarding house at 330 Carlton Street, Winnipeg, next to the Manitoba *Free Press* building. His story writing labours were rewarded with the publication of "The End of the Trail" in the New York *Tribune* Sunday magazine of March 24, 1907. While the sale of this article was highly profit-able, it made him question his career choice. He reminisced later that "It was more than I could earn teaching school. I didn't quit my job. But I filed away the information on a shelf of my brain that I could write. I would be a naturalist writer."[18]

It would be several years, however, before he could realize his ambition. First, he had to make a living; with his professional cer-tificate to hand he returned to the Runnymead School at Oak Lake from January to July 1907. This was his last rural school. After a brief teaching visit at Dunrea, Manitoba, in 1908, he moved on to Oakwood High School at Oak Lake where, following six months with the entrance exam class (grade VIII) he was appointed school principal, a job he held until 1911. Even as principal he was not content with his second-class certificate. He therefore returned to Winnipeg in July 1908 to sit the qualifying exam, and in 1910 he presented the obligatory essay which earned him a professional first-class Manitoba teacher's certificate, grade A.[19]

As principal at Oakwood he involved himself in the provincial committee on Elementary Schools, where he contributed much good advice and counsel.[20] His predecessor, Francis Mayers, moved to Vancouver in 1908 but, before his departure, he and Mack struck up a lasting friendship based on a mutual love of hunting and of the outdoors. So strong was their friendship that following the publication of *Out With the Birds* in 1913, Mayers sent him a congratulatory letter, which reads in part:

I have just got it — your book. When I think of all it has cost you, in time and labour, and even in actual capital, and when the memory of our happy days comes up why woman-like, out of pure joy, I could almost shed a tear or two. It is needless, Mack, to tell you my feelings but they run deep. For you, there dwells within me that feeling that has gone to but few men in this world, and may I tell you how my faith in you has grown from the morning I met you first in an Oak Lake classroom. While your book was a complete surprise, yet my hope in you was great and I am indeed a happy man to-night.[21]

In 1909 Mack made his first visit to British Columbia. He visited Mayers in Vancouver and with a party of teachers took a steamer up the Sunshine Coast to Capilano Canyon and Powell River. In 1977 he recalled the ornithological novelties of British Columbia.

July 19 [1909] left Oak Lake C.P.R. for Vancouver taking my mother to give her a holiday while I finished my vacation with a camping trip with a party of three teachers at Powell River. . . . Across the vast prairies I was glued to the coach window seeking new birds. I was rewarded by first sight of Avocet, black-necked Stilt and prairie Curlew. The mountains to a plainsman were very wonderful to the eye but to the naturalist they were almost a vacuum. . . . Later at Powell Lake our camp was almost birdless. Kinglets, chickadees, some sky thrushes whispered from the tall evergreens but none were friendly. For the most part the coast crow, raven and bald eagle and osprey had the stage to themselves.[22]

Between 1908 and 1911 Mack continued drawing, photographing and shooting the wildlife of Oak Lake, as well as acting as principal-teacher of a sizeable school. He also became a soccer player and baseball coach and started one of the first Boy Scout troops in Canada. In spite of these other interests he was a very effective teacher. In 1950, ex-pupil Bill Alford wrote to him expressing a sentiment common among his former Oak Lake pupils: "Whether you know it or not you had a profound influence on the older members of the Alford family for much good."[23] Part of his effectiveness came from his enthusiasm for extra-curricular activities such as the Boy Scouts, which enabled him to combine teaching with the outdoors. Mack believed that a teacher's work should not be confined to the classroom. In 1919, for example, he lamented to

39

ornithologist Percy Taverner that Canadian children were not learning an appreciation of nature at school.

As I am a pedagogue — or used to be, I think I know the situation
fairly well and I'll say this. It is difficult for the teachers to teach what
they know nothing about — and care less. They don't know Nature.
They have no chance to learn it. . . . Anyway, naturalists must be born,
not made in schools. But a love of Nature may be kindled very easily
in the young; but *they must be taken young* as Cardinal Somebody
once said about a certain religion I know. . . .[24]

Mack seems to have abandoned his own Presbyterian brand of
Christianity while teaching school in favour of outdoor sport and
natural history. At some time in his early life he copied out some
quotations from a favourite author, Robert Louis Stevenson. One
reads: "Every man is his own doctor of divinity in the last resort,"
and another: "What religion knits people together so closely as
common sport?" These lines seem to reflect his own independence
in religious matters.[25] While at the Collegiate he found that church
clashed with sport and nature study, and that Presbyterian Sunday
School "interfered a lot with ornithology." He was understandably
opposed to Manitoba's "Blue Laws" that prohibited the discharge
of firearms on Sundays.[26] Although in later life he never went to
church, he did keep a Bible full of newspaper clippings containing
hymns, biblical commentary and contemporary news, such as the
discovery of the Dead Sea Scrolls in the 1950's. He seemed more
interested in the hymns — which reminded him of his childhood —
than in the ritual or substance of the church. The few religious
references in his stories appear in an outdoors context. For example,
after a hectic day of outdoor work at Comox in 1922 he wrote that:

In the evening the wind fell away and calmed with an air from the
North-west, so that the sunset came to a bay so glassy that great rafts
of colorful clouds were painted on the water and a silence and peace
settled down like the hush that used to follow the benediction in the
old fashioned Presbyterian Kirk. And this benediction to the day I
took to be my own, to my camp under the big trees on the shore by
the rill, and to my bird adventures in a delightful land.[27]

Mack's decision to quit the comfortable life as school principal
resulted from a career crisis in 1910. His secret and greatest ambition
was to be a writer-naturalist. His public ambition was to teach art at

the Collegiate in Winnipeg, and to do this he had to acquire a specialized training in art. Secretly, however, he knew that such a training would give him the expertise with which to illustrate his nature writings: it would also give him the opportunity to see something of the wider world. In 1977 he recalled the crisis that ended his schoolteaching years.

In 1910 I decided to change my lifestyle. If I was to be a teacher I needed to specialize on one subject instead of teaching the usual dozen of an advanced curriculum. But on what would I specialize? I found I had too many natural talents to make the selection. In Collegiate life, History and English were my pet subjects but I figured difficult to teach. Science and mathematics — no! The crusty Principal of the Collegiate hated my guts and never lost a chance to assure me that I was a dunce. Physiology, no. That would lead me to an M.D. which practice would interfere terribly with my hunting and fishing — I was born a hunter.

Music? I knew I was strongly gifted — my father played his violin most all day Sundays — but teach it?— Though in my early teens I could sing, read music both vocally and instrumentally and played 3 instruments, I harbored a firm conviction that unless you are born with music in you, you never get anywhere with it. Drawing — I hesitated there always. I was strongly gifted. Had drawn naturally almost as early as I went to school at five. Had made pencil portraits of some of my friends for fun. Used the hand sketch of birds in recording new records as I met new birds. Judging by my own progress self-taught I believed it could be taught if there was anything at all to work on. My father had a smoldering talent he never developed. As to instruction we took still life in Form I. It was not easy to forget that Miss Stewart more than once had picked out my effort as the best in the class. So an artist I would be as a teacher. In June 1911 I gave up my principalship of the Oakwood Intermediate School, 4 teachers, Oak Lake Town, and primed by the advice of a local artist went to the Pratt Institute, Brooklyn, N.Y. and enrolled in the general course of Art in a class of 45 students.[28]

When he gave up teaching in 1911 Mack's intellectual development was largely complete: indeed, his years of teaching had also been years of learning. He had taken a commercial story writing course in 1904 and sold his first piece of fiction in 1907. And before leaving Oak Lake he had sold a goose-hunting story, "With the Wiffle Wings in Manitoba," to *Recreation* magazine of New York. As a schoolteacher he had also learned taxidermy, photography and nature drawing. Since its appearance in 1897 he had read *Recreation*, the magazine of the early conservation movement; and he was an avid student of the popular and scientific writings of the Manitoban naturalist Ernest Thompson Seton. Moreover, the Boy Scout movement had allowed him to satisfactorily blend his love of the outdoors with his teaching vocation. Yet at the basis of his outdoors ideology, there always remained the game warden mentality formed at Spring Bank Farm, Clearsprings, where he had learned the economic advantage of hunting and the potentially disastrous influence of pests and predators on the farm economy. And beneath all his subsequent experience and education was the conviction that he was a born hunter and naturalist.

Mack would spend the rest of his life acting out the lines he had learned in his first twenty-eight years in Manitoba. Predatory animals continued to obsess him; hunting remained a passion of pure enjoyment; writing — through which he taught his philosophy of nature — became his livelihood. Whether he was clearing land at Baybrook, hunting deer at Constitution Hill, tracking panthers with Cougar Smith, or writing stories for outdoor magazines, his reference point remained always the Manitoba of his youth.

IV

The Young Writer
1905-1913

REALITY MUST BE SERVED, FOR TRUTH IS SACRED.[1]

— *Hamilton Laing, 1979*

Mack Laing enjoyed a long and distinguished writing career: he began keeping a nature diary at "about the time my whiskers did," in 1901, which he continued, on a daily basis, until shortly before his death in 1982.[2] The material recorded in these nature journals formed the basis of virtually all his publications, both popular and scholarly. His first publication appeared in 1907 and his last in 1979. In the intervening years he wrote some nine hundred popular nature stories which earned him — especially in the interwar years — an enthusiastic and dedicated audience right across Canada and in the United States. Yet the forces that shaped his development as a writer were at their strongest as a student in Winnipeg and as a teacher in rural Manitoba between 1898 and 1911. He was influenced, first, by writer and naturalist Ernest Thompson Seton; second, by the naturalist John Burroughs, whose charge of "nature faking" against Seton and his followers precipitated the appearance of a new philosophy of natural history writing; and third, by such early proponents of the conservation movement in the United States as Gifford Pinchot, Theodore Roosevelt and G. O. Sheilds of *Recreation* magazine.

Ernest Thompson Seton (1860-1946) was overwhelmingly the major influence of Mack's early life and writing. Indeed, though a generation apart, there were many parallels between the two men.

43

Of Scots Presbyterian background, Seton was born in the north of England and immigrated with his parents in 1866. They lived on a rural farm in Ontario before moving to Toronto in 1870. After studying at the Ontario School of Art and in Europe, Seton returned to Canada and joined his brother on a farm near Carberry, Manitoba. Here, in 1882, he began keeping a natural history journal. He published his first story, "The Life of the Prairie Chicken," in the *Canadian Journal* of February 1883 — the very month of Mack's birth. Appointed Provincial Naturalist of Manitoba in 1892, Seton had published *Mammals of Manitoba* in 1886 and *Birds of Manitoba* in 1891. In the 1890's Seton moved to New York, where he studied art and where he began to write his famous animal stories based on his experiences as a naturalist.[3] In the winter of 1896-97 Seton met G. O. Sheilds, the editor of *Recreation*. In his autobiography Seton recalled that through Sheilds he "came in contact with the world of letters and men and things. Many new opportunities were presented."[4] Their meeting led to the publication in 1898 of Seton's immensely successful *Wild Animals I Have Known*, which according to W. J. Keith — the historian of Canadian nature writing — initiated a "popular vogue for the animal story" throughout the English-speaking world.[5] Seton soon went on a very lucrative lecture tour known as the Chautauqua Circuit. The best known of Seton's many followers was his contemporary, the Canadian writer Charles G. D. Roberts (1860-1943). One of the many other Canadians who avidly read Seton's scientific and popular writing was Mack Laing, who on the publication of *Wild Animals I Have Known*, was an impressionable sixteen-year-old at the Winnipeg Collegiate.

The *genre* of animal adventure story popularized by Seton and Roberts can, according to W. J. Keith, "with justice be regarded as the one native Canadian art form."[6] Seton fictionalized his animal subjects and gave them pet names such as Ragglybugs, the Cottontail rabbit and Lobo, the cunning and powerful wolf. The popularity, however, of these articles was of short duration — at least in critical circles. In 1903, the respected American naturalist John Burroughs attacked Seton, Roberts and their followers in an article called "Real and Sham Natural History." Burroughs argued that animal stories might be legitimate as fiction, but "true as natural history they as certainly are not." Burroughs was joined by American President Theodore Roosevelt, a big-game hunter, naturalist and incipient conservationalist, who ungraciously termed the nature story writers the "yellow journalists of the woods."[7]

One observer of this acrimonious dispute was Mack Laing, who subscribed to *Recreation* where the argument was played out between the so-called "nature fakers" and the serious naturalists. In his biography of Allan Brooks published in 1979, Mack recalled the controversy:

First I recall the furore over *Wild Animals I Have Known* when Seton ... wolf-howled his way on the Chautauqua Circuit across the continent. For this, some naturalists said, he was prostituting the sacred truth of natural hitsory, and some artists said he humanized his animals in his drawings, and, anyhow, no such rabbit as Ragglybug, Grizzly as Wahb, or wolf such as King Lobo, could exist except in the author's imagination. There could have been some fire below the smoke of both accusations. Much of these accusations were mere green-eyed envy.... Yet no one today could deny the good influence on the youth of the land on Seton's popular work, or disparage his serious efforts such as *Lives of Game Animals* which came later.[8]

It was only natural that Mack would follow in the footsteps of Seton, who had written the basic textbooks on Manitoban natural history in addition to his animal stories. As a schoolteacher Mack had made copious critical notes on at least one of Seton's books, *Northern Mammals*: "Note Seton gives little evidence that this mouse [Grasshopped mouse] is found in Manitoba ... Seton's notes [on Nebraska Deer-mouse] inconclusive. No records on this mouse of semi-arid plains."[9] Later, Mack heard Seton lecture on the Chautauqua Circuit and found him a "platform spellbinder."[10] Moreover, as Provincial Naturalist of Manitoba, Seton maintained close ties with Winnipeg, the provincial capital.

To the rural schoolteacher in isolated parts of Manitoba, Seton became the role model — the local boy who made good. It was up to Mack to acquire the tools of a naturalist's trade. First, he read everything he could find by Seton and Burroughs. Second, he started a nature diary and learned to draw the birds he shot. "I didn't trust my artistic temperament," he recalled, "but held the buggers down and traced around the coastline."[11] These one-dimensional bird silhouettes are now housed in the Provincial Archives of British Columbia. A naturalist, of course, must be able to write and in 1905 he received a diploma in story writing from the National Press Association of the United States.

From the perspective of the 1980's it is curious that Mack's focus was the United States and not Canada, and it is even more curious in light of his genuine love for Canada. Speaking of Allan Brooks as a youth in the 1890's he wrote:

There was of course in his day no Canadian nationality except the Native Indian. "This is my own, my native land," then to people of Canada had a hollow ring to it. On immigration and census forms you were English, Irish, Scotch, Hungarian or what not.... "Where was your father born?" This was the crux.[12]

Seton, of course, had set a precedent by going to New York — ultimately he became an American citizen. New York was also the capital of natural history publishing and the centre of the conservation movement in North America.

Mack began writing fiction in 1905 or 1906, soon after qualifying as a journalist. "The End of the Trail," possibly his first story, appeared in the Sunday magazine of the New York *Tribune* of March 24, 1907. Cast solidly in the tradition of Seton and Roberts, the story is based on one of his father's wolf-hunting experiences in early Manitoba. Over a century later, in 1980, Mack recalled in detail the incident upon which he based his first publication:

In early Clearsprings years my father accounted for two wolves, one he trapped, the other he poisoned. The trapped wolf gave him quite an adventure. His trap set for coyote with the drag well frozen down disappeared without trace on a rough snowy night. That his victim had torn the trap loose where two coyotes had failed, suggested a more powerful victim and that could only be a timber wolf. And if his guess was right, a wolf in trouble would head in only one direction: east into the no man's land of swamp and gravel ridges, scrub and timber. So he took his snowshoes and went east and made a big circle round the last cultivation and sure enough came on the trail he sought. The wolf had been hung up some time during the blizzard. A much fresher trail led away from the tie-up and the battle seemed nearly won. Father figured he was about twelve miles from home when he came up with his wolf, again snagged, and a shot from the Remington ended the chase. But not the end of the story. To skin a big wolf, even hot, on the snow, on a below-zero winter day was a herculean job for a man who had hands like my father's. He had a disability of circulation in his hands; in the cold the blood would leave them and he would suffer a lot of pain. He had just decided that the first thing on his present program was a big fire when he heard a noise nearby and right out of the blue came two Indians and a shaganoppy (pony) with it two-pole drag. They had heard the shot and veered a little to investigate the possibility of fresh meat. How right they were! The white trapper knew no Indian beyond a word or two and they shook their heads when he tried them in French. But they understood the universal language of signs, and when father indicated he wanted that wolf-skin, the one Indian whipped out his knife and went to work while his comrade hurried to a nearby willow clump for kindling and soon had a fine fire, and all father had to do was to keep warm and do the heavy looking on. The skinner took that wolf out of its hide in jig time. Then with some heavy string and babiche he rolled the skin into a pack and rigged the burden for a shoulder pack and soon my parent was on his way home. In telling this story my father never forgot to admit his luck in having those natives arrive at the very moment they were needed most.[13]

In the New York *Tribune* story Mack has inverted the plot so that the white man rescues the Indian from certain death. A Cree trapper named Kashawamp comes across a trail of blood left by an injured wolf that is dragging a coyote trap around by its leg. Kashawamp examines the prints and recognizes "the unmistakeable foot pads of an immense timber wolf." He then finds wolf hair — blue wolf hair — in the snow and it suddenly dawns on him that the wolf must be the same one that ten years earlier had made off with one of his children. Suddenly "transformed from a lethargic old Indian into an excitable savage," Kashawamp mutters to himself:

The Blue Devil at last. None other could make such prints. These ten lonely years I have not lingered here in vain. Hitherto, old friend, your trail has been very long; it has crossed the snows of many winters; but now it is becoming short, and the end is almost in sight. You shedder of innocent blood, destroyer of my own kin, think you well of your misdeeds now, when Kashawamp the avenger is on the trail so close behind! A Cree father does not live to forget the slaughter of his child. I have not forgotten! Those blood-stained footmarks, those tell-tale blue hairs, that dishevelled snow — all is plain as on that terrible morning ten years ago! Bright Eyes, my pretty one, the debt

47

shall be paid! Hear me, Spirit of my fathers! I will see the end of this trail, and the end shall be very red!

After tracking the wolf for several hours Kashawamp suddenly realizes that he has forgotten his food and has only one bullet left in his rifle, but it is too late to turn back, and he is determined to shoot the wolf. He prays: "Spirit of my father give me strength for the long trail! Give me food to sustain me until my work is done! Must this destroyer of my blood and kin go free because Kashawamp has not strength to fulfil the will of his body?" After seven nights and seven days on the trail Kashawamp finally shoots the wolf with his single bullet, but not before the wolf makes a final desperate charge at the Indian, who slashes at the wolf's neck as the beast attacks him. The mortally wounded "Blue Devil" collapses on Kashawamp pinning him to the snow:

There in the snow lay the grizzly Kashawamp on his back. Across his legs lay the huge body of the Blue Wolf, gasping out his last choking gurgles through a ghastly slash in the side of his neck. The trap was still on his front foot, and the leg swollen to three dimensions told of his terrible journey. The long chase was over; here was the end of the trail.

But it is not quite the end of the trail, for a Scottish trapper named McLennan providentially stumbles across the tragic scene:

At first McLennan thought the withered old hulk before him was dead — many a dead man looked more like a live one. But a little spark of that life, which had held so tenaciously to his frail body, yet remained, and the sturdy Scot kept it aflame until he got him back to the settlement.

The story has a happy conclusion; Kashawamp recovers from his ordeal and decides the time has come to retire from trapping: "Then the old Indian left for the West, to spend his remaining days with his relatives. He would hunt no more for his mission was fulfilled. He had seen the end of the long trail."[14]

After the publication of "The End of the Trail" Mack wrote no more fiction — at least none that was ever published. Instead, he turned to the writing of realistic, descriptive and unsentimental nature stories. Why he abandoned such pieces as "The End of the Trail" is not clear. He later said that the experience of getting such a large cheque from the Associated Sunday Magazines was so unexpected that he "got scared and never did it again."[15] It may also be that the "nature fakers" controversy coincided with his first success at friction and frightened him away from such endeavours and stifled, or redirected, his creative energies. Certainly, Seton and Roberts, while they did not stop writing animal stories after Burroughs' charges, made doubly sure that their characters were true to life.

Interestingly, the "noble savage" character is what makes "The End of the Trail" appear dated. Kashawamp is modelled after his father's old friend at Clearsprings, Kawawap, referred to in Mack's reminiscences as "a surviving Indian of the earliest population."[16] Kashawamp is a standard late-nineteenth-century fictional Plains Indian in sentiment and diction. If the nature fakers charge cautioned writers and naturalists not to ascribe human characteristics to wild animals, no such controversy prevented the stylized and stereotyped portyal of Indians in twentieth-century fiction.

In spite of the nature fakers controversy Mack still wanted to be a writer. When he finally uprooted himself and went to New York, he did so with the expectation that his art school diploma would enable him to teach art at the Winnipeg Collegiate. Instead, he found that his courses in journalism and commercial writing, his considerable and original knowledge of natural history, and his photographic expertise gave him a combination of assets that would make him a highly successful nature writer. Soon after his arrival in Brooklyn he met several influential editors, including his contemporary Edward Cave, the new editor of Recreation magazine. Cave was born in 1878 in Simcoe County, Ontario, where his parents farmed. Cave, himself a nature writer, later became editor of Boys' Life and Field and Stream. Mack recalled in 1977 that Cave had been a "pretty good" friend to him: "Just before I went to art school in Brooklyn, New York, I had sold a story to editor Ed Cave of Recreation Magazine. When he heard I was in Brooklyn, he asked me to call. Ed was a Canadian too."[17]

Mack's descriptive, well-written and illustrated articles secured him another important patron, G. O. Sheilds, the former editor of Recreation and the popularizer of the work of Ernest Thompson Seton. Just as Seton had come under Sheild's wing in 1896-97, so

49

did Mack fifteen years later. He later recalled the decisive influence on his young life of Sheilds and *Recreation* magazine:

The material for the little magazine about hunting and fishing was supplied by amateur writers and photographers. It was the first magazine to which in my youth I subscribed and I read it while it lived. In 1911, while an art student in Brooklyn, I met its founder and editor, G. O. Sheilds, then retired, and several times had dinner in his bachelor apartment in the Bronx. Naturally I discussed the art work published in Recreation. He said he had paid very little for anything but cited the rise of E. T. Seton from a start in his magazine. As Sheilds told it to me, Seton Thompson, then unknown, had brought in a story and drawings. The editor recognized the merit of both [and soon] E. T. Seton was sliding down the ways of fame and fortune.[18]

Mack clearly saw himself in Seton's shoes, and indeed his next few years as a successful writer were the most exciting of his life. Within a few months he was selling articles to the other pre-eminent outdoors periodical, *Outing* magazine; he recalled he "earned a good deal more than pay my board."[19] He sold so many stories that he was able to buy a motorcycle. His photographs, like Seton's drawings, helped make his stories acceptable to publishers. He recalled that Edward Cave had examined his photographs on their first meeting in 1911.

In the course of our conversation he asked me who did my photoprinting? I pleaded guilty of course. He said "Look here!" and pulled my story out of a drawer with two sets of photo illustrations. One set was mine; the other set was made by the professionals — I had the latter beaten by a mile! ... He was a good customer. I sold him several stories through the years.[20]

The nature fakers controversy was not lost on Mack. As a result of it he adopted a highly descriptive and accurate style similar to that of Charles G. D. Roberts. W. J. Keith, in his analysis of Roberts' prose, calls this the "anecdote of observation." This is "a sketch rather than a story, and attempts no more than a straightforward presentation of a simple natural occurrence."[21] The result is a somewhat detached prose that often avoids the use of the first person altogether. Mack refers for example to himself in one early story as "the naturalist," "the sportsman," "the hunter" and "the human intruder." Ultimately he carried the "anecdote of observation" to its logical conclusion by excluding human beings altogether from his outdoor stories: this was the ultimate reaction against nature faking.

Yet it was exactly this detached but highly descriptive and entertaining style that ensured the success of his stories. In late 1912 or early 1913, just about a year after his arrival in New York, *Outing* magazine commissioned him to write a book on the birds of Manitoba. The result, *Out With the Birds* published in 1913, emphasizes all his best qualities that as a naturalist would typify his later work. The reviewer for the New York *Nation* called *Out With the Birds* an "uncommonly good book":

Mr. Laing is a close and sympathetic observer and he writes well about what he sees. His description of the "dancing" of the sharp-tailed grouse, illustrated by photographs taken at short range, is a contribution of considerable value to the literature of that subject, and one must admire his candor in saying "What that long daily 'hoe-down' means to the birds I am unable to state. At one time I thought I knew. That was before I had learned to get right among the revellers; now after many hours spent with them I am much wiser but still mystified." Mr. Laing is evidently not one of those nature-students who finds it convenient to read their thoughts into the actions of animals they observe.[22]

Mack took this praise to heart. As a mature writer he completely departed from such fictional stories as "The End of the Trail," and made a conscious decision to avoid the charge of untruthfulness to nature that was frequently levied against the Setonian school of natural history writing. In one of his early books on geese he makes quite explicit his desire to avoid what to him was an old-fashioned kind of literature:

I almost hesitate to write of the Canada Goose, a bird for which I have so much admiration that if I tell of him as I feel I might be dubbed sentimental, a nature faker, or put in that class of those who must see in their wild things all the attributes of the human being. All of which heaven forbid! For were I to inject into my goose too much of the human I would be flattering the latter! Wawa [the Canadian Goose] is the exponent of all virtue in wild things.[23]

Ultimately perhaps he went too far by omitting altogether the human element from his stories. Writing to ornithologist J. H. Fleming in 1920 he set forth his philosophy in these succinct words:

"Take them in the aggregate and by and large the two-legged things in human shape masquerading around the woods and trails as outdoor folk here are for the most part pigs!"[24] Yet discernible in some of his stories is a Setonian or Edwardian element that he did not disregard as "fake," or even sentimental, and that is the use of pseudo-Indian or pet names as story titles. This tendency has been referred to by biologist Ian McTaggart Cowan as the "personalization cult" that characterized so much natural history writing at the turn of the twentieth century. It was appropriate and acceptable that writers, emulating Seton in Canada and Rudyard Kipling in British India, should give their animals pet names. To the modern eye some of Mack's story titles appear affected and quaint, such as "Garoo, Chief Scout of the Prairies," "Mowitch to the Minute," "Page Mr. Bubo" and "Spying on the Tribe of Wawa."

In the years immediately preceding the First World War, Mack enjoyed considerable success writing about Manitoban natural history for the major North American magazines. He soon mastered his own distinctive voice, writing for a new audience with new tastes. His camera work combined with his own descriptive, realistic prose style was "state of the art." By divesting the nature stories of Seton and Roberts of every trace of overt sentimentality, he helped carry the Canadian nature story into the twentieth century.

V

Anxious to get all he can
The United States, 1911-1917

I RECALL HOW YOUR MOUSTACHE CRACKLED
WITH FIRE WHEN YOU FOUND OUT THE TIRE
WAS FLAT. THE FACT THAT IT WAS
ONLY FLAT ON THE BOTTOM SIDE, SEEMED
TO MAKE NO DIFFERENCE TO YOU.

— *Smith M. Johnson to Hamilton Laing*
May 26, 1930[1]

As a boy Mack had been able to draw with skill and realism. "I drew quite well too at an early age," he wrote. "When just a kid I used to make pencil sketches of my friends. They looked like the subjects too who thought it was fun. So did I."[2] Later, at the Winnipeg Collegiate, he received two years of drawing instruction from art teacher Miss B. F. Stewart, who praised his efforts as the "best in the class."[3] At Christmas 1910, the Manitoban artist Beverly Sharman had advised him to apply to the Pratt Institute in Brooklyn, New York, where several of her friends had gone. Mack recollected his decision of Christmas 1910: "Now it was that I determined to shape my life by steering a new course. If I was to teach — and I was very successful and liked my work, I felt that I wanted to teach only one or two things, and chose drawing because I had always been good at it."[4] Formerly a rural schoolteacher in Manitoba and a mistress at St. John's Ladies' College, Winnipeg, Beverly Horsman had married Francis Sharman, a sheep farmer, in the 1890's. The Sharmans lived with their three children just south of Oak Lake, where Mrs. Sharman kept alive her love of teaching by giving private lessons in French and art. She met Mack in 1903 when her son, Eddie, one of his pupils from nearby Runnymead School, invited him home for the weekend. She took a keen interest in the talented young naturalist and taught him a very

53

representational, realistic style of drawing and painting. Ada Dillon, another of her pupils, contended that "She was particularly clever in portraying animals. The horses' heads which she did were so life-like and beautiful. A lion and lioness were so realistic that a visiting dog barked at them."[5]

Mack journeyed to New York in the late summer of 1911, having resigned from his comfortable and well-paying job at Oak Lake. He found an apartment at 73 St. James Place, Brooklyn, and settled in for what he considered "three of the most pleasant years of a long life."[6] But they were also agonizing years, when he juggled teaching, painting and writing as possible careers.

Despite his twenty-eight years Mack had no trouble fitting into Brooklyn's student life. He recalled:

At school I had pleasant companions. You had to be high school graduate or better to be enrolled: there were three college graduates. Age made no difference, nor sex, though females were in the majority. I was the oldest male and the boys called me "Gramp." Two female greyheads worked on easels and I heard them called "Aunty" by their juniors. One thing I liked about my companions was that the office management had accepted the application of students from about every state in the Union as well as the one from Canada. When in the course of getting acquainted I asked a little blue-eyed beauty where she hailed from, she replied "I reckon you ought to know!" Texas. Good humour always prevailed. I never heard a student express any opinion on another's work; that was left to the instructor.[7]

The Pratt Institute at the time was as much a technical school as an art school, offering courses in everything from silversmithing to architectural design. The Institute was proud of its practical, non-academic character.[8] Mack enrolled in the School of Fine and Applied Arts. He participated in the Life Class, the Pictorial Illustration Class and the Commercial Illustration Class. According to the Assistant Director of Alumni Resources at the Pratt,

Mr. Laing appears to have been a serious student whose grades ranged from C to B+. Various comments from his instructors written on Laing's registration card include "serious," "eager learner," "anxious to get all he can," "hard worker," "very wide awake," "clear headed" and "very reliable."[9]

Mack's journals give no indication that he was interested in women before he met his future wife Ethel in 1915; indeed, if we take his word for it, he did nothing but paint, write and take photographs. "My Pratt Institute days slipped by quickly," he recalled, "I described them as 'painting nudes by day and whacking a typewriter by night,' exaggeratiton of course as I usually stopped for six hours shuteye."[10] He preserved, however, several photographs of a Pratt contemporary named Jessie MacDonald, a dark-haired woman in stylish dress always posed in Brooklyn parks. Another friend was a Newfoundlander named Archie Ash who died in 1917 fighting in France. Another two close friends were his former pupils from Manitoba, Ada Dillon and Edna Burns. He wrote to Ada in January 1914 recording the misery of the Brooklyn unemployed and homeless.

A strong wind blowing from the North. Zero weather here causes as much suffering as 40° below in Man. Houses are not built for it; people do not clothe as warmly. Yesterday there were over 2000 homeless came to the Municipal Lodging Houses for shelter here. Think of it. Think of it — and no one is admitted more than three times in a month. A city like this is a cruel place. Not long ago a chap stopped me as I was on my way to school and asked me for something to get his breakfast. Said that he was down and out and was from Montreal — was a French Canadian. I had my doubts by his tongue; but he was blue with cold and I gave him a quarter.[11]

Several of the drawings and portraits completed by Mack at the Pratt Institute are technically very good. They show sound composition and display a careful, sensitive portrayal of his subjects. But he seems to have been less than enthusiastic at all times about his painting. As he explained to Ada Dillon in 1914,

I am in the deep water these days with my oils. Started my first life study in oils last week. It is very hard. Thought I was going to make my masterpiece in portrait too, and today I worked like a Trojan and found that the darned thing got worse the longer I stuck at it. It is not so hard to get the first frank impression of a face, but finishing it is the rub. I "finished" it alright.[12]

In the last few years of Mack's life the Town of Comox arranged an exhibition of his early portraits and painting. Gerald Tyler, a Vancouver art expert, came to assess the paintings and called Mack Laing a "portrait painter of considerable excellence" who "could have been Canada's greatest portrait painter."[13] It is perhaps surprising therefore that he confessed little interest in the course of modern art. Indeed he showed considerable hostility toward the new artistic developments that were sweeping the western world before the First World War. In 1913 he visited the epochal "Armoury Show" in New York when the painters Picasso, Kandinsky and Braque, among others, displayed their work.[14]

I recall with a shudder that around 1912, in company with several art students, I attended the first public display of the new Cubism in New York, where I saw the famous "Lady Descending the Staircase" and a plaster cast of a Venus with the neck of a Trumpeter Swan. I would not sully a fair name by calling this show an art exhibit. I paid "two bits" to see it and felt terribly swindled at that.[15]

Mack could not stand for any painting that was not strictly representational or realistic. It was not that he was simply old-fashioned or reactionary; his attitude towards Cubism reflects his attitude towards writing and existence in general. He felt he had to write about things or paint things strictly as they were, or as he perceived them. However, he lacked the confidence and perhaps the imagination to transform the fundamental visual reality of a model or a Trumpeter Swan into something other than that which met his eye, because he believed in what he called the "sacred truth of natural history,"[16] that is, the realism and integrity of the world as it is.

The art of photography was particularly suited to Mack's temperament because photographs, or at least the photographs that he desired, captured the predictable, truthful visual reality and nothing more. He had the ability to isolate the simple beauty of the natural world. However, his clear and tidy mind made him a devastating critic. Throughout his career he habitually clipped magazines for his own reference use. No bird artist escaped his censorious pen. For example, as a young man Fenwick Lansdowne did a series of bird paintings for the *Star Weekly* of Toronto. Mack wrote on them such comments as "Head not falcon. Bill too small. Eye too low in head," and "Pose not good — Right wing wrong." Similarly, a pair of Baltimore Orioles by John Bates Abbot were "Very poor. Head too large. Tail too short. Feet too small." Some geese by Hans Kleiber showed "very good anatomy." On an inoffensive-looking photograph of Princess Alexandra he wrote, "The smile of a Goshawk — cold as ice."[17] He even found fault with some of the plates submitted in 1924 by the bird painter Allan Brooks — whom he worshipped — to Percy Taverner's *Birds of Western Canada*. "I surely thought the pictures by Brooks were fine," he wrote Taverner, "but two I did not like at all — 3 in fact. The Band-tail pigeon, the hooting blue grouse, and the g-wing gull. Latter was too dark. The other attitudes were not good, to my notion."[18]

Every summer while at the Pratt, Mack returned to his camp at Oak Lake which he called *Heart's Desire*. His parents, meanwhile, had retired to Oregon in 1911 because of its mild winters and because his sister Nellie Waddell had settled there. At Oak Lake he experimented with new camera techniques, reactivated his Boy Scout troop, wrote prolifically, and impressed his old teaching friends with his progress. Fanny Sharman, the daughter of his old tutor in art, recalled that in the summer of 1914 "He came over on his motorcycle from the lake, bringing his collection of sketches made at the Pratt Institute, Brooklyn, N.Y., chiefly in oils, and they were put up all round the room for our enjoyment. We could see that great progress had been made during the period at Pratt."[19] His major reason for returning to Oak Lake was, however, to gather local nature notes for use in his winter writings: for in New York he was known as a Canadian nature writer. After a couple of years at art school he began to look on painting as his winter pastime and nature writing as his passion. Between 1911 and 1915 his well-written, educational and well-illustrated nature stories appeared in the leading American outdoor magazines — large circulation magazines patronized by other Canadian nature writers such as Ernest Thompson Seton, Charles G. D. Roberts and Bonnycastle Dale. His stories were so popular that, in 1913, the Outing Publishing Company brought out his first book, *Out With the Birds*, a compilation of articles on the bird life of Manitoba. Mack's photographs were a major reason for the success of his stories. Previously, nature writers had to provide their own illustrations, usually drawings. At *Heart's Desire* he constructed a darkroom made of prairie sod in order to develop and print his plate glass negatives in the field.[20] He recalled:

In holidays I hied me away from the stifling city back to the Manitoban prairies and Oak Lake where at my beloved *Heart's Desire* I camped and spent my time with some new camera equipment making negatives of the interesting life of the marshes and wildlife generally, anything that would make an illustration of wild life. For now I was a writer.[21]

In 1914, on the eve of the First World War he completed what he not very graciously called his "art spree" and, with the income from his writing bought a 1914 Harley-Davidson motorcycle.[22] The motorcycle would be his trademark until he joined the Royal Flying Corps in 1917: it gave him the mobility, the freedom and the inclination to visit remote areas for hunting or bird life. He soon became a "motorcycle naturalist" — a job description of his own invention — and traversed a large part of North America on the novel machine. In the summer of 1914 he made his first major motorcycle expedition. He drove from New York to Manitoba, and wrote up the story of his trip in *Outing* of May 1915. He gave the story the swashbuckling title "How a Greenhorn Rode from New York to Winnipeg and Enjoyed the Whole Way." After a stop at Oak Lake, he rode on to Winnipeg where he applied for a job teaching art on the staff of the Winnipeg Collegiate. When he walked into the office of the Provincial Superintendent of Schools he fully expected to be welcomed back to Manitoba and offered a job which would have been a fitting end to his hard work and study in the United States. But the Superintendent told him that owing to the "filthy new war depression" they were not hiring any new teachers; instead, they were firing them.[23] For once Mack was in a quandary. He was determined not to go back to rural school teaching. He spent the rest of the camping season at Oak Lake before returning to art school. On his arrival in New York, two of his former instructors "asked me what I came back for and I had no satisfactory answer."[24] Eventually, they allowed him to take six months of postgraduate drawing and painting, though this only postponed the question of what to do with his life. Presumably he did not relish the idea of leaving neutral and peacetime United States for mobilized and depressed Canada, especially when his writing was proving so successful. On his final graduation in 1915 he decided to stay in the United States and write.

1915 was a notable year for another reason: I came to the Y in my way of life. Over the left branch there was the sign ART. Over the right way there was a very different sign! Natural History which really meant writing. It didn't need a judge of the Supreme Court to decide

58

which branch I would take. Art, though I loved it, had let me down. The other branch had paid my board and tuition for the year and bought me another Harley Davidson motorbike.[25]

Yet another factor hastened the abandonment of his art career. In the spring of 1915 Mack's life class had taken their model to the Central Museum, Brooklyn, to "paint her seated among the pillars of the big entrance hall." While doing so, he happened to see in the background some rare Eastern Warblers, whose range did not extend to Manitoba and were thus unknown to him. He was perplexed but determined, at lunch time, to learn the identity of the strange bird.

The director of the museum was a famous ornithologist, famous mainly for his work in the South Seas. I figured he would know the birds in his own back yard, but though the reception of a green ornithologist was doubtful I resolved to try it. I was still smarting a little after being turned over to the office boy when I tried to meet the world-famous Frank Chapman, the author of my ornithological bible. The director was not on duty but his office understudy was very affable and set in to help me. Dr. Francis Harper, a young man with a southern tongue, was a man about my own age.[26]

Harper had graduated in 1913 from Cornell University with a degree in ornithology and in 1914 had worked with P. A. Taverner on the Geodetic Survey of Canada as a naturalist in the Lake Athabasca-Slave Lake area. Harper, on his return, had managed to persuade the Smithsonian Institution to allow him to lead an ornithological expedition to Lake Athabasca. The expedition was planned for 1916. Harper was "affable" and set out to learn more about the enthusiastic young nature lover. In later years Mack delighted in recounting the conversation that got him out of art and into museum work.

HARPER: Laing, did you write that story in *Outing* about White Geese?

LAING: I did.

HARPER: Hell! You did that article on the Rufous Hummer for Doubleday, Page in the present number!

LAING: Guilty as charged.

HARPER: You're master of camera.

LAING: Mebbie part way.

HARPER: Can you skin a bird?

LAING: I've never skinned anything larger than a whooping crane or smaller than a hummingbird.

HARPER: Can you paddle a canoe?

LAING: I own a nice Lakefield. I spend a lot of my holiday in it.

HARPER: And you can shoot, I know. You were the author of that slaughter of geese on the prairie published last fall in *Recreation*.

LAING: There were four of us. I invented the decoys.

HARPER: So you can shoot. What about the rifle?

LAING: I'm dead eye!

HARPER: What are you doing down there daubing paint in an art class?

LAING: I'm a schoolteacher changing over to art. Maybe I'll give it up for Natural History and writing.

HARPER: What are you going to do next summer?

LAING: Heaven knows. Probably camera and typewriter.

HARPER: You're coming with me. I've got an expedition to Lake Athabasca and you'll be my assistant bird man.

After this conversation Mack "went back to daubing paint at a striking young lady in commanding still life surroundings."[27]

By early summer 1915, with his formal education finally behind him, he decided to join his family in Oregon for the winter, fully expecting to join Harper in Athabasca the following summer. In June he bought a new 1915 three-speed eleven-horsepower Harley-Davidson with a top speed of thirty miles per hour, which he named "Barking Betsy." With a waterproof army poncho, an army blanket, an air pillow and his Boy Scout hat, he set out across the United States for Oregon. He left Brooklyn in July 1915 and met his younger brother Jim, a manual training teacher in Winnipeg, at Fairmont, Nebraska. Jim was driving Mack's "rejuvenated" 1914 Harley-Davidson which he had left behind in Winnipeg the previous fall. The brothers were accompanied by a young Californian, Smith Johnson, for the duration of the final leg of the trip across the southern desert to San Francisco.[28]

By all accounts it was an extraordinary trip. In places the "Pacific Highway" consisted of no more than dabs of paint marked on a fence alongside a sagebrush trail. Ravines, in places forty yards across, had to be forded, and in other places the riders plotted short-cuts on their map regardless of terrain. Every day Mack got up at dawn because Barking Betsy's twin motor "always purred most contentedly in the cool morning." He took photographs and notes at every stage because "of course I knew I would do a couple or three stories on travelling light on 2 wheels, sleeping out."[29] And he got much good story material from his trip. In the "backwilds" of Nevada, for example, he met a grizzled old prospector driving a team of mules. "When I asked him what he did to keep his body and soul within hailing distance, he said his business was 'locatin' gold-mines."[30] He slept in a bed only once during the trip when, after bedding down one night somewhere in Illinois, a swarm of mosquitos visible "in the failing light against the sky," began to descend upon him. The worst part of the trip were the rainy "black dirt states" when the motorcycle had to be pushed through axle-deep mud," he remembered, "but after we hit Colorado our troubles of that sort were over; and the American Desert — Colorado, Utah and Nevada — were great for I met some *new birds* and heard some *new* songs."[31] Predictably, his book about the trip, *The Transcontinentalist, or The Joys of the Road*, contains as much natural history as it does travel description. He faithfully recorded every bird seen or heard: "When I was young I had the ears of an owl," he recalled. "I built up in my head a dictionary of bird songs, chirps and noises so I was 'at home' with birds from coast to coast. Transcontinentalizing I could hear familiar birds in the woods over the popping of my Harley."[32]

After a stop at the World's Fair in San Francisco, where Smith Johnson stayed behind, the two "sun-baked rough riders" headed north to Oregon where after 4,654 miles on the road, and only nine miles from his parents' door, Mack's Harley broke down. He later called it the worst "stall in my life"; he had to be "bailed" into Portland.[33] He had forgotten to adjust his carburetor, tuned to the high and hot desert altitudes, upon reaching the moist sea-level air of the Pacific. Later in the day he and Jim finally reached home. A day or two later he went out to Jenning's Lodge, fourteen miles up the Columbia River from Portland, to visit his sister Jean and her husband Harry Robinson. As he approached their house he saw a woman on the veranda holding a baby in her arms. She was Ethel

May Hart, a nineteen-year-old Oregonian hired by the Robinsons to babysit their adopted son John.[34]

Mack was now aged thirty-two. There was a war in Europe but the United States was still neutral. As an exiled Canadian he spent the next two and a half years waiting for the Lake Athabasca Expedition to materialize; from 1916 it was postponed to 1917, and in that year, when both Mack and Francis Harper enlisted, it was postponed indefinitely. In the meantime, with the help of Barking Betsy, Mack had perfected the art of being a motorcycle-naturalist. Prior to his enlistment in 1917 he wrote for *Recreation* and *Outdoor Life* on a regular basis. His two new magazines were *Canadian Magazine* of Toronto and *Sunset: The Pacific Monthly* of San Francisco. For the Canadian magazine he continued to work up material from Oak Lake and from his old nature and hunting diaries: such pieces as "Little Warden of the Prairie Fields" and "My Manitoba Marshes." For *Sunset*, however, he wrote an extraordinary series of fifteen invigorating articles between 1916 and 1920 based on mountain climbing, hunting, and trips of exploration in the American Pacific Northwest. Some of these outrageously titled escapist stories are "On Barking Betsy to the Mountain," "Barking Betsy and the Chilled Volcano," and "By Motor and Muscle to Mt. Hood." He also contributed more staid articles to such magazines as *Tall Timber, Country Life in America, St. Nicholas* and *Scientific American* between 1915 and 1918. In 1917, he bought his third Harley-Davidson from the sale of these articles, which made him, on the average, about $35 each.

In 1916, when the Pratt Institute asked him to state his occupation for its annual yearbook, he replied "Magazine Writer and Illustrator."[35] But Mack's swashbuckling days in the western States were drawing to a close. The United States joined the war on Canada's side. Still expecting the war to carry on for several more years, in November 1917 he travelled to New York to the British Army Recruiting Mission, where he signed on to do his "belated bit" with the Royal Flying Corps. The officer in charge raised an eyebrow at him when he said he was a magazine writer, so he amended his occupation to "Motorcycle Rider."[36]

Mack's six years in the United States had taken him from a tentative start as an art student in New York to a successful and prolific nature and travel story writer in Portland, Oregon. But he had also returned to Manitoba during the holidays to camp at Oak Lake, and he had made contact with the museum world. Apart from his articles for *Sunset*, his focus had remained Canadian. Though the United States had been good to him, his Manitoba training as a naturalist, photographer and writer stood him in good stead. He had demonstrated his writing durability with one book and about fifty articles published by the outdoor magazines. His career had only just begun, but first he had to return to Canada to help defeat what he termed "a strong and ruthless foe."[37]

Laing: The Early Years

PLATE 1   Mack's father, William Laing, soon after his arrival in Canada. PABC 96730

PLATE 2   Mack's mother, Rachel Melvina Laing, as a young woman. PABC 96731

PLATE 3 The Laing family, Winnipeg, 1905. *Top row, left to right*: Rachel (Nellie), Mrs. Laing, Mack. *Bottom row, left to right*: James (Jim), William Laing, Jean (Jennie). PABC 96630

PLATE 4   Spring Bank Farm, Clearsprings, Manitoba, August 1939. Photograph: Mary and Willie Laing. PABC 96626

PLATE 5   The Clearsprings Literary Society, 1898. Mack is standing at the extreme upper left. His cousin, David Laing, is kneeling at front centre. Provincial Archives of Manitoba, N7017, Mrs. Margaret Turnpenny's Scrapbook.

PLATE 6   Student in Winnipeg, 1906, at the home of his parents. PABC 96717

PLATE 7   Winnipeg Collegiate Institute, *c.* 1910. Mack was a student here from 1898 until 1901. Provincial Archives of Manitoba, N5222

PLATE 8 The soccer player, at Oak Lake, 1908. PABC 96716

PLATE 9   The school principal, Oak Lake, about 1910. PABC 96718

PLATE 10   A Manitoba goose hunt,
about 1908. PABC 96698

PLATE 11   Scout Henry Stevens at Pipestone Creek, near Oak Lake, Manitoba,
about 1910. PABC 96715

PLATE 12   Mack with his Boy Scouts, Oak Lake, about 1911. PABC 96707

PLATE 13   "Heart's Desire," Mack's island camp at Oak Lake, about 1910. *Left to right*: Jacob Norquay, Mack, Dr. Andrew Alford. PABC 96724

PLATE 14 Painting class at Pratt Institute, Brooklyn, New York, about 1914. Mack is seated at left. PABC 96718

PLATE 15 Class at Pratt Institute, 1914. Mack is standing at left. PABC 96635

PLATE 16 Roadside lunch with "Barking Betsy," his Harley-Davidson motorcycle, 1914. PABC 96638

PLATE 17   An early field camp. PABC 96732

PLATES 18-20 The *transcontinentalists* tackle the American desert, 1915. PABC 96639, 96641 and 96640

PLATE 21   The motorcycle naturalist: Crane hunting at Ebor, Saskatchewan,
1914. PABC 96637

PLATE 22 Near the observation tower, wearing the pith helmet and uniform of a Royal Flying Corps Instructor. Camp Beamsville, Ontario, 1918. PABC 96769

VI

Back to Canada
1917-1919

I DON'T SUPPOSE ANYONE EVER HAD MORE VARIETY
IN LIVING THAN I HAVE. I'VE NEVER MADE ANY
MONEY, BUT I HAVE HAD AN AWFUL LOT OF FUN
OUT OF THIS OLD WORLD.

— *Hamilton Laing to Percy Taverner*
May 6, 1936[1]

On November 13, 1917, Hamilton M. Laing, naturalist, motor-cyclist and magazine writer, visited the British Army Recruiting Mission in New York City where he did "the necessary stunts to be pronounced soldier of the King."[2] He was told he could expect to be overseas within six weeks.[3] That afternoon he visited his old art school haunt, Prospect Park, Brooklyn, where he wrote gloomily in his diary:

Prospect under warm sun, leaves down, fountain playing in Vale of Kashmir — recalls other days and folks. The Statues at the entrance above the Triumphal Arch recall Archie. The Vale recalls others. In the Wistaria Arch in warm sun I sat awhile. Sparrows (English) came to be fed. Sparrow voice (wild) talked from the shrubbery: the rhododendrons below me — and a fox sparrow dug away industriously in the leaves where he thought he was hidden. A single ray played on his ruddy coat at times. He dug a hole in the leaves.[4]

The next day he returned to the Recruiting Mission where he swore an "oath of Allegiance to his Majesty." He remarked despondently: "To one who has lived 6 years in a Republican country, such an oath would seem to need revision — sounds like the feudalism of William of Normandy — which it is."[5]

On the afternoon of the fifteenth he arrived at the Royal Flying Corps (R.F.C.) Recruits Depot in Toronto for three weeks of basic

65

training. Here, he met recruits from as far away as New Zealand, British Columbia, the United States and England. Every spot on earth seemed represented. "Is it a war or a crusade?" he wondered.[6] By the nineteenth, he and hundreds of other recruits were being drilled on the grounds of the University of Toronto by a Sergeant-Major Brewer, an Englishman with a "voice like a Siberian tiger."

"Goosestep, about! Form fours! ... By God! Don't you know your right foot from your left?" "Never saw the like of you, by Christ!" "Take him away, Corporal, and see what you can do with him!"[7]

During both world wars Canada served as the Imperial and Commonwealth Training Centre, drawing recruits from all over the British Commonwealth and North America. The First World War Canadian Air Training organization had its headquarters in Toronto and its training and maintenance establishments elsewhere in Ontario. At the Armistice it numbered just under 12,000 staff members and trainees; ultimately Mack became a member of the staff. At the age of thirty-four he was four years too old to qualify as a pilot, but his practical talents and teaching experience meant that he rose quickly through the ranks of the R.F.C.

From his arrival at the Recruits Depot until his transfer on December 4, 1917, to the Airplane Repair Park, also in Toronto, he spent entire days on stove fatigue, sweeping fatigue, cookhouse fatigue, sanitary fatigue and parade ground drills. He recorded with dismay in his diary the appearance of a "Sergt — new one — a beauty, a fuzz on upper lip — O my God!"[8] Sanitary Fatigue (referred to by the recruits as S—— house fat-i-gue) was his least favourite activity; his diaries reflect a genuine disdain for the English officers who ordered him to wash out toilets, mop floors and polish brass. "Doubtless all very necessary," he wrote, "in the King's army but going somewhat against the grain of Canadian timber. Have been used to see Englishmen take orders not give them!" He was so disgusted that on Christmas Day he wrote in his dary: "My first Xmas in jail." On Boxing Day his English friend Scotty joked to him: "Daddy, what did you do in the Great War?" "Oh, chiefly sanitary fatigue."[9] On December 28 he developed measles — a serious disease for an adult — and spent the next three weeks in quarantine. The only good thing about it was that he was served toast.

On March 2, 1918, after three months at the Repair Park, Mack was posted to the R.F.C. School of Aerial Gunnery which at that time had its winter quarters at the Leliaferra Camp in Dallas, Texas. Here, as an Instructor of Gunnery, he was given an opportunity to exhibit two of his latent abilities: his skill and knowledge of weaponry and his experience gained through ten years of teaching. The School of Aerial Gunnery was the last school the potential pilot had to attend before being sent overseas. The three-week course taught the trainee flying, manoeuvring and air tactics.[10]

But even here he had to perform cookhouse and sanitary fatigue before receiving his instructional papers. "Serving meals is a study in human animals," he wrote. "One takes 3 slices and a whole bowl of jam . . . another is too stiff to forage and takes what comes with a sneer; one coaxes for more jam, another turns up his nose, another goes to the kitchen and uses his pull . . . the animal in the mob is very close to the surface." Sanitary fatigue was the most miserable part of his work. In mid-March 1918 he wrote:

Nothing new in the job. Dwell mentally on man's ways as a so called social and civilized being and sanitary fatigue doubtless was accountable for views. When an intelligent human has to spend a day picking up match moxes, cigarette butts, toilet paper and mop up and scrape out after his brother animals, there is something wrong either with the system, the man himself or his brother animals. Sanitary fatigue convinces a man that his fellows are not a little lower than the angels but a shade higher than plain pigs.[11]

Why was this educated and "intelligent human" with ten years' teaching experience given such a job? In part, any new recruit might expect these duties; but in part also, the class system of the British army may have worked against him. The R.F.C. advertised that its ideal officer was a "clean bred chap," bearing "the ear marks of a gentleman," able to "speak the King's English" and ideally possessing a little university education.[12] Mack was a practical man with a belief in individual merit and no time for such niceties. The oath of allegiance to the King had made him wonder "Why does man cling so desperately to outworn traditions — mostly fake?"[13] He might have inherited his antipathy towards the Anglo-Canadian officer class from his Irish-Canadian mother and his Scottish father; his six years in populist and progressive America may also have influenced his attitude. In June 1918 he committed his thoughts to his diary:

Someone today talked on democracy of the Army. It is a favourite topic with disgruntled ones. For a very good and valid reason that there can be little democracy in the army — any army. At least the prevailing idea is such. As proof he gave the facts that the rookie gets the short and dirty end of the stick; that the private is not treated with the respect that a commission is; that a Sergeant is better fed han a private yet works less; that the former is also paid more and does less; that the whole system is an absolutism comparable in every respect with the most conservative of States and churches — Germany and Papal respectively, that an army was undemocratic, etc., etc. And he was right ... when one gets a crust or heel of a loaf with every slice to each meal, 3 times a day, it induces thought.[14]

In spite of all this Mack progressed rapidly through the instructional ranks of the R.F.C. In April 1918 the School of Aerial Gunnery removed itself from Texas to the town of Beamsville on the southern shore of Lake Ontario, opposite Toronto. By July Mack had attained the rank of Instructor of Gunnery; at the same time, the R.F.C. changed its name to the Royal Air Force. According to Professor S. J. Wise, Camp Beamsville at the time "consisted of three squadrons with a total establishment of 54 aircraft. From the start the school introduced new flying techniques. Shooting at static targets on the range was discarded in favour of travelling targets, so that students could immediately become accustomed to deflection sights and deflection firing."[15] Mack's first job at Camp Beamsville was as timekeeper in the main aerodrome, but on July 19, 1918, he was posted to the observation tower on the shore of Lake Ontario. Here, far from sanitary fatigue, at last he had a responsible job. On July 25 he described his situation to a friend in Manitoba:

Out from shore at half a mile are several silhouettes of planes floating on the water. The cadets practice shooting at them from the air. They use a Vickers machine gun synchronized to shoot between the revolutions of the propeller. They come along high, then nose down, steer the gun by steering the whole plane and cut loose in bursts of ten shots. There is a tall tower on the lakeshore and it is the duty of 2 of us to stay in the tower alternately and take note of where the bullets land.

Of course they usually land in the lake, but more complete data are required at the aerial office. This work is much easier than the drome. It is hard on the eyes and demands good sight and a ready use of the binoculars, but we have only about 6 hours each a day. We live on the range, 8 of us; camp here is free and easy, — a sort of cross between military life and a Sunday School picnic.[16]

There were other benefits to living away from the main base at Beamsville. The first was an eighty-three-year-old named Philip Tifford who lived in a brick house at the base of the observation tower. "He is so firmly rooted to the soil that when the R.A.F. tried to move him from his quarters," wrote Mack, "he told them to go ahead and shoot; his walls are 18" thick. He has a wonderful memory. Told me of the days of primeval forests — not a stump of which remains."[17] Mack also got to know the neighbouring farming families who invited him to tea and provided him with fresh fruit at his lakeside location.[18] He was permitted to go up in airplanes and enthused that: "This country is beyond words when seen from above, with the eyes of the eagle!"[19]

Yet the job was marred weekly by tragic airplane crashes, many of which he witnessed from his observation tower. For example, at 6:15 in the evening of July 17, 1918, a Lieutenant Glendenning crashed his plane. He died at seven o'clock the next morning. Mack wrote:

How the world goes on mindless of those who live in it, — live and toil and fight, love and hate. Last evening I saw a fearful horrible tragedy, a fellow being and a prince of men; swirl his machine with a spin, crash horribly and then burn as we sought to draw him from the flaming ruin. What a fierce unconquerable thing is fire when it is master and knows it! The best we could offer, our best prayer for him when finally we dragged him out and deposited his disfigured body in the ambulance was that the end might come soon.[20]

Life in the R.F.C. also had its advantages, and Mack did not neglect his interest in natural history any more than necessary. Because he had little chance for bird study at the Recruits Depot in Toronto, he was reduced to describing human behaviour in ornithological terms. For example, in November 1917:

Men as well as women are like geese. Before lights out, nightly a hullabaloo arises. One chap across the hall makes loud-voiced quacking, as

I have heard a honker do when the assembled flock finds night quarters at dusk. Sleepy cries of "O shut up!" "Rest y're face!" "Close your yap!" "Quit your barking" all had no effect on the yapper.[21]

Texas, described by a friend as "a never-ending delight to one of your ilk," offered him the opportunity to study the birds of a part of the continent entirely new to him.[22] An unexpected surprise with far-reaching consequences awaited him on his return to Ontario in the spring of 1918. An anonymous friend — possibly Francis Harper or G. O. Sheilds — put a notice in the *Auk*, the American ornithological journal, that "H. M. Laing No. 170004 R.F.C." was stationed in Toronto.[23] This short notice changed Mack's life by bringing him into contact with three of the major figures in twentieth-century Canadian ornithology: Hoyes Lloyd, J. H. Fleming and Percy Taverner.

The first was Hoyes Lloyd (1888-1978), then Chemist in Charge of Milk Production at Toronto's Department of Public Health — but soon to be hired by the Dominion Parks Branch to administer the Migratory Birds Treaty of 1917.[24] On May 3, 1918, Lloyd introduced himself in the following way: "I notice in April 'Auk' that a bird man has taken to flying and was stationed in Toronto. If this should reach you and if you are still in Toronto I would be pleased to see you at any time convenient." Ten days later Mack replied from Camp Beamsville: "Were I still in Toronto I would be very pleased to meet you . . . I am not a flier; am a machine gun instructor. At present I am having a most interesting time on Saturday afternoons with the Ontario birds."[25]

The second ornithologist was J. H. Fleming (1872-1940), a wealthy Torontonian whose collection of bird skins, later deposited at the Royal Ontario Museum, eventually numbered 25,000. He too extended Mack a "pressing invitation" to visit.[26] On the weekend of June 15-16 Mack took the train to Toronto. He visited Lloyd on Saturday and on Sunday he visited Fleming, whose collection he found particularly impressive. In a "wawa" — a talking session that lasted twelve straight hours — Fleming solved about twenty-five ornithological riddles, some of which had been in the back of Mack's mind or in his notes since 1903. Fleming was also familiar with Mack's pre-war nature articles and used his connections at the Toronto *Globe* to land him a job in journalism. In June he wrote

Mack that "Mr. Joffray [of the *Globe*] asked me if I could suggest anyone who could write nature articles and I told him I would think it over, and last night I sent him your address, of course I probably should have asked your permission, but I trust no harm has been done anyway."[27] Mack's articles appeared regularly in the *Globe* from 1918 to 1924 and were met with almost universal praise by naturalists across Canada. They were reprinted in newspapers from New Brunswick to British Columbia.[28] Mack later considered Fleming his most valuable patron, and in 1920 he thanked him for his help. "I'll not soon forget the pleasure of my first visit to your museum. It was such a relief after that bloody camp that I wanted to camp out right there."[29]

By July 1918 Hoyes Lloyd and Mack Laing had become close friends and were exchanging letters on a regular basis. Shortly after meeting Lloyd, Mack was promoted from the timekeeping job at the Beamsville aerodrome to the observation tower on the lakeshore. He wrote to tell Lloyd that with his telescope and binoculars, "I can see across the lake and determine what you are having for breakfast." Lloyd replied, congratulating him on his promotion: "I am glad you have a better job. I suppose brains are appreciated in the end even in the R.A.F."[30] Both Lloyd and Fleming encouraged Mack in his bird watching, and he began to compile a systematic list of all the birds visible from his tower. "I think my most enjoyable find," he explained to Lloyd on August 24, "was the little Green Heron."

Had never met him previously. Below the tower is a slight depression — an old creek bed — and here on the 16th I met him. 1 pair — 2 f. rather, were fishing and frogging about the pot holes. A truly magnificent bird. From above he was strikingly so. Am reminded of John Burroughs' expression regarding the bluebird — "sky on his back."[31]

Mack's bird observations resulted in his first formal contribution to science, "Lake-shore Bird Migration at Beamsville, Ontario," published in *The Canadian Field Naturalist* of February 1920.[32] He also began a series of articles on the natural history of Beamsville for the Toronto *Globe*, to which Fleming's response was: "Your Beamsville articles are away and ahead the best things you have done. They have been a delight to read not only because they treat of birds I know but your use of simple language is enough to make me envy such powers."[33]

The third eminent Canadian ornithologist to discover Mack was Percy Taverner (1875-1947), the flamboyant and brilliant ornithologist at the National Museum of Canada in Ottawa who had just, in 1919, published the first of his three great works on Canadian ornithology, *Birds of Eastern Canada*. Taverner had been familiar with Mack's articles in *Recreation* and *Outing* since as early as 1915; and, like Lloyd and Fleming, he was anxious to find work for him in Canadian ornithological circles.[34]

Mack finally "emerged from the Beamsville mud" on December 14, 1918. With two kitbags, a haversack, a violin and a music holder on his back, carrying a pair of sturdy army shoes, a swagger stick, a "half-baked discharge," and $35 of "Imperial Bounty," he boarded the train to Exeter, Ontario, to visit his mother's Mack relations. The train was jammed with returning soldiers but "thanks to Darwinian ancestry," he wrote, he managed to clamber aboard.[35] He reached his parents' home in Portland in time for Christmas, and received his final demobilization papers on January 11, 1919. He would never again set foot in Ontario.

His stay of fourteen months in the R.F.C. and R.A.F. was worthwhile, not only on account of the valuable and lasting contacts he had made in Canadian ornithology but also, as Percy Taverner pointed out, because he "assisted in training many of our fliers who later made a good account of themselves at the front."[36] In doing so, he was joined by two other well-known Canadian naturalists, Charles G. D. Roberts and Allan Brooks, both of whom served as instructors in England and France. Mack would later write approvingly of Brooks: "His greatest contribution toward helping to win the war was not in the spectacular, but in the instructional field, teaching his deadly technique to his comrades in arms. There is no tape to measure such war service."[37]

On Mack's return to Oregon at Christmas 1918 he picked up where he had left off before the war, churning out articles based on his wartime nature diaries for the Toronto *Globe*, the Manitoba *Free Press* of Winnipeg, for *Sunset* of San Francisco and *Canadian Magazine* of Toronto. He did all his writing in an upstairs room in the spacious home bought by his parents in the suburbs of Portland, where, among other things, he was only too happy to continue his lifelong war against crows. He wrote to Hoyes Lloyd describing his return to civilian life: "I have been accused by some of my neighbours of breaking city ordinances. A crow used to make himself very busy around here and he doesn't any more. He perched on a telephone pole across the street about 47 yards from my window, the other day, and about that moment the earth rocked."[38] At Portland, his parents and friends helped him with his articles. In one of the very few references to his father in all his writing, Mack related in 1978 that:

Before Ethel came by my father helped me quite a bit. Especially in my newspaper work while I lived with my parents in Portland. I was doing then a newspaper Nature Story for the Saturday editions of two papers: Manitoba *Free Press* and the Toronto *Globe*. I always figured to have a newspaper story ready for typing by lunch time. They were always about 1,200 words each and my first draft of my story was always done in pencil and my Dad was about the only one who could read it! After lunch I would get him up to my room to read aloud the script to me.[39]

But Mack did not plan to stay in the United States. He had made several important and exciting contacts in Canada. Right through the spring of 1919 he was aching to get out of rainy Portland and "back to the Canadian West, where light is good and birds are numerous."[40] One of his best friends in the R.A.F. had been Gus Murchy of Princeton, British Columbia. Mack described him as "a forest ranger, bronco buster and general bad man."[41] He was also a hunter and sportsman. The two had talked late at night in their bunks about the western mountains: Mack about his motorcycle trips in Oregon and Washington, and Gus about the Similkameen Valley and the Liumchin Basin of southwest British Columbia. They had decided that, if they survided the war, they would undertake a full-scale riding and hunting expedition into the Coast Range of British Columbia.

By June 1919, with large batches of articles sent in advance to publishers across North America, Mack was ready for the trip. He boarded "Betsy III," his 1917 Harley-Davidson, and motored north to Vancouver where he visited Francis Mayers, his old teaching colleague from Oak Lake. From Vancouver, he first made a trip to

Vancouver Island to visit curator Francis Kermode and biologist Edward Carter at the British Columbia Provincial Museum in Victoria. After a day and a half there he returned to Vancouver before heading up the Fraser River Valley. At Hope, at the foot of the Coast Range, he wheeled Betsy onto a train which took them over the Hope Range to Princeton, situated in the "land of the big trout" and grizzly bears. Mack found that Gus Murchy had invited a couple of friends along for the trip, namely the Chief Forester of British Columbia, M. Allerdale Grainger, and Mr. Christie, the District Forest Ranger, described by Mack as "good fellows and delightful companions." They spent two weeks in the mountains and three weeks in the low country, travelling altogether 150 miles in a big circle that eventually brought them back to Princeton.[42] Mack kept careful notes on the birds and mammals observed along the way and sent this information to Francis Harper at the U.S. Biological Survey.[43]

He arrived back in Portland in mid-August to find a pile of letters awaiting him. One was from Hoyes Lloyd, who asked him if Barking Betsy was named in honour of an old girl friend. Mack replied: "I never had a sweetheart of that name. If it hadn't been Barking Betsy it would probably have been Growling Gertrude or some other sweet and euphonious name."[44] Another letter was from Francis Harper, who wrote that the U.S. Biological Survey's expedition to Lake Athabasca, postponed since 1916, had finally been approved and would take place the following summer. The expedition was to consist of Francis Harper, Mack Laing and Lord William Percy, an English aristocrat and ornithologist of considerable distinction.[45]

Hoyes Lloyd, meanwhile, was trying in Toronto and Ottawa to find Mack a permanent job in the Canadian Civil Service. No longer a chemist at Toronto's municipal Board of Health, Lloyd, an amateur but respected ornithologist, was now Supervisor of Wild Life Protection in Canada. He was charged with the administration of the Migratory Birds Convention Treaty of 1917. This landmark Canada-U.S. treaty was intended to establish uniform game laws governing the protection of bird life in North America. Migratory bird flyways in much of North America run north-south and many migratory birds instead of dutifully feeding on insects that destroy crops were being slaughtered indiscriminately by market hunters and over-zealous sportsmen in both the United States and Canada. Lloyd's job was to administer the Act, create bird sanctuaries, and "publicize the importance of bird conservation to the Canadian people."[46] It was in his role as publicist that Lloyd tried to bring Mack to Ottawa. He wrote on November 8, 1919, outlining his plan.

Unofficially and without making any promises I would like to know if you would consider a proposition of some kind to be my bird publicity editor or something of that nature. The idea is that I am so busy with manifold duties that not enough newspaper articles and pamphlets are being distributed. . . .[47]

Lloyd later streamlined the job description to read "Editor in the Migratory Birds Division of the Dominion Parks Branch." Mack's job would have been to write "propaganda to acquaint the public with the terms of the Migratory Birds Convention and the need for bird protection in Canada." Mack was encouraged to take the job by his friends Francis Harper, Percy Taverner and J. H. Fleming. In December 1919 Harper — whose father had been brought up on a farm in Ontario — wrote regarding the Ottawa job: "It looks to me like an unusually fine opportunity to do something not alone for yourself but for the great cause of conservation in Canada."[48] Percy Taverner wrote an equally patriotic letter from Ottawa:

Lloyd tells me unofficially that you are considering coming here? Also *sub rosa* that you are contemplating going with Harper and Lord Percy up north. It's none of my affair but I have an interest in our local ornithological circle and I think you would be a valuable acquisition. In fact we have several places where you would be distinctly useful to the [Ottawa Field] Naturalist hence to Canadian ornithology in general and a congenial spirit to us. Hence I think you will readily admit that I have got some stake in the question. I hope that you will not let this proposed expedition prevent you from coming.[49]

Mack did not get the job. It did not materialize. In early 1920 the order went out in Ottawa to economize and the proposed position of Editor in the Migratory Bird Commission was abolished.[50]

At about the same time Lloyd wrote Mack a confidential letter notifying him that the position of Federal Game Officer for Nova

Scotia, New Brunswick and Prince Edward Island would soon be filled. The job of the Game Officer was to enforce the Migratory Birds Treaty in the Maritime provinces; to supervise the work of the Deputy Game Wardens; and to act as a policeman in the cause of bird conservation. The job called for "executive ability," a sound knowledge of ornithology, and preference was to be given to ex-soldiers. Lloyd pressed Mack to apply but the Civil Service Commission awarded the job to a local man, Robie Tufts.[51] Mack was understandably upset because "it would have given me a look at a corner of Canada I have not so far invaded."[52] It is clear from these job possibilities the high regard with which Mack was held as a writer and ornithologist.

By early 1920 things were looking good for Mack: his summer trip to the Similkameen had helped put his wartime R.F.C. experiences behind him, his newspaper columns were making him a household name right across Canada, and it seemed only a question of time before he found a government job in Canada. In the meantime, he got to work busily preparing in advance the dozens of newspaper articles for his six-month absence at Lake Athabasca. He would return to Canada as an oarsman in a Peterboro freight canoe.

VII

Expeditions
1920-1926

HERE WERE NEW WORLDS TO CONQUER, NEW
BIRD VOICES AND OLD ONES WITH NEW ACCENT
OR INTONATION, TO BE INVESTIGATED
ON EVERY HAND.

— Hamilton Laing
Comox, British Columbia, 1922[1]

Mack welcomed the many advantages of his work as a museum collector. There were several good reasons to go out in the field every summer. Museum work offered him the opportunity to visit remote parts of Canada that he could never have visited by motorcycle; allowed him to record and collect new birds, plants and mammals; brought him in contact with amateur and professional naturalists across British Columbia and Canada; permitted him to take specimens and photographs for his private use; provided him with stories and experiences for his winter writing; gave him capable university students to train as field collectors and naturalists; and, most important, museum work paid his travel expenses on top of a reasonable salary. In short, museum work allowed him to apply and combine the various skills he had learned as a hunter, game warden, teacher, naturalist and writer. In spite of all these benefits, his museum work would be tinged with controversy, owing to his involvement in the most acrimonious personality conflict in early twentieth-century Canadian science: that between National Museum rivals Rudolph Anderson and Percy Taverner. Yet he would also find time to settle down at Comox with what he called "a female of the species," Ethel Hart of Portland, Oregon.[2]

In the fall of 1919 the Smithsonian Institution's expedition to the Lake Athabasca region of northern Alberta was finally authorized. Dr. John C. Phillips of Boston, Massachusetts, a wealthy

77

patron and conservationist with a large private collection of birds, agreed to contribute partial living and travel expenses to a party of three naturalists. The purpose of the expedition was to examine the main breeding grounds of migratory North American waterfowl at or near the Athabasca delta; the sponsors hoped to learn the number, distribution, and migration patterns of waterfowl, all of which would, theoretically, enable them to administer more effectively the Migratory Birds Convention Treaty of 1917.[3] Francis Harper, now a Ph.D. candidate at Cornell University, was appointed expedition leader, and he selected Mack as one of two assistant naturalists. He wrote to him early in 1920 advising him to read some of the recent books about Lake Athabasca, including Warburton Mayer Pike's *The Barren Grounds of Northern Canada*. Harper also notified an American friend of a "comparatively tame and dull" book by "some Canadian official" named "Stewart or Fitzgerald, or somebody like that." This was probably Angus Buchanan's *Wild Life in Canada*.[4] The most recent books of a scientific nature were Edward Preble's *A Biological Investigation of the Athabasca-Mackenzie Region* and Ernest Thompson Seton's more readable *The Arctic Prairies*.[5]

The third member of the expedition was originally to have been Lord William Percy, whose shoulder blade had, however, been "badly smashed" during the war. Although he crossed the Atlantic with a "wired together shoulder," Percy's condition worsened and he returned to London.[6] His place was taken by J. Alden "Pop" Loring. Harper notified Mack of the change in personnel in March 1920:

Another still better collector may turn up however, in the course of a day or two, in the person of J. Alden Loring. You may never have heard of him, but he is one of the best, fastest and most experienced collectors in the world. Among other things he was in Africa with T.R. [Theodore Roosevelt]. Years ago he collected for the [U.S. Biological] Survey in Alberta, Florida and Oregon. He once went on a collecting trip to Europe, and farmed in specimens at the rate of 300 per month. If he goes, we'll have to look out that we don't exterminate the Athabasca fauna![7]

Mack recalled that the three naturalists left Fort McMurray, Alberta, on May 11, 1920, and paddled northwards, down the Athabasca River to Lake Athabasca, in two canoes:

One canoe a 20 ft. freight Peterboro to carry 1000 pounds was skippered by J. Alden Loring in the stern. I was its power plant amidship working by means of extension rowlocks a pair of short oars — the smaller canoe, a light 16 ft. model Peterboro was the pet of our chief who was to carry little beside himself.[8]

There are other indications that Francis Harper was the unpopular member of the party. A few years later "Pop" Loring referred to the "serious experiences" they had with Harper, who had served with an American machine-gun battalion in France in 1918.[9] It is not known what these were, but it is known that Harper could not keep up with the highly competitive collecting instincts of Loring or Laing, who recalled that "Loring was high man":

With a few birds added to his mammals he had catalogued well over 500 specimens. I catalogued few mammals but had over 500 birds — twice as many as my chief. Also I had kept a plant press busy all season and taken a lot of photographs with my 5 x 7 illustration camera.

Mack later complained that Harper tended to be "wrong an awful lot when he has to deal with just folks like me."[10] Generally, however, the expedition was a great success. From their headquarters at Chipewyan covered the entire Lake Athabasca region. Harper later told Mack that their "plunder" was the "biggest haul of scientific material in birds, mammals and plants that has ever come out of the Canadian north-west."[11]

The Blackfly was one specimen they did not care to collect, for it plagued the expedition. Mack asserted that "most anything is preferable to having one's neck swelled and corrugated after the manner of an amorous male walrus — as Seton says they did to him."[12] A few years later while collecting at Belvedere, Alberta, Mack discovered a pesticide called "Flytex" which was very effective when used against Blackflies. "I really enjoy the fly now," he wrote to J. H. Fleming, "to see him fill the tent fills me with happiness":

I just shut the door, blow a few whiffs of the dope and then gleefully listen to 'em squeal and fall. When I make my million I am going to outfit a barge at McMurray [with] cargo, Flytex, high pressure firefighting equipment for spraying, and just drift down the river and clean up the fly pests of the region to the 15th or 16th generation removed. I'll invite Harper along. Not Pop Loring, because he didn't

79

mind flies anyhow and used to be devoured with apparent nonchalance.[13]

Much to Mack's disgust the expedition report was never written up and published. In March 1921 Harper's already strained relations with what he called the "bootlickers and bureaucrats" at the U.S. Biological Survey reached a "breaking point" and he notified Mack that he had quit: "Incidentally," he wrote, "I had to turn in all my original notes of last summer's trip — So, as matters stand, there is no chance of a report ever being written on our work."[14] Mack thought otherwise. By 1923 he had completed a semi-popular account of the expedition that carried the confusing title *Three Moniases Down North*. "Monias" is the Cree word meaning Damned Fool White-Man.[15] In later years Mack managed to prod Harper into action, and during their retirement the two of them wrote *Birds of Lake Athabasca 1920*, a monumental 450-page work. Neither book was ever published.

Mack returned home to Portland in the winter of 1920 and continued to write. He had been paid $700 for the seven-months' work at Lake Athabasca. News of future work soon arrived from Taverner who, like Lloyd and Fleming, was anxious to find work for Mack in Canada. Mack recalled:

Toward spring [1921] I got a letter from P. A. Taverner, Chief Ornithologist of the National Museum, Ottawa, asking if I would be available for his assistant in the midsummer field work in S.E. Saskatchewan. I said I would be. Field work was my meat. I had found my niche — and writing about it was [as] exciting as painting pictures.[16]

He replied favourably in March 1921 to Taverner's request to visit his old prairie hunting ground, saying, "I am just as ambitious as I was then and probably a trifle more capable. I have spent so much time in the field on my own hook, that I can't afford to turn down any chance to get paid for going on a picnic."[17] Mack finally met the tall, lanky Taverner (nicknamed P.A.T.) in late May at Cypress Lake, Saskatchewan. He recalled:

I saw across that wondrous prairie what distantly resembled an approaching locomoting ladder. It proved to be P.A.T.... We had scarcely unclasped the friendly grip when there was a loud shout on the air near me, and my new comrade exclaimed "Shoot!" — and

I was barely in time to swing my gun and put down my first big prairie long-tailed curlew. We were on a breeding ground. A male had come to dispute our right.[18]

Shortly afterwards, Taverner informed Fleming that Laing "makes a fine camp mate." Nineteen twenty-one would be the first of five short but productive seasons when Mack would work directly for Taverner. In 1927, in an act that perhaps precipitated his feud with Taverner, mammalogist Rudolph Anderson "stole" Mack from Taverner and turned him into what Taverner termed a "mouse-catcher."[19]

The third member of the 1921 party was summer student and cook D. Alan Sampson of the University of Regina. They visited Cypress Lake and East End, Saskatchewan, and spent the end of the season at *Heart's Desire*, Mack's old camp at Oak Lake, Manitoba, where they were visited by Hoyes Lloyd in July.

Ornithologically and socially the expedition was a great success. Armed with a shotgun as well as a permit to take migratory birds, Mack collected a total of 590 birds, the first of several thousand specimens he would obtain for the National Museum. At East End, Saskatchewan, the collectors stayed at the Gower Ranch, owned by Laurence B. Potter, an active naturalist well known in ornithological circles. Characteristically, he and Mack remained regular correspondents into the 1960's. He recalled that at Oak Lake he was "among former and generous friends." The first was William Beveridge, a School Inspector and a friend from Mack's early teaching days. On weekends, Beveridge took him to such birdy places as the Assiniboine Valley. They travelled in Beveridge's "flivver." Another friend was teen-ager Herman Battersby — a "very keen young naturalist" — who collected for Mack several specimens of rare pouched mice from his farm near Oak Lake. The Robert Alford family of Runnymead, with whom Mack had boarded in 1903, took him shooting as of old and placed their car at his disposal. A fourth friend was his old Boy Scout trooper Henry Stevens. A trooper indeed, as it was Stevens who paddled the canoe while Mack sat in the front with gun or camera. Finally there was Edna Burns, formerly Mack's student at Oak Lake school, where she had been "the star of the nature study class." She helped him collect the first Say's Phoebe after a mile-long chase across the prairie. Clearly, "Miss Burns" and Mack became close friends. "She has helped me in many ways this summer," he wrote Taverner at the end of October, "from actually getting specimens to driving me a few hundred miles in pater's Henry [Ford]."[20] A month later he sent Taverner a curious description of Miss Burns: "A young lady with a gun and band of sharp-tails may not be of much scientific interest to you but always an interesting specimen full of possibilities and tendencies to me."[21]

Edna and Mack renewed their acquaintance forty years later when she and her husband retired to Victoria. She later recalled the "glorious wild fall" of 1921 — the "best in my life." She remembered: "I think September 5th was the day I shot into a flock of crows missing all, near *Heart's Desire*. How you laughed, I didn't, for I'd used your heavy gun, my tam flew off, and I spun round, left with a welt on my shoulder!"[22]

After the weather worsened, Mack moved into the Burns' cottage at Oak Lake. Finally, at the end of November he tore himself away and returned to Portland by train, via Vancouver. Though now aged thirty-eight, he moved in once again with his aged parents at 1277 East 32nd Street, N. As he complained to J. H. Fleming the next April, all was not well and he longed to be back in Canada. "Don't talk of lack of sunlight," he grouched. "We have had 2 good days in succession only once since last November and I am sick of this d—— country and its mud and gloom. Think I will stay up in Canada next winter. The infernal rain gets my goat."[23] Meanwhile, job offers poured in from Canada. In October 1921 Taverner and J. B. Harkin, Commissioner of Dominion Parks, nearly succeeded in finding a Parks-related job for him in Ottawa, but for reasons of economy the proposal was abandoned.[24] A month later, Mack got a letter from A. Rafton-Canning, Chief Fire Ranger and Migratory Bird Guardian at Fort McMurray, Alberta, and a keen naturalist. The two had met the previous summer; now Rafton-Canning wanted Mack to go fire-ranging at Fond du Lac, where he would see some new country. Mack's response was: "I dunno," largely because Taverner had promised him more ornithological field work.[25]

The summer of 1922 was Mack's real introduction to British Columbia. Although he had visited the Sunshine Coast in 1909 and the Similkameen in 1919, his knowledge remained limited of the enormous Pacific province with its impressive geographical and natural variety. His two great discoveries in British Columbia in the summer of 1922 were a man and a bay, both well known in Canadian ornithology. The man was Major Allan Brooks, D.S.O., of Okanagan Landing; the bay was Comox Bay, the ornithological mecca of the east coast of Vancouver Island.

Allan Brooks was born in India in 1869, where his father was an engineer. He spent his early years in India, England and in Ontario, where his parents immigrated in 1881. In 1887, his widowed father brought his family to a farm at Chilliwack, British Columbia. At Chilliwack in the lower Fraser River Valley, he became a market hunter, big-game guide, naturalist and bird painter. By 1920 Brooks had become by far the best-known bird painter in Canada.[26] In 1921 J. H. Fleming informed Mack that Brooks was "probably the best informed field man, now living, on North American birds ... his knowledge of our birds is so far and away ahead of anything we here in the east can offer you." Mack had followed Brooks' work in *Recreation* and elsewhere since 1900 and considered it "gospel."[27]

In 1922, as Assistant Ornithologist with the National Museum's British Columbia field party, he finally had the chance to meet the legendary Brooks. This occurred on May 6, 1922, at a cabin on the Val Haynes Ranch, Osoyoos Meadows in the southern Okanagan Valley. The two were introduced by Taverner, whose bad stutter Mack mercilessly ridiculed in his biography of Allan Brooks:

Taverner launched into introductions. He coasted over Hamilton Laing without a hitch, but at Major B— B— B— his speech impediment ran into a bottle-neck that grew embarrassing. [Brooks] popped up straight as a phone pole, and with "I'm Brooks" extended his hand. "Brooks!", exploded the liaison, letting out pent breath and tension. For Percy Taverner was no quitter; once he had put his shoulder to the wheel of speech it just necessarily had to turn out even if a bit late.[28]

The two naturalists immediately became close friends. Soon after his first meeting Mack wrote to J. H. Fleming, "Can't tell you much about dear old Brooks. ... It — he — is too big a subject. I worship humbly at his feet. You are right. He is a wonder." Brooks had a correspondingly high opinion of Mack as a writer. After

Taverner sent him some of Mack's *Globe* articles in 1923, Brooks responded: "Laing's stuff is good, the last clipping the best you have sent me of his work. A really fine piece of descriptive writing without any gush or waste of words."[29]

The basis of the Brooks-Laing friendship was a mutual admiration based on the similarity of their backgrounds and experience. Both were "born" hunters and naturalists, both had farmed in western Canada, both were amateurs who had reached the top of their profession without the advantage of a university education, both had been weapons instructors in the war, and both shared a virtually identical philosophy towards natural history — and towards other naturalists. Moreover, each possessed a powerful love and appreciation of life and nature. Finally, Brooks was a prolific and successful bird painter: Mack was a prolific and successful nature writer. Brooks' advantage was that he knew the birds of British Columbia better than anyone else alive: Mack remained a prairie specialist in 1922. Indeed, Brooks was such an object of wonderment in Mack's eyes that he spent the final thirty years of his retirement writing the biography of his hero. In 1922, Brooks was at the peak of his powers and could answer any of Mack's questions. "Of course," Mack wrote to Fleming, "the first question I asked him was the one I asked so many — probably you. My mystery bird in the bull pines [yellow pines] of the dry belt. He just smiled and whistled the call. Poor will. I have heard it many times since."[30]

The naturalists spent the first half of the 1922 British Columbia field season in the Okanagan and the second half at Comox. From their first camp at Osoyoos the field party — consisting of Brooks, Taverner, Laing and summer student Sampson — moved to Vaseux Lake and finally to Brooks' house at Okanagan Landing near Vernon. Mack was most impressed by Brooks' field knowledge, and wrote that:

Brooks knew where to find the good stuff: which cliff had the Duck hawks, or the *rare* white-throated swift, or which sage flat harbored the equally rare sage thrashers or which mountain top was home to the still rarer Williamson's sapsucker,... our field catalogues grew rapidly.[31]

It was also a summer for making social contacts. The naturalists stayed in a cottage on the Val Haynes Ranch, Osoyoos, owned by

Allan Brooks and naturalist Charles de Blois Green. Haynes, the son of Judge Haynes, "The cattle king of the south Okanagan," had earlier taken an interest in bird conservation. From the veranda of his ranch home, where the group often socialized, they could see Canada Geese, sandhill cranes, White-tailed deer and beaver — all within the space of an hour or two.[32] In 1922 the Okanagan was full of English immigrants — "remittance men," eccentrics and naturalists. Charles de Blois Green, formerly a surveyor, was an amateur ornithologist, sheep farmer, and longtime friend of Allan Brooks. This "delightful character," Taverner wrote, was "disgusted with sheep and talks of going in for raising rattle snakes for their poison." The naturalists were joined for a time by ornithologist Frank Farley of Camrose, Alberta, who according to Taverner was a "dandy fellow," and by George Gartrell of Summerland, a fisheries inspector and Brooks' former big-game hunting pal.[33] The social aspects of the summer culminated when Farley, Taverner and Mack visited rancher Reginald Hody of Okanagan Falls near Vaseux Lake. Hody took them on a tour of his cellar where they sampled his homemade cider. The four men spent the rest of the day sampling the cider: their drunken condition on this occasion was so uncharacteristic that the incident in "Mr. Hody's cellar" remained an item of gossip for the winter months to come.[34]

Less social was their reception by H. J. Parham, the owner of the orchard across the road from the Val Haynes Ranch. Parham had left England in 1890 and had subsequently worked as a wheat-farmer in Iowa, a homesteader in Saskatchewan, a stenographer in Vancouver, and a trooper with Lord Strathcona's Horse in the Boer War. In 1905 he had finally settled down as a gentleman fruit-rancher near Osoyoos where he spent his time in the gentle and contemplative appreciation of nature. A champion of the study of living birds in their natural habitat, in the summer of 1922 Parham prevented the ornithologists from collecting a fine series of twelve Canada Geese that nested on the Haynes property in view of the Parham Ranch. Mack wrote that their "ungodly rumpus at dawn every a.m." woke him up, and that only Parham's love of the birds prevented him from silencing the "guilty ones."[35] Later, Parham lobbied against collectors such as Taverner, Laing and Brooks who, armed with federal collecting licenses — termed "death warrants" by Parham — ranged the Okanagan Valley destroying bird life in the name of science. Parham expressed his preservationist views in his book, *A Nature Lover in British Columbia*, published in London in 1937, which was met with a cool reception by Taverner and others.[36]

In late June the party, "like Moslems to Mecca," travelled north to Allan Brooks' home at Okanagan Landing. Here Brooks maintained a private bird park where owls, crows, magpies, hawks and other undesirable birds were shot on sight; in addition, Brooks had a private collection of about 10,000 bird skins.[37] They also visited Brooks' neighbour J. A. Munro, Federal Game Officer for the western provinces and longtime bird collector. Also at Okanagan Landing they were visited by Dominion Parks Commissioner, J. B. Harkin. Mack was so impressed with Brooks, Munro and with the location that he selected a twenty-five acre lot at Okanagan Landing adjacent to the Brooks residence.[38] After ten days here they continued to Comox on the recommendation of Brooks, who had stayed there at all seasons and had told Taverner: "It's the right place for birds."[39]

After a few days in Vancouver the trio of Taverner, Sampson and Laing boarded the Canadian Pacific Steamer *Charmer* for its regular overnight run to Comox. The next morning, Mack was appalled by the changes at Powell River, the site of his 1909 vacation.

The boat whistle blew for a stopping and I came out to wave a greeting to Powell River, place of pleasant memories. But — could it be? Where now was the old log wharf, the river rushing out of its gravelly banks into the sea, the towering forest growth, the croaking ravens on the shore, the bald eagle on the dry tips of firs? My lovely wilderness of a dozen short years ago — gone! Before me on the cleared slopes lay a town of several thousand souls, great mills, trim residences and stores — the answer to the great call of civilization for wood pulp to feed its hungry presses.[40]

By noon of that day, June 28, 1922, the *Charmer* had arrived at Comox. Following a day spent with Ronald Stewart, the naturalists hired a boat and rowed with their gear to Widgeon Point, about a mile east of the town, and camped in the rain forest on the shore of Comox Bay. Underfoot was a sprawling shell-midden, excavated

86

a few years before by Harlan I. Smith of the National Museum, and where, Mack wrote,

...we found the things necessary to the devotees of tent life and settled down to live on the shore. The place was romantic as could be — it reeked of the past. Those clamshell banks had been built by the hand of man; the creek when on the rampage in winter had cut into three feet of shells: an acre of ground raised by the litter of the ancient camp of the Siwash. His tools, his bones were buried at our feet."[41]

After two months of collecting at Comox, Point Holmes, Denman Island Spit, and on the Seal Islands, Mack cancelled his plans to settle at Okanagan Landing. He had fallen in love with Comox. In October 1922 he bought the five-acre lot on Brooklyn Creek where he, Taverner and Sampson had camped all summer. At the age of thirty-nine he had found his home: he would spend the next sixty years living on the same shell-midden. With Taverner's permission he borrowed the sturdy National Museum field tent and turned it into a winter home and office and with the help of neighbours John and Norman Pritchard he set about clearing bush and slashing salal. He also had to continue the articles demanded by the Winnipeg and Toronto newspapers. In late October he wrote to J. H. Fleming:

Instead of sitting down again and speiling off another thousand of copy — I work by the yard you know — I'll attend to some of my badly neglected correspondence.
    We are getting a real south-easter and a real coast rain. The woods are roaring; the bay is raging; rain is pelting; but thanks be, I can sit at my little tent door, beside the big camp stove and feel so comfortable that it hurts. Watch the gulls go by and the big yellow leaves getting banged down from the big broad-leaved maple that next year will be at my back door — I hope.[42]

In 1923 Mack stayed home to clear the land and build his house. In doing so he refused a job with the Dominion Parks Branch as a Nature guide at Jasper Park. The refusal, he wrote, "pretty nearly broke my heart."[43] Though he often spent sixteen hours a day clearing his "ranch" he was blissfully happy, drawing on his work, his surroundings and his view of the Beaufort Range for inspiration. "The view across the bay toward the glacier and the snowy ridges of the interior of the island is just splendid," he wrote Fleming the next spring.

The grass everywhere in my yard is green as Ireland and decked out in too many dandelions also more welcome erodium and shepherd's purse. The woods around my little clearing have the trilliums and adder tongues nodding and the red-flowering currant is fading from its earlier magnificence — the hummers buzzing merrily in it. My creek sings a merry tune — came up 2 or 3 inches since the rain. Woods resound with the songs of winter and Seattle wrens. The winnowing of old phleotomus the pileated, with flickers and downies and hairies sneezing and snickering and drumming — though most drumming is over now. Ruffed grouse thumping and sometimes a distant "hooter" (blue grouse). Kingfisher catching my troutlets. Bay full of waterbirds — just have to lie down on the clamshell bank with my glasses and take in the view: ring bill, short-bill and glaucous wings, loons, red-throats and I think Pacifics on hand today. W. W. Scoter, surfs, American, old squaws, pintails, golden-eyes, buffle-heads, all courting and raising thunder — grebes of 3 kinds hollering (horned, Western, Holboell) — But why tell you any more; I'll only make you feel bad.[44]

In the summer of 1924 Mack declined an offer to join an outing to the little-known Atlin area of British Columbia. This ornithological expedition was originally to have consisted of Laing, Taverner, Brooks and Harry Swarth of Berkeley, California, but eventually only Brooks and Swarth took part.[45] Instead, he accepted a surprise offer that Brooks had turned down: to work as a naturalist on the H.M.C.S. *Thiepval* expedition to Japan via the North Pacific ocean, the purpose of which was to supply fuel to the ill-fated British round-the-world flight under Captain McClaren.[46] Mack owed this job to Taverner who recommended him after Brooks decided to go to Atlin instead.

After receiving such short notice that he was barely able to pack, he left Comox at the end of February 1924. When he reached Esquimalt he wrote to his fiancée Ethel describing the route of the proposed voyage and hinting at his fear of seasickness.

We have a real expedition. The *Thiepval* is a little steel ship aobut 120 feet long, used to be a patrol boat, mine sweeper, etc. Carries crew of about 30 men. Has an awful cargo. We are carrying supplies for the round the world flight. Will call at all points up the coast and skirt all around Alaska and cross to Asia and end up in Japan. We stick pretty close to shore most of the way, for which I am truly thankful. I expect to be awful liberal to the fishes when we get up near the Queen Charlottes or run into Pacific swells. However I'm not going to cross the bridge before I come to the river and I'm not going to let the fish have my dinner as long as I can keep it below my teeth. Get your atlas. We call at Bella Bella, Prince Rupert, Juneau, Cordova, Aleutian Islands, Kamchatka, Yalsatat, Hakodate Japan, etc.[47]

News of the expedition caught Ethel entirely by surprise. "I can hardly believe it yet you are on your way to Japan. When your mother phoned me, telling about your letter, I sure got weak in the knees — no fooling. I couldn't think what was taking you way off there. . . . What wouldn't I give to have had the chance to go along too. As Mums says it would have made a peachy honeymoon."[48]

But the voyage was not peachy. Far from it. Mack had to share a small cabin with a hard-drinking, chain-smoking Scot named Lieutenant Shipley. And his worst fears concerning seasickness were confirmed — though he blamed the ship's cook for much of the trouble. In April he grimly wrote to Taverner from the Aleutian Islands: "It is positively up and down. Every lap seems worse than the last. Our wake is getting to be a streak of bile. From Atka to Kulak Bay and thence to Kiska most everyone was sick. About 4 men were heads up last stretch." Taverner sympathized with Mack but replied that he had to suppress "a little smile behind it all" at Mack's discomfort of the "rolling deep." Allan Brooks also teased Mack about his awful experiences in the converted trawler: "You must have had a rough time, it wouldn't be quite so awful if you had a room to be sick in, but to have to puke in a passage with other blighters trampling all over you must have been Hell."[49]

His troubles were not over when he reached Japan. First, he found waiting for him a telegram from his mother telling him that his father had died in Portland at the age of 83, after a month's illness.[50] Then one of the *Thiepval* crew members took a violent dislike to him, caused when he was awarded one of the ships' cabins for the storage of specimens. Growling with rage, he wrote to Taverner from Hakodate, Japan.

Had a rough one handed me yesterday. . . . I found my shelf stripped. My two big slatey-backed gulls from Petrop. and the fulmar gone. I had pinned them through feet and hammered pins into wood to hold them if the ship stood beam end. They were just yanked loose and thrown overboard I guess. . . . One low down cuss on this ship — only one capable of it. Has been trying to get me out of there I think since I started. . . . By God if I could get the goods on that fellow. If you get a certain ship's carpenter roughly skinned, you will know that we have got the goods on the cuss.[51]

The *Thiepval* encountered more serious problems than seasickness. The ship tried to enter the port at Kamchatka but, owing to very strong winds and high seas, was forced to spend a night waiting outside until daylight. To lighten the load they were forced to jettison some of their fuel. So bad was the storm that when they finally entered the port the next morning they found that many townsfolk had waited up all night in church praying for their safe entry into harbour.[52]

From a scientific point of view Mack was considerably frustrated by his inability to secure a collecting permit from the "obstructionist" Japanese officials, who would not allow him to take photographs. The best part of the stay in Japan came when the Denbigh family of Hakodate and Dr. Baba, a local dentist, took him to see a wonderfully illustrated Japanese book on birds at a rural girls' high school. Moreover, there was little point in shooting birds from the *Thiepval* when he had no way of retrieving them. All he could do was observe the birds through his field glasses. In the waters off Japan he wrote: "The most noteworthy thing I found was a duck with an orange bill — the monstrosity I saw in the Kurils and it would seem a spectacled eider. To think I had to pass that up for the mere purpose of laying gas for a world flight!"[53] Despite these difficulties he collected over 200 birds, including seventy-five from a brief overland excursion at Kamchatka where he told Fleming, "I walked those bird-clad hills to a finish."[54] He later described his finds in "Birds Collected and Observed During the Cruise of the Thiepval in the North Pacific 1924," published by the National Museum in 1925. He delighted the National Museum anthropologist Marius Barbeau by forwarding rare examples of Asiatic and Eskimo flints and pottery.[55] He was considerably relieved on August 22 when, after six months living aboard ship, the *Thiepval* returned to Esquimalt.

Meanwhile Mack's repute was growing in local ornithological circles. In 1924, he received an offer from Francis Kermode, the controversial director of the British Columbia Provincial Museum, to apply for the post of Assistant Biologist at the museum in Victoria. Two years earlier Taverner had written Kermode to "congratulate you in having acquired another good ornithologist in your province. My Assistant of the last two years, H. M. Laing has determined to settle down in Comox. He is a very good bird man and will do much to help along B.C. Ornithology."[56] Mack did not respond enthusiastically to the director's offer, probably owing to the animosity with which Brooks, J. A. Munro and most other ornithologists in the province displayed towards Kermode. Mack was familiar with the Kermode-Brooks feud, and his response was an unqualified "I'm not going to put in for it."[57] Eventually, William Newcombe of Victoria was awarded the Victoria job, only to be scandalously fired by Kermode in 1932. Mack also joined the British Columbia Ornithological Union and contributed to its circular newsletter *The Migrant*.

The summer of 1925 again found him in exceptional circumstances. Originally, Taverner, R. M. Anderson and Dr. Malte, the National Museum botanist, had asked him to go on a collecting trip to Hudson Bay via The Pas. Stitll later, firm plans were made for him to work for the Museum in Alberta; but at the end of March 1925 Taverner and Anderson jointly recommended him as naturalist to the Canadian Alpine Club's Mount Logan Expedition.[58]

Mount Logan, situated in the southwest corner of Yukon Territory, was named after Sir William Logan (1798-1875), the first chief of the Canadian Geological Survey. At 19,850 feet it was Canada's highest peak and it had never been climbed. During February, March and April 1925 an advance party of climbers travelled 950 miles overland to cache four and a half tons of supplies on the mountain, much of it at the base camp "Hubricks'," so-named after a prospector and his wife. Mack, meanwhile, had been sent to Seattle to learn motion picture photography under Asabel Curtis of Curtis Studios and Mr. Will E. Hudson of the Pathé Exchange, Inc. He was authorized to shoot 4,000 feet of film. After training in Seattle with a "Universal" movie camera he boarded an Alaska Steamship Company vessel for McCarthy, Alaska, the nearest port to Mount Logan.[59]

Here, he was met by the mountaineers including the leader, Captain Albert MacCarthy of Wilmer, Lake Windermere, British Columbia; Lt.-Col. W. W. "Billy" Foster, D.S.O., formerly British Columbia's Minister of Public Works; and Allen Carpe of New York, representing the American Alpine Club. On May 12, 1925, the party of ten climbers and the naturalists left McCarthy by trail, and on May 18 reached Hubricks' Camp at the head of the Upper Chitina River. Mack stayed behind collecting birds, mammals and plants for the duration of the summer while the others tackled the mountain; or, as he put it, "I did the collecting down below while the fellows climbed and did the heroic stuff." Earlier, R. M. Anderson had written: "Taverner is telling what he wants in the line of birds, and in mammals, anything that grows hair will be acceptable."[60]

Soon after the departure of the climbers had left him in complete isolation, he wrote to Ethel describing his view from the tent camp at Hubricks'.

Can you get a picture of this camp? Imagine a valley 1½ miles wide — the floor a desert of level gravel with a dozen small rivulets coming across it — muddy, soupy glacial stuff. Both sides of valley a mountain range up to 8 or 9 thousand feet. I am on N. side. S. side is very steep and colder. This is the best, earliest side. Green timber lines the lower slopes. I am camped in this belt. Spruce, green moss about their feet. Black poplars on all the sides and here and there on the hills. Deep ravines cut into the mountain — precipitous. Behind the green timber about the tent rises the sudden little hills and benches. Cliffs cut across here and there. There is a variety of burns, cliffs, green timber in clumps, bushy slopes, until finally you get beyond the line of timber and have only alpine vegetation up to the yellow cliffs and the eternal snows.[61]

After their six-week, successful ascent of the mountain, the triumphant but weakened climbers arrived back at base camp on July 6; Mack recalled that they had an insatiable desire for only one thing: sugar.[62] Six of the climbers had actually scaled the summit in the long trek, which in the words of the expedition's biographer Paddy Sherman, "qualifies as perhaps the most outstanding epic of endurance in Canada's rich and vibrant frontier history."[63] The climbers had such sore feet on their return that they elected to float down the Chitina to McCarthy on a rakishly constructed raft. Mack wisely sent his specimens out by pack-train.[64]

Meanwhile he had collected 245 plants, 203 birds and sixty-one mammals on the mountain: from a scientific point of view the expedition was a great success. The botanist at the National Museum, Dr. Malte, had insisted he take along a plant press after hearing that Mack had "a sharp eye for a new plant."[65] When in 1939 the plants collected from the Chitina Valley were finally examined, one was found to be new to science. The plant, an antennaria, was named *Antennaria Laingii* in honour of its discoverer.[66] Mack returned to Comox late in 1925 and wrote up his bird and mammal collections jointly with Anderson and Taverner as "Birds and Mammals of the Mt. Logan Expedition, 1925."[67] Over the winter of 1925-26, some 500-600 of the nearly 4,000 feet of film he had shot was incorporated by Allen Carpe into the film, *The Conquest of Mount Logan*. The remaining footage was supplied by Carpe, who had taken a movie camera up the mountain with him. Mack's footage consisted of group shots, panoramas and views of hawks, beaver and a sandpiper. Anderson paid him the compliment that, "As far as we could see, a professional movie man could not have done any better on most of the scenes."[68]

Two unusual experiences had occurred during his six-week hunting and collecting vigil in the Chitina Valley. The first came while he was exploring a muskeg. "I dug up some plants, then picked up my gun from sort of beside me, and it went bang and the powder smacked my left hand," he recounted to Fleming. "The gun flew out of my grasp and landed behind me — safe. I don't understand either what fired it, or how it got safe after one barrel went off. Made me stop and think a minute." Months later he reiterated: "I have never found any explanation for the near accident with my gun. It just went off and that is all I will probably ever know."[69] At the age of ninety-eight he recalled the other incident in an interview.

I was going up — in Alaska — up a stream, up a deep, deep ravine, and the sheep trail was along the high edge. Wherever you went — moved — you went on the sheep trails. Wild sheep, white sheep. And I heard a "click" and I was in a little park of very small timber, stuff not much higher than my head. I said "That's an animal." And I stopped and I looked but I couldn't see him. I said "That's either a grizzly bear or a sheep, but sheep don't go into those kind of places, so if it's not a sheep, it's a grizzly bear." And I was pretty careful when I was around a grizzly bear. Well, I went in there, in farther, and farther, and farther, and I still couldn't see anything. And then, I turned around, and I was looking into the face of a big horned owl sitting at about the height of my head of a small little tree. "Well," I said, "I'll try him with this," ... And I shot him right in the chest. Well he fell down, and he died in a minute.[70]

In 1926 Mack returned to the prairies for the last time as a member of the National Museum's field party at Belvedere, Alberta. His boss was Percy Taverner and the third member of the party was Winnipeg ornithological enthusiast Cyril Guy Harrold. Harrold, known to his friends as "Chingachgook," was born in England in 1895 and came to Canada in 1914 where he took up farming and ornithology — a combination both familiar and desirable to Mack. He had met Harrold in Saskatchewan in 1921, and considered him a tireless and keen ornithologist "with lots of pep. I have seen few more active fellows." Tragically, Harrold died early in 1929 in New York, where he had gone to join the American Museum of National History's expedition to Madagascar.[71] From Belvedere, Mack, Harrold and Taverner were whisked around the Alberta countryside in the car belonging to the noted ornithologist, Professor William Rowan of the University of Alberta. Early in October 1926 Mack returned to Comox from his last prairie visit.

Up to 1926 his unofficial sponsor at the National Museum had been P. A. Taverner. Their productive relationship grew from the fact that both were western Canadian bird experts. Taverner's classic, *The Birds of Western Canada*, published in 1926, owed much to Mack's work of the preceding five years — indeed, Taverner asked for and got Mack to write "a few points on the various species of ducks" for inclusion in the book.[72] It is therefore somewhat surprising that the two men ended their collaboration in that year. For several years, however, Mack had been collecting plants and animals for Dr. Malte and Dr. Anderson. Beginning in 1927, Chief Mammalogist Anderson had made clear his own designs on Mack Laing — who subsequently became a pawn in the jealous professional rivalry between Anderson and Taverner.

94

Taverner and Anderson were two quite different kinds of men. Taverner had trained as an architect, but had drifted into ornithology. In 1905 he and J. H. Fleming had been instrumental in founding The Great Lakes Ornithological Club, which in turn formed the nucleus of twentieth-century Canadian ornithology.[73] From his beginnings in southern Ontario, Taverner had cast a wide net over the country, culminating in the 1920's with his western Canadian expeditions. With no formal university training, Taverner was technically an amateur, as were Mack Laing and Allan Brooks and many of their contemporaries.[74] Far from letting this fact deter him, Taverner resolutely directed his considerable productive energies towards the reconnaissance, classification and synthesis of the birds of Canada. Physically, he was an unorthodox character: tall and thin, bearded, but with great personal charm. He shared with Mack a passion for music and for writing long, articulate and entertaining letters.

Dr. Anderson was Taverner's antithesis: a cool, humourless professional scientist who despised Taverner for his lack of a university education yet resented the extraordinary success of his bird books.[75] Anderson was intensely, even pathologically jealous: in a series of scurrilous private letters written to Mack in the 1930's he accused Taverner of "cribbing and sponging on other men's work for a lifetime." For his part, Taverner replied in 1936 that Anderson was "obsessed with jealousy of me because I have received some little recognition and he has done practically nothing to obtain it in his 18 years here."[76] To his credit, Mack stayed out of the destructive feud at the National Museum. In 1936 Taverner wrote to say that word had reached him that Anderson "has been writing in a most derogatory manner of me to my friends." Mack replied, "Yes, I have known things between you two were not running amicably for a long time. No, I don't believe much of what I'm told about anybody — they're never as good or as bad. But I do object to getting between the upper and nether millstones."[77]

Anderson's jealousy of Taverner first emerged in February 1927, when he acted alone in hiring Mack to undertake a mammalogical reconnaissance of southwest British Columbia. Previously, on the Mount Logan expedition, Anderson and Taverner had acted in tandem in recruiting Mack and sending him into the field. Taverner

VIII
Ethel and Baybrook
1922-1927

THERE WAS A TIME WE USED TO CHASE A WOBBLER
IN THE BAY
AND CATCH A TYEE — UMPTY POUNDS — MOST ANY
KIND OF DAY
THE WAY THEY CHASED THAT WOBBLER ROUND —
IT COULDN'T GET AWAY
"THEM DAYS IS GONE FOREVER!"

— Hamilton Laing to Percy Taverner
September 24, 1922[1]

In June 1922 Mack had selected twenty-eight acres of lakefront property at Okanagan Landing adjacent to the estate of J. A. Munro, another well-known ornithologist. But he abandoned the ornithological centre of interior British Columbia in favour of the coastal bird mecca, Comox Bay, where he settled and eventually brought his bride.

The Comox Valley had been settled in the 1860's by adventurers returning from the Cariboo goldfields, lured by the less speculative but more secure prospect of the valley's fine agricultural land. The townsite of Comox itself was not laid out until 1910. When Mack arrived in 1922, the district was still in the process of changing over from a farming to a logging economy. The desirable farm land was located on a bench a few hundred yards inland from Comox Bay; the heavily forested land was on the mountain slopes behind. As a result waterfront property was both available and inexpensive. After a good deal of bargaining with the owner, farmer Leo Anderton, Mack bought five waterfront acres for $150 apiece. Taverner allowed him to keep the Museum tent for the winter and Mack lived, worked, and slept in this while he built his house ten yards away. When he finally took down the tent he nostalgically built a storage shed and later a garage on the very spot the tent had stood.

At Comox, Mack hoped to repeat his family's pioneering experience in Ontario and Manitoba. To the end of his life he felt that British Columbia was a "frontier," for the simple and legitimate reason that, as a newcomer, it was a frontier to him. "But the west has little or no traditions and historical sentiment," he wrote, "it is all of the future; the eye here is ever turned upward and forward."[2] Like many other British Columbians with eastern Canadian roots, he naïvely believed that British Columbia had been settled by like-minded easterners who had pioneered their way steadily westward across the continent, subduing nature as they went. At Comox he found, instead, a large community of first- and second-generation immigrants who had come more or less directly to British Columbia by sea or by the transcontinental railway. These settlers therefore had little knowledge or interest in the harsh eastern or prairie winters, or in the "frontier" philosophy that such conditions produced. But there was nothing stopping him from repeating his family's frontier farming experience at Comox, and he quickly set about levelling the bush and blowing up stumps.

Mack's friends supported his move to Comox. Allan Brooks had tried to buy Anderton's Brooklyn Creek property as early as 1903 and considered it a "little heaven": "I always pictured that site as a home for myself," he wrote, "it is certainly one of the very choicest spots I ever saw." Mack spent his first winter at Comox clearing land and walking to Comox townsite or to the neighbouring town of Courtenay for supplies. "Courtenay," he proclaimed to Taverner in October 1922, "is inhabited by a bunch of business men who ought to take down their signs and unfurl the Jolly Roger. Mostly a bunch of bloody robbers. I'll buy nothing but postage stamps here when I get established."[3] Every few days he walked the mile into Comox to collect his mail. The walk took him through woods and fields abundant with grouse and pheasant, so he carried his shotgun in order to collect his dinner. Often he invited Ronald Stewart along for these short hunts. He then returned to his camp where he cooked the birds in Taverner's big wood-burning tent stove. He even committed his grouse recipe to posterity in one of his hundreds of enthusiastic letters to Taverner:

Wish you could have supper with me tonight — or last night — or night before, etc., etc. Have eaten a rooster for supper every night for sometime. Last night I didn't manage it but then I wasn't feeling well. I stuff them well fore and aft with bread and onions, then put 2 in the granite ware mixing basin with tight lid and put them in slow oven for 2 hours. Put a rock on lid to hold down when occupants grow active. Gosh I never cared for grouse roasted till I tried them this way.[4]

He may have lived an isolated and rustic camp life far from town, but he was free to carry on with his fishing, shooting and collecting. In 1923, for example, he shot a bald eagle that had recently feasted on rotten salmon. He attempted to rid the carcass of its smell by hanging it up outside overnight. The bird, however, was so rank that he wrote to Taverner: "If my good little mother stepped in here she would whale about once, turn a double hand-spring backwards and go to the angels."[5]

Mack soon got to know some of his neighbours. Most notable were Comox Valley game warden Ronald "Martukoo" Stewart; local hunter Cecil "Cougar" Smith; Theed Pearse, the Courtenay lawyer, alderman and ornithologist; Cyril Piercy, the Comox postmaster; and Jim Curtis of Nob Hill, a student at the University of British Columbia, described by Mack in 1923 as "an enthusiastic bird fellow."[6] His nearest neighbour was Quebec native Eugene Croteau who settled next door to him in 1922. Croteau shared Mack's passion for music and came over regularly to hear his Beethoven phonograph records. Haldor Eiriksson, possibly his closest Comox friend, arrived in 1922 from his native Manitoba. Haldor was a carpenter and a sports fishing guide. Haldor's future wife Elsie, also a Manitoban, arrived at Comox in the early 1930's.[7]

In 1923 Mack refused all summer work to complete his house, a mail-order, pre-built Aladdin home on the "Forest" plan. It cost him $710. Taverner — who had trained as an architect before turning to ornithology — offered him help in house building as in much else. Taverner wrote:

In any event, don't be stingy with the overhangs of your roof. Make 'em good and wide, even if you have to use poles for look-outs — not a bad idea in any event. Nothing I would like better [than] to build a nice snug little home in that location in keeping with the surroundings and your tastes. Could make a little jem [sic] of it. I'll design the chimney if you like and hope that you follow the constructiton.[8]

Taverner, however, found Mack's tastes stingy and conventional. His golden rule of house design came from a sign he had once seen hanging in a hairdresser's window in Detroit which read: "Preserve the likeness and accentuate the beauty." For this reason he advised Mack to nail rough slabs of local wood onto the outside of the house. "Am sadly disappointed in you," Taverner wrote in April 1923. "Afraid of slabs because they are unconventional . . . of course the residents would stare when you got it done and be a little critical at first but finally you would have the show place of the community." Mack replied, "Why Man, if some of my friends found me in a slab shanty — well fancy my mother, for example. She would have a hemorrhage of green paint at the very suggestion." Taverner continued to tease Mack for his conventionality: "Well, I suppose it will be another nice shiny chromo in a good frame but at least it will be smug and eminently respectable but I thought better things of you."[9] Taverner concluded by warning Mack that "Someday when I retire I will have to go out there and build next to you and show what can be done without money but with brains and a little ingenuity. You will all be green with envy, and then I will chortle." Mack's curt rebuttal was: "Come along and retire but you can't come next to me because I want that [lot] myself as soon as I can find the necessary $." Taverner was appalled at Mack's rough-and-ready land clearing methods. The most economical way, he found, to remove large stumps was with dynamite. In 1922 one large fir stump took nineteen sticks of dynamite to uproot. "But," he assured Taverner, "I have preserved the likeness and accentuated the beauty."[10] Taverner was apparently serious in his threats to retire to Comox, where he would be near his bachelor ornithological cronies. Both he and Martukoo were heavy smokers. In 1923 he outlined his retirement plans to Mack — who was violently opposed to smoking:

Tell Martukoo when I retire and come out to Comox and buy Widgeon Point from under your nose I will keep a special tobacco box on the shelf for him and a box of matches to hand. For you I will have a bottle of perfume and a box of chocolates and a fume-proof chamber for you to retire to. For Brooks I will have a series of perfectly made up Dickcissels and Black Merlins to admire.[11]

Land clearing in British Columbia was, according to Mack, a "he-man's game" and he found it necessary to hire at various times Cougar Smith, Eugene Croteau and neighbour Norman Pritchard. He also got help from Ronald Macdonald Stewart, an Englishman of Scots ancestry, who had come to British Columbia originally to hunt big game. Stewart had once been in charge of a sugar plantation in Tonga where he earned his peculiar nickname "Martukoo." In 1910 he married Ellen Holmes, daughter of the pioneer Comox merchant J. B. Holmes. Another of Stewart's several nicknames was "Spike-buck Stewart," earned because when on deer hunts he liked to stay in camp until everyone else had left, and then go out and shoot a small buck (a spike-buck) which entailed much less effort. His third nickname was Ronald "Good-God-Yes!" Stewart, earned because of his enthusiasm for all things to do with ornithology and hunting. Allan Brooks, who had been Stewart's early hunting friend on the mainland, wrote to Mack shortly after his move to Comox in 1922: "Stewart's enthusiasm is inspiring and it is a good thing to have such a man to talk over any new capture with."[12]

Meanwhile the members of Mack's middle-aged bachelor fraternity were growing increasingly suspicious of Mack's intentions. Taverner, Brooks and Mack were unmarried. Mack at one point likened marriage to "Leander stroking the Hellespont with a grindstone tied to his neck."[13] His attitude towards women was probably no more Victorian than that of his contemporaries; nevertheless it is striking from a 1980's perspective. In 1918, for example, his Oak Lake friend Edna Burns sent him a newsy letter at Beamsville. He wrote pompously in his diary:

Letter from E.B. — gives details of Manitoba birds and nature in more ways than one. A young woman's nature turned perhaps into strange paths. Women have never been great naturalists, never will perhaps, but they can appreciate Nature on the surface of things. The emotional and imaginative faculty of the woman is adapted to appreciation; the systematist with his 5000 odd skins from Australia and the Far East — that is another kind of thing.[14]

The role of "the woman" was clearly defined to Mack. Women were put on earth primarily to help men in the struggle for existence. Only after they had accepted their subsidiary or service role by getting married could they expect something approaching equal treatment or respect from men. In 1919 Mack wrote Fleming: "Nearly took brain-storm typing all those dates and figures and jaw-breaking names. If I ever get hitched up tight to a female of the species, pray heaven she may be a stenog. I'll never be able to hire one; will have to marry one." Soon after moving to Comox he informed Taverner that: "First live stock on this ranch — barring the wife, of course — isn't going to be a setting hen, but a dog like Martukoo's to catch those winged pheasants." And after his return from Japan in 1924, he remarked: "Gosh! have just scrubbed the floor — first time since I moved in. I don't see why I didn't buy a Jap woman when I had the chance. You can actually buy them for years over there, body and soul, bag and baggage." Mack and his ornithological brotherhood found it ludicrous that women should be involved in ornithology. In 1919, for example, J. H. Fleming wrote Mack about a naturalist named Miss Durand who had gone on the lecture circuit in Ontario, wearing trousers — which at that time were worn only by the latest fashion models. This led Fleming to ponder: "What chance has a boy to get to know the living truth when all the models have trousers?" Mack's response was, "I don't know, unless he feels underneath. A lot of us learned some nature study that way!"[15]

Mack's friends knew there was a woman in his life; now that he was building a house their suspicions seemed confirmed. Fleming, for example, teased him early in 1923 that: "In your last letter you mention digging a cellar, in other words you are preparing a place of safety when domestic troubles become too great for a mere man to endure, is my guess right? Anyway I trust the building of a home is the assurance of a happy future for someone besides yourself." That other person was Ethel May Hart, a 25-year-old native of Michigan, who lived with her mother at Jenning's Lodge, Oregon. She was nineteen years old and acting as babysitter to Mack's sister Jean Robinson on August 10, 1915, when Mack arrived in Portland at the end of his transcontinental motorcycle trip. He later recalled that Ethel was "the first girl I met in Oregon." On the day they met, Ethel was holding Jean's adopted son John in her arms.[16]

It is unclear when Mack and Ethel started seeing each other. Their earliest surviving letters date from Mack's return from the

R.A.F. in 1919; by the spring of 1920, when he was on his way to Lake Athabasca, they were clearly in love. In May of that year, Ethel wrote to him as follows: "You see I am already beginning to think of the time when you will be back here it cannot come too soon for me. I'm just loving you as hard as ever I can and think of you most all the time." Mack's protestations of love were rather more reserved. He invariably ended his letters with a formal phrase such as "With best of good wishes and all kinds of love and I hope your neck is better."[17]

By 1920 Ethel had found a job as a stenographer with the Portland Light and Power Company. She spent much of her time typing up contracts between the company and its customers. It was an unrewarding, mechanical job that depressed Ethel but she was determined not to let it defeat her. In June 1922 she wrote Mack dishearteningly that:

I suppose they will be moving my office to the 4th floor tomorrow. Just makes me sick to think of having to work down there. Can you imagine having to work all day with scarcely no other light than by strong electric light? Well, that is what they expect me to do. I don't know what will happen to my eyes.... I don't think I deserve such treatment after the way I have always kept the work up. Just you wait maybe I'll have the chance to put one over on them yet ... I have said all I'm going to — never seems to get you anything — likely would if I was a man — seeing that I'm only a girl — they think I don't count.[18]

Ethel was a sensitive, intelligent woman with a love of needlework, music and the outdoors — especially gardening and hunting. She also collected butterflies and moths. She found the Portland suburbs too crowded and supported Mack in his search for a home in British Columbia in the summer of 1922. "You know any place would suit me," she wrote, "just as long as there be lots of wild flowers and good places to go out shooting and not very many *people*. It's getting altogether too civilized and populated here to suit me. Good Lord, getting so you can't go or do a thing, but the whole neighbourhood knows of it in short order." She longed to escape from the dreary and patriarchal office into the outdoors:

Had my first swim in the river night before last, the water was real warm and nice. I felt quite "puffed up" over the fact that I could swim man-fashion — never could before — always had to paddle along dog-fashion. With a little more practice I'll be a regular swimmer.[19]

Theirs was a difficult, long-distance romance both before and after their engagement in 1922, especially for Ethel, who saw Mack only when he journeyed to Portland for the Christmas season. She was most upset with Mack's summer expeditions which lasted generally from May until October. In 1921, for example, he stayed at Oak Lake until the end of November with Edna Burns and other old friends. While he was chasing rare birds across the Manitoba prairies with Edna, Ethel was writing: "Have you made up your mind yet when you are coming here? I know all your friends will want to keep you just as long as they can — but then you know I want you too — seems like you have been gone a terribly long time."[20]

The next summer, however, when Mack was at Osoyoos or Vaseux Lake with Allan Brooks and Percy Taverner, he sent her an engagement ring. Ethel thanked him:

I don't have the words to express how happy I am with that lovely ring. You are an old dear to get me such a pretty one. If you were here I sure would give you a great big bear hug — it feels real tight, but I think it's best to have it that way. I think it just as pretty as can be. I was so surprised when I opened the box, I didn't have any idea what was in it.[21]

Their engagement lingered on for the next five years. This may have suited Mack for awhile, but Ethel was clearly impatient with the unsatisfactory relationship, as well as with her unrewarding office existence. Meanwhile she had started acting as Mack's secretary in his absence. He supplied her with articles and lists of magazine addresses, and it was her job to send each article to each magazine on the list until it was accepted or finally rejected by them all. She even offered to lend him some of her savings to buy the land at Comox in 1922.[22] Still the engagement lingered on and on. She was teased at work for still being single. "I have a good joke to tell you," she wrote Mack in 1923:

One of the men here (at work) asked me the other day how much longer I was going to work for the PRL&P Co. I told him I really couldn't tell him — now he was trying to find out something all right

— then he asked me "Is *the* young man connected with the Smithsonian people?" I told him no. Can you beat that for nerve?[23]

In 1923, when he was building his house, he did not invite Ethel to come and help clear land, lay out the garden, or pound nails. Far from it. Ethel did not visit Comox until 1927. With a hint of frustration in her voice she wrote in 1923: "So all the ladies in Comox approve of the new house — well that speaks well for it. You know I can hardly wait to see it myself. I know it is real nice." Still Mack did not ask her to visit. In August 1923 he wrote to Taverner: "So you are still saving up for that happy day of mine. Keep right on. Think I'll keep postponing it!" And postpone it he did. After spending the Christmas of 1923 in Portland he returned again empty-handed. He wrote to Ethel: "Martukoo came in the other morning and told me he had been commissioned by P.A.T. to kick me in the slats. I don't know what I was to have my slats busted for; perhaps for coming back alone!" Only occasionally did he let his affection for Ethel show. While in Hakodate, Japan, in 1924 he made a telling remark to Taverner who had kidded him about his sea-sickness. "Yes smile on!" Mack wrote. "Sea sickness is like love sickness: all very laughable when you see the other fellow in the throes. Both at once make a hell of a combination, I believe."[24] The Mount Logan Expedition of 1925 postponed the marriage even further, though it appears that in the spring of 1925-26 they finally expected to marry. But then Ethel's mother was sick for awhile, and then Ethel and Mack got their wires crossed somehow. In September 1925 an infuriated Mack wrote to ask Ethel:

When am I coming to Portland, did you say? When are you coming to Comox? is what I am more interested in. I can go down any time you are ready, but we may have to make it short and snappy if I am to write a Logan report ready for publication in October. I have been hoping we could get married this fall for sure. How about it? All the folk here are dreadfully disappointed that I came back alone. Let's not disappoint them *too* much longer. I know I'm asking a lot of you but if we are ever going to make an end of a most trying situation why not now? I'm ready when you are.[25]

Yet a full year later it was Ethel's turn to admonish Mack.

How does it happen you are going to do all that visiting and collecting all this fall? Why can't you come down sooner than Xmas. Don't you know I told you last time you were here I would go home with you on your next trip — well I hope I was telling the truth. Mums seems all right now so I don't see why we should wait any longer.[26]

Finally, on January 19, 1927, they got married at the Congregational Church at Jenning's Lodge and immediately returned to Comox a married couple, to their friends' and their own mutual relief. "Brought the mate back with me this trip," Mack related smugly to J. H. Fleming, "and she seems to like Comox about as much as I do, I am of course frightfully happy and excited. Was mighty glad to get back to God's country." He wrote a similar note to *Province* columnist J. W. Winson who replied: "You are a most unsociable beast! I don't know how you managed to make yourself agreeable enough for a woman to decide you were worth living with!"[27]

Both before and after his marriage Mack had to put up with a great deal of similarly good-natured (and not so good-natured) teasing from his bachelor naturalist friends. J. H. Fleming was most blunt. "If you are going to marry a typewriter," he had written in 1919, "wait for a silent one to be put on the market. My advice is marry a young one if you expect to get a companion interested in your work." Taverner feigned dismay at the break-up of his bachelor brotherhood in the late 1920's when both Mack and Allan Brooks threatened to marry. When, in early 1926, rumours of Brooks' impending marriage reached him, Taverner wrote to Mack: "It does rather shake my complacency however. If Brooks falls on whom can we depend? The sooner I can get you to the bush the sooner you will be safe." On Brooks' marriage to Marjorie Holmes later in 1926 Taverner wrote, "Who would have thought that Brooks would ever side step birds for a woman? Wonders never cease. There are still greater wonders to come. Look out!!!" Even after Mack and Ethel's marriage the teasing did not stop. Taverner wrote, "Bless you my children. Am eaten up with curiosity to get to Comox and see the newly established family and how quickly the bachelor crankisms are being eliminated." And a few months later Taverner continued: "You certainly seem to have your wife well trained. Always supposed you had to catch em young to do that, — I mean very young of course — infantile almost, — don't let her see that break of mine or I will be ruined in your house completely."[28]

Perhaps Ethel's most valuable asset in Taverner's eyes was her ability to type:

You are lucky having a typist. Wish I had one. It would be very pleasant to be able to sit in my arm chair with my feet on the desk and my head enveloped in contemplative smoke while I listed to the merry rat-a-tat-tat of the keys and felt that the drudgery was being accomplished, and the words spelled correctly. You are a lucky guy to be able to watch your eagle tree while the work does itself.[29]

But Taverner's interest had evidently been piqued when Brooks and Mack got married within a few short months of each other. Early in 1928 he wrote: "P.S. The most interesting thing about your recent information is your wife. A typing, bird-skinning camping and good cooking wife is a pearl without price, — are there any more at home like her? I am interested." Ethel and Mack, and Marjorie and Allan Brooks, had the last laugh early in 1930 when Taverner finally got married. Taverner's arch-enemy R. M. Anderson took the opportunity to announce in April 1930 that: "Mr. Percy Algernon Taverner surprised all the natives on last Saturday the 29th March by getting married to a very estimable lady, Mrs. Martha H. Weist of Detroit an old friend of the Taverner family." Mack promptly wrote Taverner a rather malicious letter concluding: "of course your ornithological career is ruined."[30] Taverner's final word on marriage reads as follows:

Ottawa, Canada
April 16, 1930

Dear Laing:

Your facetious and utterly inconsequential letter received and promptly consigned to the waste basket without consideration where it belongs. If you think or thought that because I am bald-headed and a grey-beard and altogether a has-been that I am quite out of the running you had or have another guess coming. I got pretty well tired of the patronizing superior airs that you married men exhibited and decided to show you how easy it all was. All you have to do is to find some poor woman who is fool enough to idealize you and the thing is done, — no superiority on your part — just capitalizing the weakness of a confiding sex. If you have enough low-down smartness to keep up the bluff the marriage is happy but woe be it if you ever let her find you out. You must be fairly clever in that line and I hope to equal you. The trouble is that I am naturally so d—d honest that I cannot tell a lie even when I hear one. In the meantime I suppose all we husbands must stand together and if you don't blow on me I will promise not to give you away.

Sincerely,

P. A. Taverner[31]

With Taverner out of the way, Mack and Ethel settled down for a happy if brief marriage. A keen gardener, Ethel was happy right from the start on the Comox "ranch," which she christened "Baybrook." She was most interested in its agricultural potential and succeeded in turning Mack into a nut farmer. While still at Portland in 1922 she had suggested: "Mums says for me to tell you not to forget to set out some nut trees when you set out the fruit trees. I told her maybe they wouldn't do well up there, how about it? Don't you think walnuts and filberts would grow up there as well as here?"[32] No sooner had they married in 1927 than Mack disappeared into the field for several months, leaving Ethel alone at Baybrook with several pencil drafts to type and mail to publishers. A year later he was sending her terse directions such as: "Will you get that copy back for [Gordon] Dallyn re Oiled Ducks right away without fail. It should be in their office now. Send it to me first, never mind waiting for the other articles."[33]

With her husband away Ethel was welcomed into Comox society by, among others, Ellen and Ronald Stewart, Flora and Cyril Piercy and Cecil and Mrs. Smith. At the end of August 1927, when Mack had been gone since May, Cyril Piercy the postmaster was joking to everyone that Mack had deserted Ethel and did not intend to return. "Seems to get quite a kick out of it," Ethel wrote Mack. "I told him to just wait and see!"[34]

IX

Life's Best Adventure
1927-1944

CLEARING LAND IN B.C. IS A HE-MAN'S GAME.
I'M NOT NEARLY HE ENOUGH I THINK. THEN
I'VE GOT TO KEEP THE SCRIBBLING GOING AND
THERE ARE ALWAYS HAWKS AND OWLS AND
THINGS ATTACKING ME.

— Hamilton Laing to Hoyes Lloyd
February 26, 1928[1]

Mack and Ethel were at their happiest and most productive in the years after 1927. Aged forty-three and thirty-one respectively at their marriage, they quickly turned to the cultivation of the Baybrook Nut Farm and market garden. In these years Mack also became known as one of the finest free-lance collectors in Canada. All these factors contributed to the variety as well as the success of his popular natural history writings.

In 1927 R. M. Anderson replaced P. A. Taverner as his sponsor and boss at the National Museum. Taverner was not pleased with the way Anderson had pre-empted Mack's field services, though he apologized for the confusion in late May:

Sorry for the mix up in the field work for the season. Suppose I should have closed up immediately I found that you were willing to go out again. If you had not been such a bum correspondent this winter probably should have. I assumed that you would want to stay home with wifie this summer. Your disclaimer was long in coming and I had no idea Anderson was dickering with you as a mouser.[2]

Mack was equally annoyed. "Well, how in heck am I to know what you fellows are consulting about down there?" he replied. "Anderson asked me if I could go as usual and said where, and as you sort of kissed me good-bye when I got married, I naturally supposed you had sidetracked me. . . . Why can't [Dewey] Soper who is a mammal man catch those mice anyhow?"[3]

Anderson placed Mack under the tutelage of Charles H. "Bugs" Young, the National Museum's veteran field collector. Taverner predicted that after a field season with Young, Mack would be making as good a mammal as a bird skin: "Young makes the best skin ever and is always willing to show others how things should be done," Taverner wrote. Anderson's goal was to collect a representative sample of mammals from right across the country, rather as Taverner had done with Canadian birds. In 1925 he told Mack there are "far too many wide open spaces in the biological map of Canada, I am sorry to say."[4] Anderson's ambitious plan was to undertake an exhaustive exploration in search of mammals, birds, amphibians and reptiles in southern British Columbia from the Pacific Ocean to the Rocky Mountains, and he wanted Mack for this job. He set forth his instructions as follows:

The primary object of your expedition is to make as complete a collection as possible of zoological material, particularly the smaller mammals, in the country for about 50 miles north of the International Boundary in British Columbia. The region is of particular interest because of the extraordinary and sharply defined variety of climate and topographical conditions that occur from east to west and because it differs in these respects from the country to the north, and these differences are reflected in the fauna.[5]

The mountainous southern part of British Columbia had never before been systematically surveyed, and was known best by prospectors, packers and big-game hunters, all of whom assisted Mack in his field work. Allan Brooks, for example, had hunted in much of the area as a young man and suggested several productive collecting areas. He also recommended two ancient books which suggest how little work had been done in the area since colonial times. These were John Keast Lord's *The Naturalist in Vancouver Island and British Columbia*, published in 1866, and Lord Milton and Dr. Cheadle's *The Northwest Passage by Land*, published in 1867. Brooks and Mack had a great deal of difficulty locating one of Lord's rare horned toads.[6]

In his first field season, 1927, Mack and "Bugs" Young explored from the coast to Princeton, British Columbia. Young was a temperamental old man who had worked for the National Museum since the days of naturalist John Macoun. "I have my own pup tent," Mack informed Anderson in July 1927. "Very necessary when camping with Young — his snoring rocks the foundations even of a tent — as doubtless you well know." Just as Taverner had predicted, Young taught Mack how to prepare a good mammal skin. "Like a cold bath," he wrote Taverner in midsummer 1927, "peeling mice isn't so bad once you get used to it." Just as earlier he had boasted to have shot everything from a hummingbird to a whooping crane, so now he could claim to have skinned every mammal from a finger-sized shrew to a bull elk.[7]

Together, Young and Mack examined the south coast mountains taking a large number of specimens. These they regularly crated back to Ottawa by rail. They also met several guides and naturalists who took them into remote areas. From Cultus Lake, Mack hitched a pack-train ride up to the Liumchin Park with E. A. (Ed) Wells of Edenbank Farm, Sardis, and Chief Billy Sepass of Chilliwack. They reached alpine country at 4,600 feet "full of flowers just breaking" in late July. At Huntingdon they met naturalist J. W. Winson who had contributed a nature column to the Vancouver *Province* since 1912. A "slight man with a slender ascetic face and a pointed beard," Winson lived on the boundary at Huntingdon on a ranch that actually straddled both countries.[8] At Hope they visited one of Allan Brooks' ornithological friends, an Englishman named Lindsay Thacker; and while crossing the coast range to Princeton they were guided by George Allison, described by Mack as a "hunter, trapper, guide, miner, tourist-wrangler — one of those who ... know that country the way our grandparents (Scotch) knew the catechism."[9]

The field season ended finally in October 1927: Young returned to Ottawa but Mack was joined at Princeton by Ethel for their belated honeymoon. As honeymoon address Mack chose "The Cabin, 12 Mile Creek, Princeton, B.C." This remote log cabin was the property of "Punk" Davis, a hunter and prospector. Every week Punk delivered mail and supplies to Mack and Ethel on his little stallion "Tulameen Gold." Mack described this character to Taverner in November 1927:

Punk is about 70 but he climbs the hills and hauls the horse up after him like a youth of 40 odd. A good old scout even though he thinks bears are hatched from eggs and that deer never lie down while the moon is above the horizon, and fries certain unmentionable parts of the buck that I give to the Whiskey Jacks. He has killed more deer in his forty years here than anyone else and I wish he would take me out and show me how.[10]

The 1928 and 1929 field seasons passed quickly by. When in the spring of 1928 Mack agreed again to work for Anderson, Taverner sneered: "So you are going mouse catching again. Better put on a set of whiskers and a long tail and say meow. The mighty have fallen and Adam's old excuse." In 1928 Mack worked alone and extended the boundary survey from Princeton to Westridge, British Columbia. In October, he travelled up to Okanagan Landing for what he termed "a few days bully shooting" with the "Enthusiast of the Okanagan," Allan Brooks. Brooks was agitating for the annihilation of the crow in the Vernon area and told Mack "half-heartedly, but with a great deal of truth, that he was 'gamekeeper' of the area."[11]

On May 2, 1929, Mack was back in the field in southern British Columbia accompanied by student assistant Elgin R. S. Hall of Orton, Ontario, a biology student at Queen's University. Together they surveyed from Osoyoos to Yahk in the Moyie River Valley. Mack flourished both as Young's pupil and as Hall's teacher. Anderson — who issued praise only sparingly — visited them during the summer of 1929 and expressed himself very pleased with their progress. He wrote from Ottawa: "I am very well satisfied with your work on the whole. Mr. Young is almost as proud of the 'make' of your skins as if he had done them himself, and talks as if his mantle had descended upon worthy shoulders."[12]

Mack spent three weeks in April and May 1930 completing the extensive boundary survey near Newgate. Finally in September he completed the survey near Elko on the eastern slope of the Rockies. For the rest of the summer, however, he did something entirely different. The Dominion Parks Branch hired him as a "Guide Naturalist" — the first Park Naturalist ever hired in a Canadian National Park. This position was the creation of two Parks officials, James Harkin and Hoyes Lloyd. It was a triumph for Hoyes Lloyd who had tried without success in 1919, 1923 and 1927 to find work for Mack in Ottawa or in the Parks system. When the Nature Guiding job first came up Mack was hesitant, but finally welcomed the change, saying it "might save several of us — as well as a lot of small mammals — a heap of grief and pain."[13] It speaks highly of his reputation as a naturalist that he was selected for this new and experimental program. The Parks Branch put out a press release entitled "Nature Guide for National Parks" which described that "Mr. Hamilton Laing, the well-known naturalist and writer of the Pacific Coast," would act as "an outdoor curator of the natural treasures and curiosities" at Jasper Park Lodge, Lake Louise and Banff. Mack's friends were naturally pleased with the news. J. W. Winson, for example, thought the job would suit him "down to the ground and up to the skies."[14] The second Parks official was James Harkin, who, as Dominion Parks Commissioner, was instrumental in the wildlife preservation movement in this country. Harkin defined for Mack precisely what his duties would be:

A nature guide is a hike leader, school teacher, lecturer, scientist and game leader all in one; in fact, he is a walking encyclopedia of outdoors information. His job is to tell you the names of the animals, birds, trees, flowers, and to discover with you nature's secrets that lie hidden to the multitudes, but in plain view of one who has eyes to see.[15]

Taverner was one of the few who understood Mack well enough not to take his endeavours too seriously, and his response to the Nature Guiding news was, as always, abusive and derisory:

I have often wondered how you likes [*sic*] showing the dear little birdies, the pretty pretty flowers and the awfully cute mountains to gushing lady school teachers. But I suppose you do occasionally strike a few brains and an occasional intelligence. It may have its drawbacks, one of them is that we [the National Museum] have largely lost your services . . . I hope you hang on to it. But of course you know best, — or think you do.[16]

When planning for the 1930 field season Anderson felt that Mack should have a student assistant during the upcoming summer — one of six that Mack worked with during his years with the National Museum. The assistants were usually enthusiastic university students who had been brought to the attention of Anderson or Taverner. Mack's fine teaching abilities ensured that the summers spent by these young men in his company would be profitable, and many remained his lasting friends. The student chosen by Anderson to work with him in 1930 was Ian McTaggart Cowan, later a famous educator and biologist. Anderson wrote:

There is another factor which enters into the plans. You are now about the only free-lance collector in the West who is competent to do museum collecting, and is familiar with the technique, and as an old apostle we want you to help pass on some of the tradition to a disciple. We have a young man in view who has been recommended to me from several different sources. His name is Ian McTaggart Cowan of North Vancouver, now a third-year student at University of B.C. I met him at Winson's place in Huntingdon last fall, and Kenneth Racey and Allan Brooks spoke highly of him, also Professors Spencer and MacLean Fraser of the department of zoology at the University. ... They say his forebears were naturalists, and he has camped and hunted all his life. Spencer says he is one of the best shots in B.C. and is a go-getter in the field. I had only a short conversation with him last fall and was much taken by him ... I think that Cowan is the real thing and used to bushing it in the West.[17]

Cowan worked that spring at Newgate with Mack, before moving on to Banff to continue his work there as Park Naturalist. Mack was clearly impressed by the twenty-year-old Cowan and later called him "a born naturalist — not one of those biologists made in college and interested only in the cheque his Ph.D. will pull in for him." Mack and Cowan were joined in late April by Ethel who had been hired by the Parks Branch as cook. Later in the summer Mack went to Jasper where he guided a "nature study riding party" from Washington, D.C., headed by Richard M. Westwood of the American Nature Association. After his stint with the "Trail Riders" he returned to his regular duties as Nature Guide at the Jasper Park Lodge and Banff Springs Hotel. He left behind no record of his reaction to his job as a "nature study wrangler," though naturally he and Cowan were disappointed that they were not hired back in 1931 owing to the Depression. When the Park Naturalist position was revived in the late 1930's it was awarded to Mack's friend Dan McCowan, the Banff naturalist and author of *Tidewater to Timberline* and other books.[18]

"Life's Best Adventure," as he called his married life at Baybrook, was interrupted not only by the Depression but by a family squabble late in 1930. Fortunately some correspondence has survived which provides a glimpse of the personalities and dynamics of the Laing family.

Mack's seventy-eight-year-old mother, who had lived alone since her husband's death in 1924, ran out of money in November 1930. She had loaned Mack's brother Jim a total of $3,500 which Jim needed to pay off the mortgage and other debts incurred on his Manitoba mink farm. When Mrs. Laing ran out of money she wrote Jim asking for the repayment of part of the loan, not realizing that Jim had gone further into debt. Jim replied saying that he would be able to pay her back only after New Year's, and suggested that Mack might lend her some money. Mrs. Laing was not pleased. She hesitated to ask Mack for money because she knew he was unhappy with the way Jim had managed his financial affairs, but she wrote him in desperation: "I would be very thankful for to borrow $90.00 if you can spare it. I never was so hard up in my life." Mack promptly sent her the $90.00. Mrs. Laing's financial predicament was, however, more serious than she thought, and she wrote back that she might have to borrow more money or rent out her house. Meanwhile, his older sister Jean, sensing Mrs. Laing was "on the rocks," sent her some unsolicited dollars.[19]

At this point Mack sat down and wrote his mother a very stern letter, telling her that he would not lend her any more money until she had investigated Jim's indebtedness. He also stated that her business sense was not what it used to be and that she should be looked after by two guardians. Soon it was Christmas and sister Jean arrived in Portland. Jean had been a rural schoolteacher in Manitoba while Mack was still at the Collegiate. She read Mack's letter to Mrs. Laing, which so incensed Jean that she wrote to him:

You say you have something to say to Jean, well she has something to say to you. And you are going to get it straight from the shoulder — a dose of brimstone without the treacle. It just spoiled my whole Christmas day for me, thinking of a lovely old mother and the shock of receiving such words from her eldest son.

Jean agreed that Mrs. Laing had made a mistake in lending Jim the money, but argued that "at the time it was quite right for her to do so." She then took the opportunity to unburden herself of some more simmering resentments.

But that wasn't the biggest mistake Mother made. Her big mistake was in raising two selfish self-centred sons. To have given her all and asked nothing in return. Thru much self-denial and at much sacrifice she schooled you and at 18 yrs. of age you were fitted with a permanent job for life [1901]. It was seldom you wrote home, couldn't even spare the money to go back and see the old folks who had given you your golden opportunity. Then came the time when you wanted to climb higher. Mother was keeping a boarding house in order to have independence in her old age — so she would not be a care to her children when she could no longer work. You returned home and she cheerfully gave you board and room for a bigger job — a year and a half probably you lived on her bounty [1906-07]. Then came New York and at the end of that time you were broke and needed money [1914]. Dad cheerfully and immediately dug down into his bank account and handed you out the necessary $300 without question and no strings attached. When you arrived in Portland [1915] Mother staked you until you got on your feet again, and when you had saved enough you built your home without a nickel of debt if I am correct.

Jean then contrasted her own experience, and that of her husband Harry Robinson — who worked for a railway company — with that of her brothers.

I want you to know I got an education at my mother's and father's expense and I have always appreciated what that meant to them and to me — But I paid them back, every dollar from my first two years earnings. That was a promise I made with Mother when I was given my schooling and I kept it and at once. When Harry and I borrowed money from mother we paid back the principal, every dollar, with *Interest*. Note the latter. Why sons should not pay their honest debts to their parents does beat me. Daughters are expected to do so. But not the sons. But I'd scorn to do anything different. Harry would no more think of using mother as you two boys have done than he would jump in front of a moving train.

Jean continued by expressing her deepest resentment of her younger brother.

Maybe shooting, killing, trapping and skinning is a wonderful work in Mack's eyes but methinks it must dull the finer feelings and take the edge off all the beautiful things which go to make the world a good place in which to live, and from thinking and knowing that the greatest thing of all things is a good mother.

And she concludes:

I never thot [*sic*] I should ever have to write a letter like this, but you deserve it all. You called me penurious one time, well I can retaliate with a worse name now, but I scorn to write it. Instead of writing those biting, bitter, unkind, thoughtless words you ought to be on your knees thanking God for giving you such a fine old mother; for giving you an opportunity to repay in small measure what she has done for you, to consider it a privilege and a duty as well to relieve and help her with her worries and burdens when she is alone, and doing everything to make her remaining years easier and happier. You and Jim remind me of the man who asked for alms and was given a stone. I feel sorry for Ethel when you think and write such thoughts to your own good mother.

Jean[20]

Equally revealing is the exchange of letters between Jean and Mack that follows, of which only Jean's reply has survived. She apologized, saying that her conscience had hurt her deeply. She had written in her first leter that Mrs. Laing had "more good business ability and common sense in her one fist than you have in your whole make-up." Mack challenged her statement that he was like their father, who had once made a disastrous loan to a Mr. Van. B. in Winnipeg. In her contrite reply Jean answered, "No, I don't think you are a bit like father. You are your mother all over again. You have father's keen mind but mother's great ambition and tireless energy. I didn't intend to bring father's name into this at all. He is gone and can't speak for himself, but mother, it seems to me, always made too much of father's mistake in lending to Van B." Jean resigned herself to the fact that Mack remained the apple of his mother's eye, in spite of his behaviour. She wrote: "Mother rose to your defence most beautifully just as mothers will and I find you are 'all wool and a yard wide' once more."[21]

Mack evidently forgave Jean, for after her death in 1962 he wrote to her son John calling her "the soul of honour and the nearest thing to an honest woman I'll ever know."[22] Mrs. Laing died in 1934; Mack scribbled "to be preserved" on Jean's letters and filed them away.

This family quarrel occurred at about the same time as the Depression — which may even have caused Jim's indebtedness. In 1931, Mack suddenly found himself out of work after the National Museum and the Parks Branch both abolished their summer work programs. He described the grim situation to Fleming in June 1931:

No job — I suppose you know no collecting for museum and no nature guiding in Parks — so I'm on my own, trying to wring a living out of an unfeeling publishing world that seems living from hand to mouth too. Lots of knocks, but I'm used to them. One of the worst was that I had all my plans laid for the Parks — having ... put $400 into camera equipment which now isn't exactly paying dividends.[23]

A year later he was getting desperate: "I've never found it so hard to earn a dollar since as a kid I taught country school at $35 a month. Last year was pretty bad but this is simply a blank." Several friends came to Mack and Ethel's aid by offering to lend them money, but this was out of the question.[24] Mack weathered the Depression in three ways: by increasing the size of Baybrook Farm, by collecting and selling birds on a free-lance basis, and by expanding his market as an outdoors writer.

Mack and Ethel poured their energies into the expansion of their farm during the Depression. Traditionally, Baybrook had been Ethel's domain: she had worked it while Mack was away on his long summer expeditions. In the 1930's, however, out of necessity Mack started to spend a great deal of his time with the farm. First, he had to clear several acres of heavily forested land before it could be planted with nut trees or other crops. Gun powder was cheaper than horse-team work: "The labour I can get out of a box of powder at $15.30 is a Corker and the B.C. Gov't gives a rebate of $2.00 per box used in land clearing." He became quite an expert at stump demolition. "A B.C. rancher without powder," he told Taverner in 1933, "is like a collector without a gun."[25] One stump took over fifty sticks of dynamite to uproot. He turned his experiences into popular articles such as "Stump-Wangling," published by *Maclean's* magazine October 1934.

In 1931 Baybrook consisted of six acres of nut trees on the upper bench in addition to fruit trees and a big garden; by 1943 Mack and Ethel had planted a total of 866 nut trees. They had captured the entire Christmas market in walnuts and filberts from Nanaimo to Campbell River on Vancouver Island, and their dozens of customers ranged from the Overwaitea and Safeway supermarkets to the "Laird of Comox," Sir Ernest W. Petter. Moreover, they had gone into vegetable and fruit farming in a big way. Their fruit orchard in 1931 included seven pear trees, two prune trees and McIntosh, Spitzenburg, Yellow New Town and Delicious apples. "Your orchard," Taverner wrote them in 1935, "is certainly doing well. Soon you will be able to sit under your fruit trees and watch the world go by."[26] Mack called Ethel a "farmerette." She canned, preserved and sold an enormous variety of fruits and vegetables including crabtree, raspberry, strawberry and Oregon grape jelly, tomato and citron juice, pear and peach marmalade, English relish, corn relish, dill pickles, plum jam, marrow preserves and spiced crabapple. The farm also offered fresh beets, corn, yellow wax beans, peaches, prunes, pears, salmon and several different kinds of cherries. Cherries presented a difficult challenge: in order to harvest even a quarter of their crop they shot as many as 400 robins a season. One year they answered the robins by covering the cherry trees and strawberry patch with nets. Mack recalled later that this created a unique problem of its own, but one that during the "dirty thirties" may have been appreciated: "We had strawberry shortcake for 31 days in succession," he wrote. "I was making up for lost time. My wife thought strawberry shortcake was about the last thing in desserts!"[27]

Free-lance bird collecting was Mack's second profitable Depression venture. Since coming to Comox he had built himself a substantial collection of bird skins under the guidance of Ronald Stewart and Allan Brooks, but his "Scottish blood" had prevented him from selling any. "I have never collected commercially and don't care to much," he wrote in 1932, "but if this damned depression keeps on growing I'll be selling the whole collection, pygmy owls, merlins and all!" For advice he first wrote to Brooks, who put him immediately in contact with some "U.S. fellows" with private incomes and large bird collections. He then sought the advice of Anderson, who assured him that he could not succeed as an independent free-lance collector. Anderson's pessimism was perhaps exactly the challenge Mack needed. He sold his first birds in October 1932 and early the next year wrote: "The $ came in mighty handy. A dollar is 100 cents these days and I've never known it so difficult to run a greenback down." Within a few years he was selling his duplicates to some twenty different collectors including J. H. Fleming at Toronto, Louis B. Bishop at Berkeley, California, and Matyas Garfinkiel of the University of Warsaw. The gems of his collection were his rare "black" adult merlins which in 1938 were for sale at $50 each.[28]

Mack was one of many writers affected by the Depression. "The lesser magazines," he wrote in 1933, "are either out of business, begging or stealing it." Several "big shot" writers had even been reduced to selling articles to the "cheap" magazines. He complained that the major American sporting magazines like *Field and Stream* and *Outdoor Life* were "the only square shooters of the lot!" To bolster his declining sales he wrote to his friends for advice. Brooks replied by steering him to "some American patrons who were still solvent and in need of Canadian articles." Brooks also introduced him to G. Burrard, editor of the British outdoor magazine *Game and Gun*.[29] He also wrote on Canadian subjects for the other prestigious British periodicals *Field* and *Country Life* during the Depression.

Less successful were the twenty pieces of fiction he wrote between 1931 and 1936. Designed as money-makers, nearly all these stories were based on his experiences as a naturalist. "Spider Love" is a Blue-Back salmon romance set in the Strait of Georgia. "In the Reign of King Olaf," describes the ups and downs of a Scandinavian logging tycoon, possibly modelled on his Comox neighbour Robert J. Filberg. "The Change of Wind" is a stump-blasting drama set on Vancouver Island, "Bobby and His Kin" concerns a natural history outing with his Oak Lake boy scouts, "The Panther in a Tea Cup" was based on a hunt with Cougar Smith. Rarely did he succeed in divorcing natural history from his fiction, but when he did, the result is hollow and awkward. For example, "The Arm of Eriksen" grew out of his 1930 experiences as a naturalist at the Chateau Lake Louise. It begins:

He was slumped down on a verandah chair of the big Chateau, a great-shouldered little Saxon giant, and at the moment I thought I had never seen a picture of more complete dejection. He had a book but he did not know it. The Lake, the wondrous peaks of the Canadian Rockies were in their glory before him under the sun of mid-forenoon, but he saw nothing. In his tanned face was the look that I had seen in the eyes of my dog when once I thrashed him for a crime he didn't commit.[30]

Perhaps fortunately, few of these stories were ever published, despite the fact that Mack hired a New York literary agent and editor, A. L. Fierst.[31]

In 1933, following two sedentary years of farming and writing, he decided to outfit his own expedition to Quatsino Sound and Cape Scott, on the northwest coast of Vancouver Island. He hitchhiked a two-week ride with the provincial game department's patrol boat, which took him to many remote inlets and settlements. He returned to Comox laden with birds which he sold to his customers around the world. He kept an up-to-date list of duplicates which he sent to his correspondents. The next summer, 1934, he finally landed work with another large-scale institutional expedition. Taverner heard that Dr. George Miksch Sutton of the Carnegie Museum of Pittsburgh and John B. Semple, a wealthy American collector, planned an expedition to British Columbia. He urged that they contact Mack. As a result he spent the summer of 1934 collecting for the Semple-Sutton Expedition on Vancouver Island, the Strait of Georgia and briefly in the interior of the province. Armed with a Federal Migratory Bird Collecting Permit, obtained from Ottawa, they collected about 700 skins which Mack sent off to Pittsburgh in late June.[32] Typically, he had also done a great deal of his own collecting in early mornings, evenings, weekends and holidays.

Meanwhile the scarcity of money for fieldwork in Canada had frustrated Anderson's wish to send a National Museum field party to British Columbia. A nationalist, Anderson wrote to Mack early in 1935 that he hated "to see all the good men working for U.S. museums." Anderson knew that the National Museum had given Mack his reputation as "the top or at least second-best field man in Canada" and it rankled that American museums and private collectors could outfit expeditions to Canada when the National Museum's fieldwork had been discontinued owing to parliamentary restraint.[33] Finally in 1935 Anderson obtained enough money to send Mack out on a thorough survey of Cape Scott, one of the little-known areas of British Columbia. Appointed as Mack's assistants were two amateur naturalists from Vancouver, architect Bob Luscher and mining company executive Kenneth Racey. Mack described his "new pal" Luscher in 1934 as "a Swiss, a good hunter and a fisher and bird man too and I get a great kick out of him."

Luscher spent the summer of 1934 at Allan and Marjorie Brooks' "summer establishment" at Comox, where he spent much time fishing and hunting with Ethel and Mack. Kenneth Racey was editor of the *Migrant*, the circular newsletter of the British Columbia Ornithologists' Union and a respected amateur ornithologist. "Racey," Allan Brooks had informed Mack in 1924, "is a fine fellow and you must meet him," he "paid me a short visit and went wild over my birds."[34] In 1936 Racey's daughter Joyce married Ian McTaggart Cowan, who had just been appointed Assistant Biologist at the Provincial Museum in Victoria.

Luscher, Mack and Racey spent three productive months on northern Vancouver Island. In mid-October they sent an impressive total of 409 mammals and 243 birds to Ottawa. Anderson unpacked the crates and after a quick examination of the mammals replied simply, "I am more than pleased with the material which you have collected."[35]

From 1936 to 1939 Mack was engaged in his most ambitious and intensive project to date, one that equalled if not surpassed his boundary survey of 1927-1930. This was his four-year faunal reconnaissance of coastal British Columbia from Powell River in the south, to Bella Coola and Tweedsmuir Park in the north, and to the Chilcotin Plateau in the east. Each summer he was given one or two promising assistants to train and make useful. The first was George Holland, aged twenty-four and a graduate student at the University of British Columbia. Though he worked only for the summer of 1936, Holland recalled ten yars later that Mack had awakened in him "an interest in mammals and bird life that has never waned since."[36] The second student was Charles Guiguet, afterwards Curator of Biology at the British Columbia Provincial Museum. Guiguet, like Cowan before him, came to Mack with good references from Anderson who wrote in 1936:

Mr. Charles G. Guiguet, 5337 West Boulevard, Vancouver, 20 years old, [has] passed senior matriculation at Shaunavon, Saskatchewan. He has collected for Shaunavon "Grand Couteau Museum" and makes good mammal and bird skins, and has sent me a number. He needs a job and some encouragement. H. F. Hughes thinks he is a coming naturalist, if he gets half a chance. . . . If you take Guiguet you will have one boy who is willing to work at anything, industrious and full of ambition, who will be able to help you turn out a good line of mammal and bird skins, and help at any kind of work around camp.[37]

As it turned out, Guiguet stayed as a member of Mack's field party from 1936 to 1939. Mack was clearly impressed by the young naturalist. In June 1938 for example he wrote home to Ethel from deep in the Rainbow Mountains: "Charles has just come in and said he had called up a black-throated warbler. He has nothing on me." Guiguet absorbed much of Mack's vast knowledge of hunting and of the outdoors, and the two became close friends. At the end of the 1938 field season Mack wrote to Ethel: "Chas. is almost swallowing a lump in his throat at the prospect of the season being over. It has been a delightful season, one of the best I ever spent." Socially and ornithologically the work was very satisfactory. And in spite of Anderson's private injunction, "Do not spend too much time collecting birds this year," Mack nevertheless located some very fine and rare birds. In 1936, for example, at Rivers Inlet he and Guiguet collected breeding pine grosbeaks, a rare breeding sparrow and breeding black pigeon hawks.[38]

During these summers Mack and Charlie visited the community of Hagensborg on the Bella Coola River where they got to know and admire the Norwegian settlers. His favourite was Herbie Hammer, a timber-faller and amateur ornithologist, who worked for Mack in 1938 and again in 1939 as camp cook. "He is keen," Mack wrote to Ethel. "He is the best young ornithologist I have yet encountered, I think."[39] In a letter to Ethel from Hagensborg of 1938 he gave one of his rare but perceptive descriptions of people:

We get butter at Sangstads, eggs at Urseths, grub at Mackay's (his wife is a Stalstad), milk at Brinks. So we are pretty well steeped in old Norway. Even the hens cackle in Norwegian. But they are fine folk. I like them all. "Kellog" is the English way of saying something like it in Norwegian and "Hammer" is English for something else in Norway. I gave Herbie [Hammer] a lesson in grafting today — apples. These people don't know their luck with fruit. About all they do to apple trees is keep the grizzlies from pruning them too severely.[40]

Mack found himself in his element in the rugged coast range, a haven for strong-willed individualists. At Kingcome Inlet, Mack and Charlie boarded with the pioneer Halliday family on their seaside farm; and at Tweedsmuir Park they stayed with Marion and

Tommy Walker, the writer, big-game guide and conservationist. They also met the guiding and hunting borthers, Milo and Frank Ratcliff, and at Tweedsmuir Lodge they met Don and Phyllis Munday, the famed writers and mountain climbers of the coast range. Below Lonesome Lake they visited Maxie Hickman, the celebrated one-armed bear hunter. And at the end of one field season Mack met conservationist Ralph Edwards, later known for his work with trumpeter swans at Lonesome Lake. Edwards did his best to persuade Mack to come and stay with him at his lakeside settlement but Mack was unable to accept the offer.[41]

Charles and Mack were collecting above Tweedsmuir Lodge when war broke out in 1939. They knew nothing of it until on their way down to the Lodge they were met by Tommy Walker who came out to meet them and exclaimed, "You don't know it, but we're at war!" The war altered their plans; Guiguet joined the R.C.A.F., and in May 1940 Anderson notified Mack that "Parliamentary estimates do not provide a cent for any field work by the National Museum." Thrown out of work, Mack did what he had done during the Depression: he found work as a free-lance collector for wealthy private collectors and institutions in the United States. These were Louis B. Bishop of Berkeley, H. B. Conover of Chicago, and Dr. Max Peet, a private collector. He recalled that he "hied me to the hills and lone-wolfed it for nearly 4 months ... trying to peddle off my plunder."[42] He was accompanied by the promising Herbie Hammer — who afterwards joined the R.C.A.F. and unfortunately abandoned ornithology. Anderson was furious at Mack, not for finding work elsewhere, but for continuing the National Museum's Rainbow Mountain field work for a different institution. Anderson fulminated in December 1940:

With all the broad open spaces in British Columbia where hardly anybody has collected, why do you have to pick up some area where the National Museum has with considerable difficulty financed the biological exploration, and go in to make a clean up for our American rivals before we can get our reports out? It takes some time to do a workmanlike monographic job, and with our handicaps of shortage of money for field work, lack of museum assistance and no money for purchase of specimens it is damned hard to compete with some of the institutions and wealthy private collectors south of the line.[43]

124

The long summers of separation were difficult for Mack and Ethel. Guiguet recalled that all he heard about were "the melons, filberts and walnuts from dawn to dusk." During his five seasons on the Coast Range, Mack took to writing newsy letters back to Ethel at the farm. One of these begins, "Maybe I have something better to do than write long chatty letters to my wife, but I don't know what it is and I'm not going to do it."[44] The summers were longest for Ethel who for six months at a time was tied to the Comox farm. At the end of each summer Mack returned with a full beard. He recalled in 1980:

I have to smile about one of my beards. It was after I was married and had been north all summer. Ethel came to meet me at Campbell River Wharf. I recognized the old Chev Sedan Delivery and headed for it to get my kiss. The woman got out, came two or three steps then stopped, suddenly turned, jumped into the Chev and shut the door till I made some explanations.[45]

Ethel had to learn the role of gamewarden when Mack was away. She learned how to operate a .22 rifle, originally in order to destroy robins, hawks, crows and other thieving birds. She soon excelled at her bird shooting, as at everything else she did. Her value in Mack's eyes went up considerably when she added new birds to the H. M. Laing Collection, Comox, B.C. In the 1970's he recalled that:

... her clever hands were easily taught to make a good bird skin. She also had a sharp eye for a bird, was a crack shot with the .22 and twice in my absence took "firsts" off the Laing hawk tree in the back yard: Rough-legged hawk and Western pigeon hawk.[46]

On one such occasion in the summer of 1940 Ethel successfully shot a rare Merlin and wrote to tell Mack about it. He replied: "You're a dear, a darling, and a dead shot."[47] She was also a keen fisherman. Tyee salmon were her favourite quarry. In May 1927 Mack wrote to Taverner:

We went fishing for an hour on the high tide this evening. I rowed the boat; wife dragged the clothesline. She caught a big-headed monstrosity. I don't know fish: the brute wears a billy goat on his chin. He rolled his large, kind eyes and smiled widely when I beat him over the bean. Wife is sure he is good to eat.[48]

Mack refused to have a modern sprinkling system installed on the top bench at Baybrook where the nuts grew, so all summer long

Ethel had to haul water barrels in a wheelbarrow from a pool in the woods near the creek that Mack had dug. He also sent her long-distance directions concerning the garden, so she was kept pretty busy during his absence. When she wasn't gardening, she was preserving fruit or vegetables, fishing or sewing. She embroidered towels, pillowcases and quilts which she gave as presents to her many Comox friends. She loved to cook: Mack referred to her as the "farmerette" or as "my cook." Ethel also acted as his secretary in his absence, so her life consisted of little apart from hard work. She also became Treasurer of the Royal Canadian Legion Women's Auxiliary at Comox.[49]

Baybrook had no radio, telephone or proper plumbing. Electricity was not installed until 1937. "Gas buggies and radios," Mack had decided in 1938, were the "curse of the age." The radio was the "bla-bla box." Nor were there any children at Baybrook. Their lack of children was a cause of great regret to both Ethel and Mack; Mack recalled in later years that although they did not have a family "it wasn't for lack of trying." This was most unfortunate for Ethel who loved children. She used to visit her friend Elsie Eiriksson on Comox Avenue. She would ask Elsie, "Can I come up and see the kids bath?" Perhaps to substitute for children Mack and Ethel acquired two Springer Spaniels named Lady and Rascal. She would complain to Elsie, "I don't know who's going to be moving out first, me or the birds!"[50]

Ethel's main love was music, and she established a fine collection of classical records. Her favourite performers were Galli Curci, Enrico Caruso, Fritz Kreisler, Mischa Elman, Jascha Heifetz and Efrem Zimbalist. Martha Taverner, formerly an opera singer, helped Mack and Ethel choose their records. Percy Taverner wrote in 1932, for example: "We were unable to recognize the music line you sent. If it had been anything in standard musical literature my wife would have known it. She knows every composer who ever composed — or decomposed."[51] In music as in agriculture, Mack and Ethel's interests happily coincided — Mack had inherited his father's and grandfather's violins. In 1933 the Taverners sent all nine Beethoven symphonies as a present. Mack listened to them all in one sitting for the first time ever. He replied:

Those eight double sides leave a fellow in a ruddy glow. I guess I have the capacity for appreciation all right — it has taken root and grown in me like a lot of melon seeds in my window-boxes. Symphonies always haunt me. I can hear the various parts in my head and feel them in me but they can't be sung, hummed or whistled, they are d—— exasperating in a delightful, tantalizing sort of way. . . .[52]

A year later he wrote Taverner, "I like Schubert better at each hearing but still cannot rise to him like the other. If he would only grab a good theme by the tail and hang on and twist it as Beethoven does!. . . . I'd like him to rub it in a bit more!" His keen ear also enabled him to recognize bird songs from afar; together he and Ethel made a study of bird songs. In 1927, for example, Ethel wrote asking him to identify an unfamiliar bird by its song. "What bird would have a song something like this?" she asked:[53]

> see - see -   - gay
>   - such a

On another occasion, in 1935, Mack wrote to Taverner expressing his respect for Ethel's knowledge of bird song:

The other evening while I was up on the bench, I heard above the jabbering of the brant and beyond the brant and beyond the Spit a note that stopped me in my tracks in disbelief. Then I heard lots of it — and a voice from the house came up "Oh Mack — geese — a lot of them — 200 — 300 of them, speckle-bellies, white-fronts — the 'queek-queekers!'" Now I think that pretty good — there are a lot of folk can't tell a goose by his squawk as well as that. I saw Harper come back one day from the McMurray Prairie and report a lot of flocks of Canada geese, when every danged one of them was a wavey![54]

After the 1940 field season Mack retired from both writing and collecting. During the war he joined the Vancouver Island Militia Rangers, and in 1943 he turned down an offer to accompany the National Museum's Rand Expedition to the Alaska Highway.[55] Instead, after 1940, Mack and Ethel settled down to what would be their first and last few years of retirement together before her tragic and premature death from cancer in 1944. On August 6, 1944, he wrote Taverner:

Dear P.A.T.

I've lost Ethel. She died in the local hospital July 23rd after a very short illness — an illness that the doctors say was mercifully short, considering the nature of the trouble. She did not complain till about 3 weeks before her death. In hospital less than 2 weeks. What the medicos diagnosed as simply fibroid tumor, turned out to be a most malignant type and a fast worker involving about everything in the lower abdomen and there was absolutely nothing that could be done for her. It was terrible to see a strong and active woman in so short a time melt away and wither like a broken flower in the sun, but it was better so when she had to be taken. She never knew I believe, that she was in real danger, "felt far better" daily — after a small operation giving temporary relief — and her last words out of the coma an hour before she died were "I'm fine!" repeated several times.

I sometimes pause to wonder just what the devil it all means and what I'm working for, but it is best to carry on as usual. Time, they say, rubs down the sharp edge of it, and maybe so. When Fern (Ethel's sister, here now) takes the mother back to U.S. I'll be settling down to old habits of 17 years ago, a chapter of my life finished.[56]

PLATE 23   Allerdale Grainger, Chief Forester of British Columbia, with western red cedars on the Skagit River, British Columbia. July 28, 1919. PABC 96705

PLATE 24 Percy Algernon Taverner, Chief Ornithologist at the National Museum, Ottawa. East End, Saskatchewan, 1921. PABC 96652

PLATE 25   The Taverner party, Vaseux Lake, British Columbia, May 31, 1922.
Standing, left to right: Allan Brooks, P. A. Taverner, Frank Farley. *Seated, left to right*: Hamilton Laing, George Gartrell, D. Alan Sampson. National Museums of Canada, 56293

PLATE 26   Mack's pupil Edna Burns, Oak Lake, Manitoba, 1921. PABC 96629

PLATE 27   Charles H. "Bugs" Young setting a mole trap, Huntingdon, British Columbia, July 1, 1927. PABC 96666

PLATE 28   Ian McTaggart Cowan packing a black-tailed deer, Constitution Hill, Vancouver Island, November 10, 1930. PABC 96675

PLATE 29   Rudolph M. Anderson with a white-tailed doe, Yahk, British Columbia, September 21, 1929. PABC 96672

PLATE 30   J. A. Munro above Okanagan Landing, British Columbia, October 24, 1928. PABC 96671

PLATE 31   Allan Brooks examining roots of a Sitka Spruce, Comox, British Columbia, April 1928. PABC 96669

PLATE 32   Allerdale Grainger, Gus Murchy and unidentified individual on the Hope-Princeton skyline trail, 1919. PABC 96645

PLATE 33   Tommy Walker and George Drainy packing a mule deer, Precipice, British Columbia, October 17, 1939. PABC 98588

PLATE 34   Moving day at Cypress Lake, Saskatchewan, summer 1921. *Left to right*: P. A. Taverner, Mack Laing and D. Alan Sampson. PABC 96653

PLATE 35   National Museum field camp at "Heart's Desire," Oak Lake, Manitoba, *Left to right*: Hoyes Lloyd, P. A. Taverner, D. Alan Sampson and Mack Laing. July 5, 1921. National Museums of Canada, 53458

PLATE 36 Charles Guiguet with black grizzly, Stuie, British Columbia, September 16, 1938. PABC 96684

PLATE 37 Charles Guiguet at field camp. Tommy Walker's cabin, Stuie, British Columbia, September 16, 1938. PABC 96685

PLATE 38 Cougar Smith with a sheep-killing bear, Comox, November 28, 1929. PABC 95560

PLATE 39   Cougar Smith with a female panther and two cubs, Anderson Lake, Vancouver Island, January 25, 1930. PABC 96661

PLATE 40 "Stump-wangling" at Brooklyn Creek, Comox, April 1928. Burning a Sitka Spruce stump. PABC 96668

PLATE 41 Mack's camp on the Brooklyn Creek shell midden, November 1922. The seated figure is Norman Pritchard who helped clear the land and build Baybrook. PABC 96724

PLATE 42   With a juvenile bald eagle, Comox, September 1922. PABC 96654

PLATE 43   Ronald Stewart at hunting camp, Forbes Landing, Vancouver Island, 1923. PABC 96695

PLATE 44   With ringneck pheasants, Comox, October 15, 1924. PABC 96647

PLATE 45   Mack's first fire at Baybrook, October 11, 1923. PABC 96646

PLATE 46　At the Chitina River, Alaska, July 2, 1925. PABC 96662

PLATE 47   Gun-valeting, Baybrook, February 10, 1937. PABC 96683

PLATE 48   Shakesides, Mack's second home at Comox, located within the Mack Laing nature park, 1985. Photograph: Alexander Mackie.

PLATE 49   Sign marking the entrance to the Mack Laing nature park, Comox, British Columbia, January 1985. Photograph: Alexander Mackie.

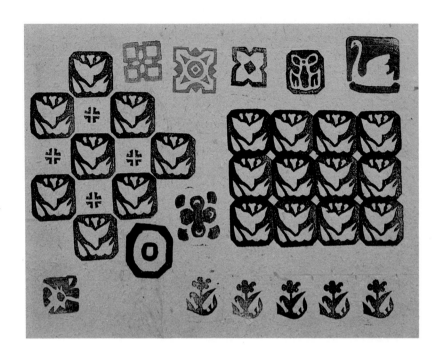

PLATES 50-51   Linocuts and pastoral scene dating from Mack's Pratt Institute years, 1911-1915. Drawings courtesy Town of Comox. Photographs: Alexander Mackie.

PLATE 52   Ethel Laing on the day after her marriage, January 20, 1927. Photograph: Nina Mayers. PABC 96657

PLATE 53   Ethel and Mack's honeymoon location: Punk Davis' cabin, Twelve Mile Creek, Princeton, British Columbia, November 6, 1927. PABC 96664

PLATE 54   Ethel Laing, *c*. 1927. PABC 96628

PLATE 55 Portrait of black woman, Pratt Institute, 1914-1915. Courtesy Town of Comox. Photograph: Alexander Mackie.

PLATE 56   Portrait of Indian woman, Pratt Institute, 1914-1915. Courtesy Alice
Bullen. Photograph: Alexander Mackie.

PLATE 57   Ethel's preserves, Comox, 1933. PABC 96632

PLATE 58   Meadow mushrooms from Baybrook, October 18, 1940. PABC 96658

PLATE 59   Baybrook cauliflower, April 1934. PABC 96679

PLATE 60   "Our worst predatory animal"—a 7 lb. 6 oz. tomcat trapped and shot at Comox, December 23, 1938. PABC 96694

PLATE 61   Baybrook Nut Orchard, Comox, January 26, 1950. PABC 96690

PLATE 62   Making salmon spoons, Comox, August 11, 1934. PABC 96681

PLATE 63   With spring salmon, Comox Bay, April 26, 1929. PABC 96674

PLATES 64-69 *Top row, left to right:* common goldeneye, pileated woodpecker.
Middle row, left to right: double-crested cormorant, goshawk.
Bottom row, left to right: peregrine falcon, surf scoter.
Courtesy James and Elizabeth Curtis. Photographs: Alexander Mackie.

PLATE 70   Autumn scene with barn swallows. Pratt Institute pastel drawing.
Courtesy Town of Comox. Photograph: Alexander Mackie.

PLATE 71   Haldor Eiriksson and Ethel Laing with 46½, 35, and 30 lb. salmon, Comox, August 7, 1932. PABC 96678

PLATE 72   Ethel and 35, 30 lb. salmon, August 7, 1932. "First of season." PABC 96676

PLATE 73   Mack and 44 lb. salmon, August 11, 1932. PABC 96677

PLATE 74   Hamilton Laing packing a grizzly through the Atnarko River, near
Stuie, British Columbia, September 16, 1938. PABC 96693

PLATE 75 At the feeder. *Top to bottom*: varied thrush, rufous-sided towhee, common grackle. Courtesy Town of Comox. Photograph: Alexander Mackie.

PLATES 76-77 Mixed media drawings, Pratt Institute, 1911-1915. Courtesy Town of Comox. Photograph: Alexander Mackie.

PLATE 78 In the nut orchard, *c.* 1970. Photograph courtesy Comox District Free Press, Courtenay, British Columbia.

X

The Hunter and The Scientist

WHOOP-LA! JUST DROPPED MY PEN, GRABBED
MY GUN AND GOT MY FIRST OAK LAKE
CHIPPING SPARROW.

— Hamilton Laing to Percy Taverner
July 26, 1921[1]

In 1935 the nature writer Bonnycastle Dale died at Riverview, his estate at Middle Clyde, Nova Scotia. A few weeks before his death he had written to his friend in Ottawa, Percy Taverner. He awaited, he said, "the Call to Workers, deeply regretting my labours were so light and my researches so immature, but I yet thrill at the very thought of the mighty spaces I covered in my field work." Dale was perhaps a little too modest, for he had spent several seasons at the turn of the century collecting biological specimens in British Columbia with William Spreadborough and John Macoun of the Geological Survey of Canada. Yet for the bulk of his career Dale had been a nature writer for Canadian and American magazines, and, apart from a valuable collection of some 4,000 photographic negatives, he left little of permanent scientific value comparable to Taverner's classic three books on Canadian birds.[2]

By contrast with Dale, Mack Laing's scientific legacy remains the most enduring of all his accomplishments. He collected perhaps 10,000 birds, mammals and plants now housed in museums, universities and private collections all over the world, though primarily at the National Museum of Natural Sciences in Ottawa and at the British Columbia Provincial Museum in Victoria. His specimens are literally in daily use at these institutions. He also wrote some two dozen scientific articles or notes for the major ornithological periodicals, in addition to about 700 popular newspaper or magazine articles on all aspects of natural history. He not only subscribed to but wrote for the *Canadian Field Naturalist,* the *Auk, Condor* and *Blue Jay.*[3] His most personally satisfying legacy to science was the two bird, two mammal and one plant species bearing his name or of his discovery. Finally, he taught an appreciation of natural history and a knowledge of collecting to his schoolchildren, to his Boy Scouts, to his thousands of readers, and to his National Museum student assistants in British Columbia.

Mack always stated that he was a "born" hunter and a "born" naturalist. Perhaps the most fundamental of the two was the hunting instinct which formed the basis of his interest in collecting and field work. In turn, his contribution to science was dependent in part on his hunting prowess. His father's wolf-hunting stories had furnished him at an early age with a fascination and respect for hunting, and as soon as he could read he discovered similar wolf stories told by Ernest Thompson Seton. As a schoolboy he became the "official farm pest trapper" and "pestwarden" of Spring Bank Farm, Clearsprings, where he graduated rapidly from slingshot to snare, to trap, to shotgun, and to rifle.[4] Hunting was in his blood, and his contention that he was a born hunter is witnessed by the unbounded enthusiasm with which he hunted geese in Manitoba with the Alford family, cougar with Cecil Smith, and deer with Martukoo on Vancouver Island. The primitive bloodlust of the hunt has no parallel in modern urban life. For example, after a 1922 mowitch (deer) hunt with Martukoo Good God-Yes! Stewart at Forbes Landing, Mack sat down and described the undertaking to Taverner:

It really was an intensive hour. Martukoo said I would have my deer in half an hour — Good God Yes! I went sneaking through those timbered jungles, forest primevals, till of a sudden on a rocky slope a little below me and 30 yds distant I saw my buck. He didn't see me. I promptly broke his neck. But he fell so that his head was up and his eye open and as I couldn't see that he had his head propped up I took another wipe at that neck and another and another and another — and old Martukoo was off in the distance saying "Mack's got the buck fever!" Well, I had, but it didn't help the deer much for he hadn't much left of his cervical vertebrae when I was through.[5]

Mack was one of thousands who enjoyed hunting. To many it was a matter of economic survival, but to some it was not. In 1926 he was inducted into an organization called the Brotherhood of Venery. Founded by Hoyes Lloyd in 1925, this élite and secret men's club has met annually ever since, usually in Toronto or New York. The "B of V" soon evolved into a venerable institution, and as the minutes of the 1970 Annual General Meeting testify, the time had come for mature reflection:

Hoyes Lloyd at that time [1925] was the first supervisor of Wildlife Protection for Canada and commanded deep respect among all. He proposed a long-considered and quietly-discused secret, fraternal order, based upon the age-old concept of hunting and the chase, to provide a focal point and sounding board where men of good will could come together and discuss mutual problems among themselves. With ten others, a creed and constitution were written and adopted. It is based on the ancient act of venery — hunting for sport.[6]

On being notified of his induction in 1926 Mack wrote to Hoyes Lloyd that

I think it a fine idea. Were you handy I might lead you forth from the ways of the devil, the world and the flesh, up to Constitution Hill where we would shoot a noble stag. The only thing I don't like about the B of V is the title. It sounds too reminiscent of a certain ward of military hospital, all too well patronized '14-'18.[7]

Though Mack never attended a meeting of the "B," it has been patronized since 1925 by several other naturalists including J. A. Munro, Ian McTaggart Cowan, Kenneth Racey, J. B. Harkin, Robie Tufts and Percy Taverner.[8]

But Mack was also a naturalist at heart, with a fundamental appreciation of the outdoors. "The bird enthusiast afield goes forth several times blessed," he wrote in 1922. "He has all the joy and pleasure of the scientist, the explorer and discoverer linked to the returns in physical fitness of the mountaineer, general hiker and outdoor lover. He has a point, an ambition to every ramble."[9] As a small boy he had learned the natural history of every square inch of the Clearsprings farm, and so strong was his desire to become a naturalist that he took a story-writing course in 1905. Like his heroes Edward Thompson Seton and John Burroughs, and countless others before them, the pen was the only legitimate way for a naturalist to earn a living. A university training was a superfluous asset: a "born naturalist" could appreciate nature, voice articulate thoughts, and earn the respect of other naturalists without any formal training in science. As a writer, Mack's trademark was a descriptive, anecdotal style based squarely on his nature diaries, which might contain, for instance, all the striking or unusual observations made on a day outdoors at Oak Lake or on a walk in a Brooklyn park. And after Burroughs' "nature faking" charge of 1903, Macks' stories were scrupulously honest and realistic. He had high standards and great integrity. For instance, in 1919 he ridiculed the naturalist Norman Criddle for his description of the snow goose in Manitoba, saying that Criddle had obviously never seen one of the birds. "I shall stick to what I *know*," he wrote proudly to Fleming. Jim Curtis, a retired forester and amateur naturalist at Comox, characterizes Mack's popular stories as "gospel" and "completely reliable" in terms of their scientific value.[10] And it was exactly this reliability that attracted naturalists and professional ornithologists alike to his writings. Moreover, as A. C. Bent's enthusiasm testified, Mack's early articles also constituted a significant contribution to early twentieth-century Canadian ornithology.

A. C. Bent was the author of the epic seventeen-volume *Life Histories of North American Birds* published between 1918 and 1939. These books remain the standard encyclopedia for many ornithologists today. Bent quotes Mack's observations for no fewer than eleven birds, ranging from the Alaskan three-toed woodpecker to the prairie sharp-tailed grouse. He quotes most extensively from an article called "Garoo, Chief Scout of the Prairies," published in *Outing* magazine in September 1915; he also obtained Mack's permission to use his excellent close-range photographs of the sandhill crane, or "Garoo."[11] Other early admirers included ornithologists Francis Harper, J. H. Fleming and Percy Taverner. In August 1915 Harper described to Taverner his meeting with Mack:

This spring I became acquainted with Hamilton M. Laing, the Manitoba chap who writes so much good stuff for Outing and Recreation, and has published a whole book on his experiences with the wild life of the prairies. I presume you know the book ("Out With the Birds"), and if not, I am sure you would be glad to get it and read it. While it is not particularly scientific, and perhaps not even accurate in a few details, it is, I believe a valuable contribution to [North] American nature writing.[12]

Given Mack's lack of a scientific education and his popular audience, his preference for the narrative and descriptive over the analytical or deductive methods of science is not surprising. One of the several aspects of his writing that appealed to both scientists and the general public was his spirited but accurate rendition of bird song. For instance, an American reviewer of *Out With the Birds* found that "Mr. Laing's syllabic representations of the songs of certain familiar species are original and quite as effective as the more familiar ones. For example . . . the White Throated Sparrow . . . says 'Oh, dear Canada! Canada! Canada!'" Mack's books and articles are full of similar renditions of bird songs; indeed, he built up a bird song "dictionary" in his head which, unfortunately, he never committed to paper. A crowd of wavies on the Manitoba prairie cried: "Woolly-head! woolly-head! Ha-ha-ha! Yelp! Yelp!" The Traill's flycatcher of British Columbia said: "Brigadier!" or "Tre-de-deer!" The olive-sided flycatcher called: "Quick! Three beers!" The wren: "Tweedle-eedle-eedle-eedle-eedle!" The Steller's jay: "Clang-clang-clang-clang-clang!" and "Wolf!" The sound of the guillemots was: "T'seeeeee r-r-r-r!" The harsh wing quills of a big bald eagle: "Whiff-iff-iff"; and the flicker (at the top of his voice) "Murder!" "In solitude," Mack wrote, "my ear is always trained on the air tensely, consciously or unconsciously for the slightest sound in the woods and every bird that speaks up within hearing is sure to register."[13] Birds expressed a whole range of emotion in their song. For example, in 1922, he took a boat to the "gullery" at Mittlenatch Island in the Gulf of Georgia, where he was met by a "bedlam" of bird song:

Oh it was a Wagnerian symphony of the birds, a chorus of lost souls crying out from some realm of the damned where the sweetest sound that echoes from the portal is a chorus of wailing. It was a savage, cruel place this nursery; discord was more than phonic; strife was in the air. . . . I came down from the nursery full of the wonderment of it all — this savage nursery where bickering and quarrelling and disaster and death were the order of every day — apparent on every hand that colossal selfishness of Nature that makes one ponder on the meaning of it all.[14]

Mack was not a serious collector of birds until 1922. Though he had learned some rudimentary taxidermy from his father's manual in 1903, his bird mounts had been savaged by Gregor Fraser's house cat at Glenora, and he preserved very few birds between 1906 and 1922. Instead of collecting rare birds he put his energies into shooting their predatory enemies such as owls, hawks and crows, and he learned photography which conformed to his early conservationist principles. The turnaround came in July 1918 when he visited J. H. Fleming's vast bird collection in Toronto. He told Hoyes Lloyd of his reaction:

On Sunday morning after my Saturday with you, I phoned Mr. Fleming and then went out. Gee Whiz! What a day I had.... I enjoyed Mr. Fleming tremendously and he turned over a fair-sized museum for my inspection. I had a glorious time among the hawks and geese.... I realise more than ever before the folly of my past years in allowing specimens to slip through my fingers. I have a lot of data, diagrams and notes however.[15]

The Athabasca Expedition of 1920 was his first opportunity to collect birds for science, and he had as mentor the formidable American bird man J. Alden Loring. He began his career as a collector at Lac la Biche, Alberta, in April 1920. He was at first hesitant to shoot certain birds, particularly nesting birds. One evening he was returning to camp in his canoe when he spotted a rare species of salt-water duck that goes to fresh water to breed. This duck was on his list of *desiderata* but it had four or five little ones with it. As Jim Curtis recalls,

He got out his gun and levelled it, and then said "I can't do it!" So he put down his gun and went on paddling. But then he asked himself "What would he tell Harper?" because he was so utterly honest and they always discussed what they had collected and seen. So the collector's instinct got the better of him and he went back and shot the whole lot.[16]

Though he collected 502 birds that summer, he was still hesitant about doing it. "I started too late to like it," he complained to Taverner in December 1920. "I would rather photograph them. You've got to catch a Scotchman young, you know." But he soon became one of Canada's most expert "collector-preparator-specialists" as the National Museum termed its field men. In 1926 Taverner kidded him over a small mistake in identification: "Am surprised that Hamilton Mack Laing cannot tell an accipiter from a falcon.

I should think a Goshawk was the last bird a Gyrfalcon should be confused with."[17] And Mack became an expert mammal collector under Rudolph Anderson and "Bugs" Young. In 1932 Anderson wrote:

You are a good collector . . . we have obtained some knowledge of the mammal and bird life of Southern B.C., and have a representative collection. . . . The gain will be an increase of knowledge of the natural history and natural resources of Canada and diffusion of said knowledge to persons interested.[18]

Mack had ample justification for his avid collecting. He wrote that the early twentieth century was an "age of discovery in Canadian science" when trails were first blazed for "others to follow and improve." It was as a collector that Mack's hunting and naturalist instincts merged so satisfactorily. "The bird man's great hope," he wrote in 1922, "always is to get something new, something he has never seen before in the region or that no other naturalist has recorded. Such a quest adds zest to his game; it is the spice of life." It may appear contradictory to the modern reader that Mack could profess on the one hand to being a conscientious naturalist seeking the "sacred truth"[19] of his subject and on the other hand to shooting, trapping and skinning practically every form of life in Canada. Yet this is exactly what he did, and he did not see it as contradictory, any more than do modern scientists who use laboratory animals in their experiments.

Until relatively recently every serious naturalist or biologist had to go out armed with a gun to collect the animals he wanted to study. This was partly because optical instruments such as microscopes and zoom-lens cameras were not sufficiently powerful, but it was mainly because much of the initial collecting and taxonomic classification had not yet been done.[20] This was especially true in Canada where taxonomists simply did not know what kind of animals were living out there in the woods or beneath the waters of the sea. Indeed, the transition from gun to optical instrument could not take place in Canada until the basic species reconnaissance had been undertaken. Naturalists like Mack Laing therefore had to shoot birds and mammals in order to study them. They subscribed to a whole range of maxims which share a common ancestry with the competitive old hunting motto, "meet them and beat them." Two of these were "Find it and get it!" and "What's shot's history, what's missed's mystery."[21] In this climate of unknowing, the best hunter made the best collector, and ultimately the best scientist was the one with access to the best collection. "Science knows too little," Mack wrote, and he continued, "Science must forget its heart, even sometimes to the point of killing a nesting bird." While certain cynics argued that the maxim of indiscriminate collectors should be "Shoot first, identify afterwards," the collectors felt sure they had won the argument.[22] Mack wrote in 1922:

If all biological reconnaissance consisted of eye-spying on the birds with binoculars, field-work would be easy — and shorn at the same time of many of its deeper meaning and worth while things. Much knowledge can be gained only by use of gun and scalpel and stuffing forceps and formaldehyde solution, and collecting of specimens is really the major part of field-work. [For example] when it comes to distinguishing several of the flycatchers, the poet who asked us to name without using a gun, asked too much. It can scarcely be done even by the most expert with the specimens before him. For two of these tiny chaps: the Wright's flycatcher and the Hammond's are classified mainly according to their wing formulas when in hand. If the first primary is shorter than the sixth the bird is the Wright's flycatcher; if the first is equal to or longer than the sixth the bird is the Hammond's. It is hard to make such fine classification when these fellows are darting after insects through the sunny openings of the shrubbery![23]

The Migratory Birds Convention Treaty of 1917 established a system whereby certain authorized collectors could continue to shoot rare birds. Permit holders now had to receive, annually, the approval of both federal and provincial wildlife authorities. Hoyes Lloyd of the Dominion Parks Branch issued these permits. In 1920 the permits stipulated that:

Permits to take migratory birds, their nests and eggs, under the Migratory Birds Convention Act and Regulations are granted for the sole purpose of scientific study and not for the collection of objects of curiosity or personal or household adornment. Therefore only such persons as take a serious interest in ornithology, and are competent to exercise the privilege for the advancement of knowledge, are elegible to receive such permits.

Finally it is urged that provision be made so that specimens taken will ultimately find their way into permanent or public collections where they will be available for study by future generations and not be wasted or lost through neglect.[24]

It was permits such as this that allowed an active group of ornithologists in British Columbia between the wars to establish large collections of birds, most of which have found their way into museum collections.[25]

Occasionally, however, some early collectors were over-zealous in their collecting. One British egg collector, for example, actually destroyed the entire osprey population of part of Scotland.[26] In British Columbia between the wars several naturalists spoke up in protest against what they saw as the depredations of a trigger-happy permit-holding clique including Taverner, Brooks and Mack Laing. One was Theed Pearse of Comox, author of *Birds of the Early Explorers in the Northern Pacific*. Pearse professed an ecological awareness and was in favour of wildlife sanctuaries. He was also Mack's neighbour. In the 1920's Pearse established his property as a "no-shooting preserve"; Mack's response was to stand on the property line at the edge of the preserve and call out the birds with his pygmy owl "decoy call" learned from Allan Brooks. Birds were so curious at the identity of this mysterious predator that they would come and investigate Mack's "magic call" — only to be collected for their curiosity.[27] Another of the handful of naturalists subscribing to the new ecological perspective between the wars was J. H. Parham of Penticton. In his 1937 book, *A Nature Lover in British Columbia*, Parham complained that collecting permits had fallen "into the hands of men who find collecting for sale a profitable business." Though he does not mention the names of these profiteers, he may well have had Mack in mind. Parham argued that collectors were responsible for the disappearance of several birds including nesting Dickcissels, Sage Thrashers, Sandhill Cranes, Wilson's Phalaropes and Lazuli Buntings from southern British Columbia. Parham pointed a guilty finger at the damage done to his Vaseux Lake "Bird-Paradise" by Taverner's National Museum expedition of 1922; finally, he pointed out that Wildlife Protection Officers from the regional to the national level were themselves hunters and collectors.[28] It was only after the Second World War that limits were imposed on the extensive powers given to most permit holders. By this time, however, pre-war collectors were dying and leaving their valuable collections to the Provincial Museum or to the museum at the University of British Columbia. The result is that many such institutions across Canada contain splendid collections which will remain useful to ornithologists for as long as birds are studied. The Victoria bird artist Fenwick Lansdowne, for example, received his only formal ornithological training amongst the British Columbia Provincial Museum's bird specimens.

As the biological map of Canada filled out in the mid-twentieth century, so did the intersts and methods of biologists change. Similarly, the improvement in optical instruments during the early years of the century was paralleled by a "takeover" of Natural History — which had been a discipline staffed largely by amateurs — by university-trained specialists such as herpetologists, ichthyologists, entomologists and parasitologists. In Canadian museums and universities this takeover took place between 1930 and 1950; in Britain and in the United States it had occurred somewhat earlier. Mack's field assistants such as Elgin Hall, Ian McTaggart Cowan, Charles Guiguet and George Holland participated in the takeover from the ranks of amateur naturalists. With his enviable interest and expertise in birds, mammals and plants, Mack was one of the last of Canada's Victorian naturalists, though it is worth noting that his scientific achievement was much more permanent than that of the stereotypical Victorian natural history dilettante.

Mack was very proud of his formal contribution to science, the more so because he had had no formal academic training. His major papers of discovery are those on the birds of the Mount Logan and Thiepval expeditions of 1924 and 1925, which were published by the National Museum. He wrote to Anderson in 1926: "I am rather pleased with the Thiepval report. As it is my first born, so to speak, I am naturally a bit proud of its appearance." His are well-written, lively reports — unlike some of the scientific papers he ridiculed in the *Auk*, which he complained were "written with a funereal air that almost is solemn enough to be funny."[29] Many of his discoveries were of a practical, unspectacular nature. For example in the late 1930's when he and Charles Guiguet were staying at one of Tommy Walker's base camps in the Rainbow Mountains, the mountain climber Phyllis Munday brought them what she thought was a mouse. Her horse had stepped on it and killed it on the way down from Mt. Brilliant, and knowing that naturalists were in the area, she kept it for them. The "mouse" was actually a Red Lemming which at that time had never been found south of Telegraph Creek in northern British Columbia. Mack and Guiguet were very excited and went into Tommy's Pass where they collected a fine series of forty Red Lemmings for the National Museum. Phyllis Munday's accidental discovery may have resulted only in a few lines of text and an amendment to Anderson's Red Lemming distribution map, but the cumulative effect of such discoveries was considerable. Similarly, Guiguet discovered that the Pika, a rock rabbit, lived at sea level at the head of Bute Inlet, at the foot of a large rock slide. Pika were thought to occur only at much higher elevations. This discovery earned Guiguet the nickname "Pika Charlie."[30]

Mack often referred to his discoveries as his "children." In addition to his *Antennaria Laingii* from the Chitina River Valley, two birds and two small mammals were named after him. One was a sub-species of the long-billed wren from Lake Athabasca named in 1927 by Francis Harper *Telnatodytes palustris Laingi*. Harper named it after "Hamilton M. Laing, in appreciation of his writings on the bird life of western Canada." In 1932 Taverner wrote: "P.S. I see the new Check List gives the new Marsh Wren, *Laingi* domain over the whole prairies — congratulations for the house of Laing." When Mack heard the news he exclaimed, "I never deserved a new bird named for me, but being human I hope he [Harper] makes it stick."[31] Unfortunately, the bird has recently fallen prey to a "taxonomic lumper" and now appears as *Cistothorous palustris* (Wilson). While working for Anderson Mack found two new British Columbia mice. The first was "Laing's White-footed mouse," or *Peromyscus maniculatus Vancouverensis*. The second was the Anarchist Mountain Pocket Mouse, or *Perognathus Laingi*. Anderson explained that he would have named the first *Peromyscus maniculatus Laingi* but "I might have been accused of playing favourites." Mack wrote to Fleming in 1933 about his discoveries: "I suppose you saw about the new B.C. mice and that I have a name sake in that line. I brought back some interesting mice last trip — plainly intermediate between the cuss here that steals my peas and the new mountain form of Peromyscus. . . ."[32]

Over the years Mack developed several general theories of bird extinction, distribution and migration. The first concerned the disappearance of the passenger pigeon — which as a boy his father had pointed out to him. According to Jim Curtis, Mack believed that "after market hunters got through with most of them, the prairie hawks cleaned up the remnants because otherwise they wouldn't have disappeared." He also felt that alcohol-soaked grain was responsible in part for their final extinction.[33] His other theory concerned the westward movement of birds on the Canadian prairies where he had seen, for example, Eastern Kingbirds and Woodpeckers nesting on telephone poles for want of trees. He expounded this theory in "Feathered Pioneers of Canadian North-West," a popular article published in 1936 in the *Canadian Geographical Journal*:

A great many species have actually pioneered with the settler, working steadily north-westerly into that whole new empire claimed by the landseeker in that invasion that, beginning in the '70s down in eastern Manitoba, has its outpost today in the Peace River. Westward and northward has been the path of the plow and ever in the wake of the furrow has followed a new tide of bird life.[34]

In British Columbia he believed for many years that Trumpeter Swans never came to salt water and characteristically refused to talk to anyone in Comox who claimed otherwise. In this he had the support of Ralph Edwards of Lonesome Lake, who in the winter would break the ice to feed the swans. Suddenly to his great surprise Trumpeter Swans were found at Comox, affirming his theories of westward bird migration.[35] Unfortunately Mack never wove together all the strands of evidence into a comprehensive publication.

Mack was a Victorian naturalist both in the range of his interest and in the variety of his scientific output. Moreover, like Seton he combined the scientific with a prolific popular literary output. He made by far his greatest contribution to science as a field collector, and by doing so, helped lay the foundations of modern Canadian biology — just as his National Museum contemporaries like Marius Barbeau ranged the country collecting the artifacts and myths of Canadian Indians. The only regret, in this context, is that he did not immediately pursue a scientific career when he left the Winnipeg Collegiate in 1900. Finally, he owed his value as a collector of biological specimens to the fact that he was a "born hunter," yet it was this same deep-rooted hunting instinct that conditioned his hostile attitude to predatory animals.

XI

Conservation and Predation

IN ARGUMENT EACH MAN SEES BUT ONE ISSUE —
HAS BUT ONE IDEA. THAT DOUBTLESS IS THE
REAL CAUSE OF THE WHOLE BLOODY WAR.

— *Hamilton Laing*
Nature Diary, November 20, 1917[1]

Like many of his contemporaries, Mack Laing was both a committed conservationist and a dedicated hunter. To most genuine conservationists of his generation, this was neither cynical nor even contradictory. The bird conservation movement was started by hunters and naturalists alarmed that slaughter by market hunters and unprincipled sportsmen posed a serious threat to the survival of certain species. Early proponents of wildlife conservation in the United States included John Muir, Gifford Pinchot, G. O. Sheilds and Teddy Roosevelt—who was a fanatical big-game hunter. These men were responsible for publicizing conservation in the United States in the two or three decades before 1914, and their views were welcomed by a public shocked, for example, by the disappearance of the passenger pigeon. This bird, once present by the millions, was extinct by 1900. These early conservationists were appalled at the methods employed by market hunters to catch their game, such as nets and machine guns; and through such organs as the League of American Sportsmen and G. O. Sheilds' *Recreation* magazine and the Audubon Society, they influenced the public in favour of conservation. The movement was at first stronger in the United States than it was in Canada, which was a much younger and more sparsely populated country, and one with a necessary emphasis on resource exploitation and development.[2] Mack spent his formative years in Manitoba under the long-distance influence of the early American conservation movement; his move from Manitoba to New York in 1911 took him to the centre of the whole movement. From New York he campaigned against market hunters in Manitoba. In *Outing* magazine in 1914, for example, he wrote concerning migratory birds. "They come to us from afar in the autumn; they return to us from afar in the spring; not a tithe of anything do they seek from mankind; they ask nothing but a safe passport through the land. Might not they have it?"[3]

Out of the clamour for bird conservation came the Migratory Birds Convention Treaty of 1917 between Canada and the United States, which signalled the final official adoption of conservationist policies in both countries. The treaty sought to control market hunting, in order to avoid the kind of destruction of wildlife that had occurred with the passenger pigeon. The treaty also placed limits on the hunting season of migratory birds and resulted in the creation of the Canadian Wildlife Service to administer the act.[4] Mack was fully in sympathy with the aims of the Treaty, and very nearly found a job in 1919 in Ottawa as Hoyes Lloyd's propaganda writer. But just because he was sympathetic to the aims of the conservation movement did not mean he threw down his guns and rifles and stopped shooting innocent animals. "It isn't the homesteader away back knocking over a goose that I object to," he told Hoyes Lloyd in 1926, "it is these well-off farmers and sports from the towns making a slaughter among birds that are tame from protection south of the line." Mack always brought his pragmatic, frontier wildlife philosophy to his attitude to conservation. As naturalist Janet Foster has shown, the early conservation movement was split between the "wise-use" conservationists and the later, more radical, "no-use" preservationists. Mack Laing was clearly of the "wise-use" generation.[5]

A final paradox of the early conservation movement is that its adherents followed strict rules of outdoor behaviour. It was very important to set oneself apart from the unprincipled mob who shot birds only for profit. It was felt that if the correct rules of conduct were followed, shooting for sport could be a healthy, character-forming exercise. These rules were cautiously expressed in 1926 by Percy Taverner in the preface to *Birds of Western Canada*.

There are certain birds which for their size, habits, and general food value are regarded as legitimate game. The pursuit of these is invigorating sport, tends to the healthful welfare of the sportsman, and teaches woodcraft, hardihood, out-of-door adaptability, and marksmanship. The true sportsman has a code of ethics founded upon economic as well as humanitarian principles. He shoots nothing without giving it a fair chance and little that cannot be used as food. He is also careful not to deplete the game upon which his future sport depends.[6]

Ornithologists such as Mack Laing and Allan Brooks exhibited nineteenth-century frontier ideas about bird conservation. In their eyes, predatory birds posed at least an equal threat to the survival of rare birds as did market hunters and the advance of civilization. Brooks had experienced pioneer farming conditions on the Lower Fraser River in the 1880's, and Mack was brought up in a similar environment ten years later in rural Manitoba. Both had discovered a whole range of "bad" animals which posed a threat to their livestock or crops. Later, Brooks likened his role on his thirty-acre estate at Okanagan Landing to that of a "gamekeeper," and professed great admiration for the controlled game shooting of British estates.[7] Likewise, Mack saw his own role both at Clearsprings and Comox as that of game warden. In each case, the right to interfere with the laws of nature was explicit. The ideology of both men was based squarely on that of another frontier naturalist, Ernest Thompson Seton, who had farmed in Ontario and Manitoba, and whose classic *Wild Animals I Have Known* (1898) shows a hatred of predatory animals. Seton's horned owl, for example, is a "murderer," and Silverspot, the crow, has a passion for eating new laid bird eggs. "There is only one bird that terrifies the crow," Seton says, "and that is the owl."[8] In his attitude to pests and predators Mack never got beyond Seton's teachings. From 1900 to 1982 his attitude to predators was remarkably consistent. Falcons, for example, were "destructive little killers"; cougars were "the greatest foe of deer conservation; magpies were "thieves" with "noisy, impudent, abusive tongues"; a horned owl was a "killer"; a camp-raiding bear was a "conscienceless vandal"; mosquitoes were "foes"; a pack-rat was a "mischievous rascal . . . unloved by every hunter or camper or rancher in the land"; seals were "these terribly destructive enemies" owing to their taste for salmon.[9] At the bottom of Mack's list were crows and house cats. He was very proud of the fact that as a schoolboy in the 1890's he had entered several crow shoots. On one shoot he shot forty crows; market hunter William Bruce bagged forty-two to win the competition. Though Mack "felt bad" about losing to a market hunter, he was cheered when a spectator commented on his "creditable massacre." In later life, crows were "black tormenters," "black pirates," and "vermin." In 1919 he growled to Hoyes Lloyd from the Portland suburbs that: "Every year they come in here and rob all the nests they can find. I hate a crow. I don't know whether this ruffles your feathers or not. But I wish I had the last one of the species in a sack. I shot 40 adult crows once in one day. I wish I could do it *every* day."[10]

At Comox, Mack waged a very distasteful war against the domestic cat. Any cat that stepped on his property did so at the risk of his life. Whether they were stray cats or his neighbours' housecats, they were all "devils" in Mack's eyes and he got no greater satisfaction than killing them. His methods were gruesome. He described to Taverner in 1937:

The place is overrun with cats again, also coons and mink along the creek nightly. As for the cats I loaned my experienced old weather-beaten box trap and had to make a nice new one and it is so nice and new that the pussies won't even go in it to get salmon. They want the weathered, Tommy-smelling old one. Guess I'll have to use a #2 shell and turn the Tom loose in the box and decease him there and see if it alters matters.[11]

On another occasion J. H. Fleming was the recipient of one of his cat-hunting stories.

A good trapper has to have a lot of low cunning. I used my stock last night. There has been a huge black Tom cat prowling here, an awful yowler, living on the grouse and quail and birds. I tried to get him but missed one shot at dawn with the rifle and he wouldn't let me use scatter gun. So last evening I set a #2 double spring and a salmon tin beside my foot bridge and by 11 p.m. he was playing with that trap. I never saw so wicked a creature, wild or tame. He was snipping off rosebushes like a beaver. It was an awful business. A flashlight isn't intended for rifle shooting even at 4 or 5 feet among bracken and rose-bushes. He took 5 .22 bullets before he decided to quit. Must have had 9 times 9 lives. I was sorry only for my wife — who held the flash-light. Had she been the kind that faints, she would have been in the creek. But I have no mercy for the brutes — they are our worst predatory animal. A lot of the game problem of the coastal west is wrapped up in the wild house cat. We have no winter to subdue them as in the East.[12]

In his drive against predators Mack was supported by all levels of government and, at first, by popular sentiment. British Columbia's Game Act contained a list of what were termed "Noxious Animals." In 1922, 17,625 Horned and Snowy owls, 7,095 Bald-headed and Golden eagles, and 2,246 magpies were shot for bounty in British Columbia. Also in 1922 the provincial government offered a bounty of 20¢ a bill on crows. But just as these were "bad" animals, so there were "good" animals in Mack's outdoor ideology. Hornets were an acceptable insect because they were the "greatest scavengers" that fed on flies inside a tent and kept a camp clean of food scraps.[13] Swallows were good birds because they ate mosquitoes. Rattlesnakes were good animals because they fed on small mammals which destroy crops. At the basis of Mack's philosophy of natural history was a very basic spirit of competition that dated from his farm days. Half the members of the animal kingdom were enemies because their activities encroached in some way upon his existence as a farmer, rancher, fisherman and collector. Quite simply, life was a battleground upon which certain animals were the opposition, and where survival itself was at stake. A competitive voice told Mack: "I'd better shoot that hawk, because if I don't, he'll threaten my rare birds which it is my duty both to protect as a conservationist and destroy as a collector." To us today, his argument appears to have been an unwarranted and unacceptable interference with the natural cycle.

Yet there was not an ounce of sentimentality anywhere in his attitudes, and like Seton's his stories were realistic and rarely had happy endings. Concerning *Wild Animals I Have Known*, Seton wrote: "The fact that these stories are true is the reason why all are tragic. The life of wild animals always has a tragic end."[14] Similarly, Seton's contemporary Charles G. D. Roberts based his stories on a knowledge of what he termed the "savage and implacable sternness of the wild" and on the "normal savagery of Nature." Such views were based on the anti-Romantic, "Nature red in tooth and claw" aspect of Darwinian scientific thought, adopted by many early Canadian nature writers.[15] Seton's theme of the wilderness "tragedy" was central to Mack's ideology. "We so often meet the term 'benign Mother Nature'," Mack wrote in 1922, but it is only rarely "that we get the correct perception of Nature and learn the savage side, the deadly war of one creature on another; the near extermination that predators bring to the weak and inoffensive."[16] Nature to Mack could be a "savage nursery," and he returned again and again to the wilderness tragedy. In 1921 at Oak Lake for example he wrote to Taverner that:

On Sat. evening as we sat down to supper I saw the most bloody-awful tragedy of the wild I ever witnessed — and I have seen a lot of them. Heard ground squirrel squealing. Ran out. In grass, 12 feet from woods, found a big squirrel in the clutches of a long-tailed weasel. I stood over it and saw it all — and have been haunted by the bloody cruelty of it ever since! The wicked little devil did it handily enough, and seemed enthusiastic over it, but it was awful to look at.[17]

By 1920 Mack's late-Victorian or Edwardian nature philosophy had aged. Even in 1917 when the Migratory Birds Treaty was passed he was thirty-four years old. His ideas were up-to-date only for the first three decades of the twentieth century; in 1930 they appeared noticeably old-fashioned, and by 1940 they were verging on the reactionary. He was unprepared for the emergence of the balance of nature theory which stated that, given a stable habitat, "mortality must at least approximately balance reproduction."[18] In other words, predators will find their niche in a protected environment and cease to pose a threat. The balance of nature theory spawned the later ecological movement of the post-war era, in which man's interference in the natural cycle was severely restricted.

As nature writer Janet Foster has shown, the emergence of the preservationist or ecological movement was the major influence on Canadian wildlife policy between 1920 and 1940.[19] On an institutional and intellectual level it divided the old conservationists from the new: the nineteenth-century naturalists from the twentieth-century biologists. The old gentlemen sportsmen and hunters constituted the conservative "right wing" while the new, university-educated, protectionist, ecological-minded twentieth-century products formed the "left wing." The controversy split the Canadian ornithological community in half. On the right there were the old amateur hunter-naturalists like Allan Brooks and Mack Laing; somewhere in the middle were Hoyes Lloyd and Percy Taverner vainly struggling to keep the peace; and on the left were ornithologists J. A. Munro, Theed Pearse and H. J. Parham. The left was joined on a popular level by Englishman Archibald Stansfield Delany, who went by the name of "Grey Owl."[20] By 1935 the press and general public had come out in favour of wildlife protection which meant sanctuaries, parks and reserves. The truth is that the advocates of each faction were in their own way dedicated to wilderness conservation in some form.

The thirty bird sanctuaries created across Canada by Hoyes Lloyd and the Parks Branch between 1917 and 1921 served as the catalyst of discontent in Canadian ornithology.[21] Collecting was forbidden in these sanctuaries. Allan Brooks and Mack took this personally: it seemed that their competitors, the predators, had been given a free rein to murder all the migratory birds they wanted, while they, the collectors, were forbidden. Brooks for one believed that game reserves were simply "sanctuaries for predatory mammals and birds." He pointed in 1932 to the Rocky Mountains National Park which apparently was "desolate of bird life except Ravens, Crows, Magpies, etc." Indeed, from a collecting point of view sanctuaries spelled disaster. J. A. Munro — the federal wildlife officer in charge of the implementation of protectionist policies in British Columbia — was aware of the contradictions inherent in creating sanctuaries where birds of prey would be given the freedom to kill. In 1923 he wrote to Mack stating the case that: "If it is desirable to put a man in jail for killing an insectivorous bird or a game bird out of season it is surely equally desirable to kill a Sharp Shinned Hawk that may dispose of 400 in a year. It is a delightful spectacle to watch but that is beside the point."[22] Munro, however, later took up the protectionist cause much to Brooks' disgust, who complained that Munro's "whole religion is to oppose anything I advocate." Though they had once been good friends and were neighbours at Okanagan Landing, Brooks and Munro fell out initially because Munro kept his arsenic in a Magic Baking Powder tin, which Brooks mistook for baking powder.[23] Brooks believed that Munro was a hypocrite because he preached wildlife protection while remaining a bird collector. In 1930 he confided to his ally Mack that:

Munro and all the Parks Branch sail with the tide & turn their sails to the favourable wind, it's easy to be profitable, the press all believe in a beneficial nature and the kindly offices of predatory animals. But the time is coming when the public will know the truth and already some of the idealists are being fired.[24]

In 1930, Theed Pearse, supported by Kenneth Racey, put forward an enlightened proposal to turn the whole of Comox Bay and Comox Spit into a bird sanctuary. Brooks was opposed to the idea because, he said — in all seriousness — "The Bay is a sanctuary right now, if no shooting is allowed it will become a hunting ground for all the eagles in the region and there will be no one to protect the ducks."[25] By 1937 the Provincial Game Commission had finally rejected the proposal, much to Brooks' delight.

What Brooks and Mack were unable to recognize was that the frontier conditions of their youth had passed and consequently that their anti-predator and pro-collecting philosophy made them easy targets. So they plunged into battle with what Brooks uncharitably termed the "infernal new crowd" of "rabid protectionists," such as the Parks Branch and the recently formed Audubon Society. In their eyes these organizations preached a gospel of hypocrisy. As early as 1923 Brooks blasted a so-called "game expert" in the Yosemite Park district of California who he believed was more concerned with showing his "bird students" how to "smell trees" than with preventing the oil spillages which had killed thousands of ducks in the area. To Brooks, preservationists were "opera glass friends," "binocular students," "indoor naturalists," "theorists," "idealists," "cranks," or worst of all, "college proffessors [sic] and desk men" who taught their gullible students that "Nature can correct anything."[26] Similarly, Mack despised "these high pressure, long-distance protectionists," these "afternoon-tea, field glass experts," who taught that "nature in her wonder" would protect the weak and inoffensive birds from predators. Both Brooks and Mack were influenced by the influential California biologist Joseph Grinnell's 1915 article "Conserve the Collector," which coined the expression "opera-glass student" to refer to desk or microscope-bound opponents of collecting.[27] But the victory of the despised preservationists was inevitable for a number of reasons. First, as Canada moved into the 1930's the frontier conditions that so many of the

148

older generation had experienced were fast disappearing. The younger, urban naturalists had no animosity for predators: all animals were of equal worth. Second, much of the basic collecting and classification had been completed by 1930. Third, the despised "university-trained" biologists were taking over the museums, universities and government departments from the gifted amateurs, and instead of looking down rifle sights they were looking down microscopes. There was simply less room in mid-century Canada for the amateur naturalist or gentleman sportsman to roam the mountains in search of rare birds or big game.

What made this a bitter pill for the likes of Brooks and Mack to swallow was that they had done good work and knew it. They were also committed naturalists with a knowledge of the Canadian outdoors that few, perhaps, will ever equal. What Mack says in his biography of Allan Brooks goes for both men:

The necessary killing in his years of field work did not cause him a qualm. That was an unfortunate necessity to ornithological knowledge; if his conscience ever dwelt on it he would have answered that the killing of all the collectors in [North] America were as one straw in a stack compared to the toll of the natural predators, not to mention the hazards of civilization: house cats, autos, ships, trains, lighthouses, fences and various high electric wires, crude oil on the waters, etc. — bird material tragically wasted. He believed that there was only one road to ornithological knowledge: get the material, preserve it for posterity, study it and interpret its meaning.[28]

Allan Brooks and Mack Laing were also prophets. In many ways they were ahead of public opinion, particularly in their concern with industrial pollution and with the destruction of the wilderness. In 1922 Mack was shocked at the fate of the Ponderosa pine tree in the Okanagan. "As for the trees," he wrote, "it was plain that they were a remnant . . . that such trees should be felled for mere firewood seemed a crime against nature and man; against the former that took hundreds of years to raise such a monument; against the latter in the generations to come that may not see such trees and may miss the joyous thrill of worshipping at their feet." Twenty years later he made a trip into the central mountains of Vancouver Island west of Comox, into a district he had previously visited to hunt deer and cougar. He wrote with anger to Taverner in 1941:

"This whole country is just one slashing. 15 miles inland the timber is gone. It was brought home to me a week ago when I went up with the logging tram. . . . What a desolation!"[29] Industrial air pollution or "acid rain" was another of Mack's concerns. In 1922 he journeyed eastward from the Okanagan into the Kootenay mountains where he reported that:

There was really a great change on every hand. My last view eastward disclosed at 2000 feet below, the desert of the Columbia Valley — blue-hazy, burning; that man-made desert that is more gruesome than any work of Nature; the blight of the poison gas from the Trail Smelter that has killed and left the blanched skeleton of the forest at its feet.[30]

In his disgust at maritime oil pollution Mack was a good forty years ahead of public sentiment. In 1928 he complained to Taverner:

Maybe you heard of our latest waterbird disaster. Logging Co. at Deep Bay, near Union Bay, pumped 2200 gals. crude oil into tank on teredo-eaten wharf — plumped the whole works in the bay. For 40 miles along this shore the place was littered — more or less of course — by oiled and dying birds — grebes, loons, ducks, murres, etc. I counted 6 oiled scoters in 100 yards in front of my house. They did not last long. Had to come ashore. Eagles just mopped them up in no time. Thousands of birds cached in. . . .

No crude oil should be stored, loaded or unloaded by pumping on wharf over water. If the federal law has teeth enough to pinch some poor guy for shooting a scoter out of season, what about a logging co. that by utter negligence will crucify thousands of birds! It is the cruelest damned thing I ever saw![31]

In the face of what they considered stupidity and hypocrisy on the part of the Parks Branch and the various conservationist groups, and ignorance on the part of the rising younger generation, Mack and Allan Brooks finally adopted a theory in the 1930's called "Practical Conservation." This theory was essentially a well-argued, articulate justification of the old frontier, game warden philosophy. The popular Ontario conservationist Jack Miner was the third champion of "Practical Conservation" in Canada. In 1932, Miner was successful in securing the complete withdrawal of hawks from protection in Ontario.[32] The two most important aims of "Practical Conservation" were, first, to bring to public notice the evil effects of modern civilization on nature; and second, to show the evil side of nature itself. Mack, Miner and Brooks desired to offset what they saw as "the fanatical harangues of the God-made-the-little-birds fellows." Miner went on the lecture tour, Brooks took to his easel, and Mack took to his pen to show the world the habits of such killers as hawks, owls, housecats and eagles. In Winnipeg, some 14,000 came to hear Jack Miner talk compared to only 7,000 who came the previous evening to hear British politician Lloyd George. Brooks did his part by painting a series called "Hawks of North America" for the Audubon Society. He portrayed the hawks with bloody talons and dead songbirds in their claws. He was enraged when the Audubon Society returned the paintings and asked that the blood be removed.[33]

It may seem unfortunate that Mack was drawn into this volatile dispute, but very few of his contemporaries were able to remain on neutral ground. One who tried was Percy Taverner, who Mack accused of fence-sitting. "I know which side I'm on," he proudly wrote Taverner in 1940, "whereas as I see it, you're straddling the top rail of the fence trying to get a foot anchored in each lot and even your long legs can't quite make it. . . . Man alive, wake yourself up, tell the truth and shame the devil as Bill Shakes [William Shakespeare] said." Mack had never held his punches, and he had always expressed to his readership the realistic frontier view of nature he had learned in rural Manitoba. When the battle lines were drawn, he found that his most powerful weapons against the "sentimentalists" were his intimate knowledge of the cruel natural world and his ability to describe the evil ways of predators in sober, vivid prose. "One thing I can do," he wrote Fleming in 1931, "and that is tell the truth as I see it. There are no strings on me; and I am grinding no axes." He therefore wrote a whole series of articles aimed at vindicating his philosophy of natural history and showing the Parks Branch and the Aubudon Society the error of their ways. "It was time some one told some truth to offset the methods of that gang," he wrote, "and I don't mind being the goat."[34]

As the 1930's progressed — and as international tension increased — Mack's predator articles seem to grow increasingly vicious. Indeed the almost pathalogical level of intolerance displayed by the "Hawkists" and "Anti-hawkists" toward each other parallels the social intolerance characteristic of contemporary fascist states. In

"Page Mr. Bubo: How You Can Eliminate This Killer," published in *Field and Stream* in December 1936, Mack exhorts the reader to call the owl out of the woods to be shot. He was affronted by the horned's owl's competition. In the article's opening paragraph he could almost be describing himself:

The horned owl, of whatever race, is usually rated as one of Nature's most efficient executioners. Few people realize his efficiency. He has the wing speed of a goshawk, and under his weather-proof coat is the muscular strength of a tomcat. In his head he carries ears of magic sensitiveness and eyes like a binocular telescope, and in his heart a killing lust that keeps him well nourished anywhere. From one of his lesser owl cousins to a turkey, he dines impartially. He is deadly to game birds — another reason why one of his kind in a landscape is generally regarded as one owl too many. Every hand should be against him.[35]

Allan Brooks encouraged him. "You," he wrote in 1932, "are one of the very few nature writers that tell the truth to the public." So successful was "Page Mr. Bubo" that Ray P. Holland, the editor of *Field and Stream*, asked for more articles showing "the sane side of the predator problem." The results were "Befuddled Conservation" of April 1937 and "Predation in the Backyard" of December 1939, subtitled "Illuminating figures on common winged predators that kill 365 days a year."[36] These articles may tell the "truth," but they are nonetheless realistic propaganda aimed at showing, at any price, the existence of Seton's "wildlife tragedies." "Befuddled Conservation" attempted to correct some of the misconceptions of the popular conservation movement. In response, Mack received a flurry of hate letters from advocates of the new school of thought which show the intensity of the controversy. One was from Hampton J. Carson, Jr., of the Zoological Laboratory, University of Pennsylvania:

Your unintelligent and sentimental baloney is what makes my blood boil. When you talk about "horror thrillers," and call the Sharpshin a "dirty murderous wretch" for merely fulfilling his biological needs for food, it is a preposterous hypocrisy. I suppose it never occurred to you did it, that the number of birds killed and as many more winged and left to die annually by the sportsman who kills for fun, might possibly be considered a "horror thriller?" No I am not a sentimentalist, I'm red-blooded and two-fisted, and have hunted and fished all my life. You're the sentimentalist — anybody that would save his poor dear little robin from a hawk — you might as well shoot the robin to save the dear little earthworm, or your butcher when he kills a chicken for you to eat.

Well, I won't waste any more of my time or yours. Frankly, I thought your article was rotten, and maybe some day you'll think so too; for your sake, I sincerely hope so.

> Yours truly,
> *Hampton L. Carson, Jr.*[37]

But Mack was undeterred. He got the idea for "Predation in the Backyard" early in 1938 when he observed eagles and hawks plucking waterbirds from the beach in front of Baybrook. He wrote to Ray Holland outlining his ideas and Holland responded enthusiastically. Mack aimed the article at a man he believed was a "paid propagandist" of the preservation movement, Richard H. Pough of the Audubon Society. "Pow, puff or peow?" Mack wondered. The article is a forceful recapitalization of Mack's 1938 Comox nature diary, illustrated with a few gory photographs of hawks and owls alongside their plucked and half-eaten victims. The article concludes:

I have not hunted for these gruesome exhibits with malice aforethought. The predation of my little shore acreage was not sought, but thrust upon me. And if in the light of man predation — autos that strew our thousands of miles of road with bird remains; lighthouses that bring death in the night; endless highwires that spread destruction across every landscape; flotsam oil that spreads cruelest fate across our waters; our drainage and tillage and pasturage that often bring slow fatality — if in the light of these things, such predators as sharpshins, Cooper's hawks, goshawks, horned owls and some others of that ilk are necessary to keep Nature in my backyard in healthy and happy condition, then my judgment in the matter is poor indeed![38]

In Pough's very calm response he set forth his belief in the balance of nature theory. "My enjoyment of the wild creatures themselves is free from any necessity to have possession of them, or to use them in any way," Pough wrote. Worse than Pough's confident reaction was Percy Taverner's response — Canada's leading ornithologist and one of Mack's best friends. Nearly twenty years earlier Taverner had questioned the validity of his anti-crow campaign: "You must have a grudge against those crows, haven't you any heart or any poetry in your soul? The soft tinkle of bells and the lowing of kine. Don't you know you should love such things? And then the way you stepped on my effusions — it was positively brutal!"[39] Later, Taverner acted as mediator in the predation dispute. In 1932 he had responded to one of Mack's more level-headed articles, "Hawks That Concern the Hunter," published in the *Illustrated Canadian Forest and Outdoors*. "Your hawk paper is just the stuff," Taverner wrote:

If we had more like it we could get somewhere on the hawk question. Unfortunately we are divided into Hawkist and anti-Hawkist and neither side ever publicly admits that there is any good in the other. Both are fanatics. If Brooks and Miner et al. would work as hard to protect the good hawks as they do to condemn the bad ones (the other side vice versa) we could all meet on common ground and perhaps do something constructive.[40]

After reading "Predation in the Backyard," Taverner decided to call Mack's bluff. He sat down and wrote a seven-page letter to *Field and Stream* objecting to the article. It begins as a plea for compromise and reason.

I have known Mr. Laing for many years, indeed I am happy to count him among my most valued friends. I know his sincerity and his ornithological competence and his wide field experience, and respect him for them. I also know the particular scene that he describes, hawk and eagle tree and all. I do not question a single evidence that he produces. However, I beg to differ from some of the conclusions that he advances or infers — particularly that predation as predation is wholly evil.

Taverner systematically cuts the ground out from under Mack's feet in an elegant defence of the balance of nature perspective.

To condemn a predator for merely beating us to the kill is hardly a sportsmanlike attitude, the less so that we do it for sport and he does it of necessity for a living. To stigmatize predators as bloodthirsty, ferocious or with other epithets because they are efficient with the only tools they have for making a living is hardly logical when we, as men, probably shed more innocent blood in our abbatoirs than all the predators put together and often when we kill show the greater animus.[41]

Taverner sent a copy of the letter to Mack, along with a covering letter. Unfortunately he sent the original by mistake to *Sports Afield* instead of *Field and Stream,* so the letter was never published. Mack replied that he had got many such letters, but "I didn't answer any of them. Some said the article was the best thing ever written in English; some said it was a putrid mass of tripe and signified a great enthusiasm for shooting me against a well. So what?"[42] Mack later said that he quite writing "perforce" in 1940. One can only wonder if he did so because of the war, or because his views on predation were making him more enemies than friends.

XII

The Writer: The Corpus

WHEN YOU TAKE YOUR PEN IN HAND
YOU CERTAINLY DO A REAL LOGGER'S JOB.

— *Edward Cave to Hamilton Laing*
May 12, 1941

Whether he was farming at Comox with Ethel or collecting for the museums, Mack was always writing or jotting down story outlines. Though his first publication appeared in 1907 and his last in 1979, his production was at its most intensive and successful between 1911 and 1941. Altogether he wrote some nine hundred newspaper and magazine articles and fifteen books, only two of which were published in his lifetime. Some of his books are educational, some are instructive, most are autobiographical, one is philosophical, and one, his life of Allan Brooks, is biographical. A major reason for Mack's success as a writer was the enormous public demand in Canada for wilderness and nature stories.

In his perceptive study of the wilderness movement in Canada, historian George Altmeyer points out that in the prosperous years of the Laurier government between 1901 and 1911, the urban population of Canada increased by sixty-two per cent and the rural population by only seventeen per cent. Altmeyer documents how this demographic change produced, in his words, "a certain uneasiness about what this new era of industrialization, urbanization and materialism meant for people on a personal level." In turn, urbanization evoked a "back to nature" response that peaked between 1900 and 1910. People turned to the wilderness in a variety of ways: nature study classes were introduced in most public schools across the country between 1900 and 1904; national and provincial parks were established throughout Canada; Canadian summer camps and cottages for children were established; Ernest Thompson Seton's wilderness-oriented Woodcraft Indians and later, Baden-Powell's Boy Scouts were formed to teach an appreciation of nature to urban and suburban children. The wildlife conservation movement spread across the country, and outdoor periodicals such as *Rod and Gun* (1899) and the *Canadian Alpine Journal* (1907) were established to provide a hungry urban public with wilderness literature.[2]

The Edwardian age in Canada produced a remarkable group of writers, painters, scientists and anthropologists who undertook the spiritual exploration of this vast country. By doing so they helped define in Canada a unique wilderness-oriented national identity. Just as the Group of Seven found a public willing to buy their landscape paintings, so did writers like Hamilton Laing find an audience receptive to their wilderness stories. As historian Douglas Cole suggests, the Group of Seven "began to paint the wilderness at just the right time to catch the enthusiasm of a generation of cottagers and wilderness buffs."[3] The "back to nature" or wilderness movement was manifested on an intellectual as well as a popular level. In English Canada, the movement was led by writers and poets: Ernest Thompson Seton (born 1860), Sir Charles G. D. Roberts (1860), Bliss Carman (1861), Pauline Johnson (1861) and Archibald Lampman (1861).[4] The second generation of naturalists, scholars, poets and artists included Marius Barbeau (1883), Wallace Havelock Robb (1888), E. J. Pratt (1883), Grey Owl (1888), Frederick Philip Grove (1879), Tom Thomson (1877) and Lawren Harris (1885). The average birthdate of the Group of Seven was 1883. Hamilton Laing, also born in 1883, belongs with this second generation.

But neither the wilderness movement nor late nineteenth-century urbanization were unique to Canada. Both developments had occurred in the United States, a country with a rich indigenous tradition of wilderness writing exemplified by naturalists Henry David Thoreau and John Burroughs. And the conservation movement — an offshoot of the wilderness movement — was initially much stronger in the United States than it was in Canada, owing perhaps to the more rapidly diminishing American frontier and larger urban population. Moreover, the wilderness movement was international in the sense that the two countries shared a common language and some common problems, so that Canadian naturalists could write for periodicals in both Canada and the United States. By going to the United States and then returning to Canada, Mack Laing bridged the wilderness and conservation movements in both countries. And though many of his magazine articles could be tailored for publication in either Canadian or American periodicals, his overall emphasis was Canadian. All but one of his books are set in Canada or deal with Canadian subject matter. As he wrote to a new friend in 1978, "Let me assure you that this is from a 100 per cent Canadian, born in Ontario, raised in Manitoba and has lived and worked in all the western provinces."[5]

When Mack began to write in 1907 the wilderness movement was at its peak. Tens of thousands of copies of Seton's and Burroughs' books were selling each year. As a schoolteacher, Mack had taken a story-writing course, started a nature diary, learned photography and taxidermy, and generally taught himself the skills of a naturalist. In his biography of Allan Brooks — which reveals as much about the character of Mack Laing as that of Brooks — he remarked that Brooks sought to escape the "bondage of youth to land-clearing and pioneer agriculture." This perhaps helps explain Mack's own enthusiastic migration from Clearsprings to Winnipeg and from rural Manitoba to New York. He later remarked that schoolteaching was a soul-destroying profession in which the teacher was ruled by the clock and by a rigid, unyielding curriculum imposed from outside. The result, he claimed, was that students inevitably were turned out as alike as factory biscuits.[6]

Mack's first known articles were written for the major American outdoor periodicals of the Edwardian age, *Outing* and *Recreation*. These were patronized by many Canadian writers, including Ernest Thompson Seton, Agnes Laut, Bonnycaste Dale, and Agnes Deans Cameron. By 1916 he had added *Canadian Magazine* of Toronto to his list. Following the lead of Bonnycastle Dale and American Herbert K. Job, Mack provided his articles with state-of-the-art photographs of live birds, their nests, and their habitat. Some of the early conservationists preferred camera-hunting to gun-hunting. According to George Altmeyer, it was hoped that the "morally and

aesthetically superior sport of animal photography" would ultimately render killing for sport obsolete. Both Seton and Roberts had
embraced the early conservation movement and had renounced
hunting on humanitarian grounds.[7] Though Mack never gave up
shooting for sport, several of his early articles (1911-17) praise the
advantages of the camera over the gun and many of them advocate
bird conservation in some form. *Out With the Birds* (1913), his
first book, is a compilation on the birds of Manitoba. One reviewer
called it: "A book that would have been impossible twenty years
ago. The author goes armed, but not with a gun. He brings home
his game at the end of the day, but it is not a jumbled heap of
blood-stained feathers. The weapon is a camera, and the game is a
truthful and sometimes exasperating dry plate."[8] It is striking how
radically Mack's philosophy changed ten years later after meeting
collectors such as J. Alden Loring, Allan Brooks, Percy Taverner
and J. H. Fleming.

In 1913 or 1914 Mack completed his second book, *The Birds of
Heart's Desire* subtitled *or The Diary of a Bird Man*. This was an
elaborated version of his Oak Lake nature diary of the summer of
1913. It is dedicated to "Scout Henry [Stevens] able assistant, who
as comrade of the out-of-doors has shared my smudge-fire and
blanket." *The Birds of Heart's Desire* was intended as a sequel to
the earlier, successful, *Out With the Birds*. It was rejected by one
Toronto publisher on account of its "more or less local interest."
Another Toronto publisher, William Briggs, returned the book in
1917 in tones that must have been disheartening to a Canadian
writer:

It is quite true that we handle a number of Mr. Thompson Seton's
books, and indeed we have had two of these within the last few months,
but his name of course is an assurance of a considerable market for
these and we are able to bring in small editions of his books from
American publishers to supply our market at a price much below what
we could produce it for in Canada.

If you are able to find some United States publisher who can handle
the material we could almost certainly promise to collaborate with a
small Canadian edition. This, however, is as far as we feel we could
go.[9]

Whatever the real extent of his conservationist tendencies, Mack never for a moment abondoned hunting. From 1901 to 1914 he hunted geese with a passion, and he turned his knowledge and expertise to the writing of three books between 1913 and 1917. These are *The Goose Trail, A Canuck Out of Doors* and the untitled *Wild Goose Ms*. At least in part, all are compilations of articles published in some form elsewhere. Houghton Mifflin and Co. rejected *A Canuck Out of Doors* in 1916 on the grounds that: "Experience has taught us sharply that we cannot count on a satisfactory sale for such papers when gathered into a book, and we feel constrained to return your collection for lack of positive Hopefulness."[10] Over the winter of 1915-16 he wrote *The Transcontinentalist, or The Joys of the Road* which represents a break from his earlier bird and bird-hunting books. *The Transcontinentalist* is the story of his 1915 motorcycle trip across the United States, and like the motorcycle stories he wrote for the outdoor magazines, it adopts the bravado, devil-may-care attitude of a rugged individualist. It begins:

They tried to discourage me, of course. They said that on such a long trip in such a short time I would shake my liver loose, that the sand-fleas and mosquitoes would eat me, that if I travelled alone and slept out of doors "just anywhere" rattlesnakes would bite me and I would be held up and robbed; also that I would lose my way. They said many and divers other things of a chilling nature.[11]

The R.A.F. put a temporary stop to Mack's motorcycle gallivanting, but thanks to J. H. Fleming of Toronto he started a newspaper column for the Toronto *Globe* while still at Beamsville in 1919. He got this job in the wake of a controversy of the kind that would typify Canadian ornithology in the inter-war years. The controversy began on December 8, 1918, when an editorial entitled "The World Safe for Birds" appeared in the *Globe*, written by a man named Buckley of the Conservation Commission. Buckley proposed the creation in Canada of bird sanctuaries like one in Washington State where, he wrote, "the birds have multiplied with great rapidity, and the reserve has become a paradise not only for the birds, but also for men and women who can see beauty without wishing to destroy it." Predictably, leading Canadian ornithologists were outraged at this article because it threatened their work as collectors and seemed to ignore the threat of predators. Fleming, for example, condemned Buckley as "some unfortunate Englishman who sometimes sends in articles." Fleming, Taverner and Mack each complained to the publisher and editor of the *Globe*, with the result that Mack was invited to write a nature column on a trial basis. Fleming had suggested his name to the publisher, Mr. N. G. Joffray. He was paid $10 for each 1,000-word article.[12] Between 1919 and 1924 he contributed several series of articles truly national in their scope, including "Nature Diary, Beamsville," "Nature Studies of the North," "Nature Notes on the Plains," and "Bird Rambles in British Columbia."

He wrote Fleming in January 1919 that he would "break in" the readers "with a real nature faker's thriller: the fliver bird singing its lays in the branches of the whang-doodle tree, or something equally startling." And to Taverner he stressed that: "When a fellow writes for the mob, he has to keep his eye on the crowd." "When I get wild," he asked Fleming, "please haul me over the coals." He continued to refer to his articles disparagingly as "hash," as "breezy, frothy stuff," and as "nature faker's stuff."[13] His friends, however, did not equate his articles with those of the nature fakers — the "yellow journalists of the woods," as T. R. Roosevelt had called them. Fleming thought his articles "fine really beyond words." Hoyes Lloyd wrote that "Your articles were fine — and having met them in several provinces they all seem like conversations with you." Boy Scout founder Sir Robert Baden-Powell was sent some of the articles and considered them "delightful." Taverner was equally laudatory. "I wish to congratulate you on the articles in the Toronto Globe," he wrote, "they note many thoughts of my own in them that I have not seen elsewhere and the points brought out are just the ones I have always thought needed emphasis. Have written the Globe to express approval."[14] The articles were reprinted in newspapers from Saint John, New Brunswick, to Victoria, British Columbia, making Hamilton M. Laing a household name among naturalists and bird-watchers from coast to coast. He owed the job to Fleming's patronage, and after Fleming recommended him again, to the Canadian Forestry Association in 1926, he replied: "You are the best booster and financial agent I ever had and my Scotch tightness relaxes to the point of sending you a black merlin skin — which goes forward this mail."[15] As well as those for the *Globe*,

Mack wrote a weekly column for the *Manitoba Free Press* between 1921 and 1931, and intermittently for the Vancouver *Province,* the Comox *Free Press* and the Toronto *Star.*

Mack's *Globe* articles were stopped in 1924 for two reasons. First, some Ontario readers had complained that western and northern bird material was taking the place of Ontario ornithology. This was the reason given by the editor, Stewart Lyons, when he "fired" Mack. The second, possibly more important reason was, that according to Fleming, the editor felt that Mack's pro-collecting articles were "misleading the grit youth of our country." His outspoken and uncompromising views on the collecting and predator questions ultimately got him fired by most papers. Gradually he found that only the popular hunting and sporting magazines agreed entirely with his views on "good" and "bad" animals. In 1923 he had written to Taverner: "It is hard to give an Editor what he wants without writing 'for' him — and that is something that Gosh willing, I will never do. I may have to burn an awful lot of manuscripts, but well, better burn."[16]

After leaving the R.A.F. Mack again found the time to write for the magazines and to write books. Early in 1919 he found that only "War, War, War" filled the pages of the current magazines. "Things in my line are devilish tight," he told Fleming in March 1919, "nature stuff generally in the bum; editors do not know what they want now under the new conditions." His return to Canada as a museum collector and "rancher" between 1920 and 1926 provided him with enough material for dozens of articles and for three books. The first book, *Three Moniases Down North,* is based on the 1920 expedition to Lake Athabasca. He sent a copy to Francis Harper, the expedition leader, who replied: "The book of the 'Moniases' put me in mind of a cross between Seton's *Arctic Prairies* and Albert Bigelow Paine's *Tent-dwellers.* Only you seem to have outdone each at his own game: the one, in giving a vivid and faithful picture of wild life in the North; the other, in wilderness humour."[17] Mack felt that *Three Moniases* was one of his better efforts. "If that northern stuff ever gets across," he wrote Taverner in 1923, "it will be rather a new slant on the North. A bit different from what the thrill-mongers put over." *Three Moniases* was rejected, however, by the editor of *Maclean's* magazine who complained that "it

would not serialize easily and there is not sufficient suspense interest."
J. Vernon McKenzie added that he was already well supplied with
wilderness material by outdoor writer Arthur Heming. Mack was
crushed by this news and stated that the book would never be
published. "They don't want it," he lamented to Taverner, "I feel
pretty damned sore, to tell the truth. It is the kind of thing that takes
the heart out of one and makes me wish I had stayed on the farm."[18]

Bird Rambles in British Columbia was Mack's first Comox book,
and it fared much better than *Three Moniases*. He wrote the book
during his first winter at Comox (1922-23) in his tent beside Brooklyn Creek. *Bird Rambles* is a gentle book and, interspersed with
philosophical musings on the meaning of life and nature, it is also a
true naturalist's book. Most of it was serialized by the Toronto
Globe between September 1922 and August 1923, and Mack as
always was modest about the quality of his contribution. "For God's
sake don't read those bird rambles," he warned Taverner in October 1922. "They will appear utterly frothy and utterly inadequate
to you that have been over the field."[19] In 1923 his efforts were
finally rewarded when the Ryerson Press of Toronto chose one of
the *Bird Rambles* for their comprehensive new anthology, *Our Canadian Literature: Representative Prose and Verse.* "In Vale of
Incaneep" recounts his first day of collecting with Allan Brooks. The
article begins:

May 12 [1922] Osoyoos Meadows. The sun rose clear with a few
wondrous dawn clouds upon the hills, and there was a racy tang in
the air — the kind of air that calls the hiker to the hills. A little lake
in the next valley eastward was to be visited, and as the trail crossed
the ridge, an early start was in order. Anticipation and expectation
were high. The writer was fortunate in the prospect of a rare day
afield in the company of that peerless field naturalist and artist, Major
Allan Brooks. Much was expected.[20]

Mack felt "a bit puffed up to be included" in the anthology, along
side Seton's story "The Trail of the Sandhill Stag."[21] Other con-
tributors included Frederick Philip Grove, Arthur Heming, Agnes
Laut, Susanna Moodie and Nellie McClung.

His second Comox book was *Rural Felicity*, subtitled *An Adventure in Living.* Written sometime between 1927 and 1933, it documents Mack's life as an eligible bachelor at Comox between 1922

and his marriage in 1927. It is a thoughtful, personal book that revolves around the themes of singleness and marriage. He asks himself why, for example, he should marry and lose his freedom when half his men friends are unhappily married anyway. The book is written from the vantage point of a self-important naturalist who sees himself as a worthy prize in the eyes of the unmarried women of Comox. *Rural Felicity* is the most frank and intimate of Mack's books because it reflects an emotional state over which he had little control, and which he chose to commit to writing.

As a successful professional writer Mack wrote on an astonishing variety of subjects for at least fifty different periodicals ranging from *Canadian Homes and Gardens* to the Boy Scouts magazine, *Boys' Life.* The secret of his success as a writer was that he was able to clothe the hard facts that were the core of each article in lively and intelligent prose. Taverner, for example, thought Mack had "a facile and delicate pen." Mack was not so sure. "I don't deserve the compliment to my easy writing," he told Taverner in 1921, "I do get a lot of stuff off my chest in a short time but usually after it gets an hour cool I don't know what it means myself."[22] His articles are far from being "scientific" in a methodological sense, even though they are always based squarely on his nature diaries. In 1931 he was asked by the editor of an anthology of magazine readings to give a short description of his writing methods. He replied:

There is really very little that I can tell in regard to writing such nature articles as this. I am a naturalist, and the stories just tell themselves. It is hard to say where the ideas for such articles come from. They keep croppng up constantly and I have a constant waiting list of them. . . .

The main thing about writing special articles is to know so much about the subject that the article writes itself. The mere writing seldom presents difficulties. It is the preparation, the enthusiasm and the study preceding the writing that counts most in work of this sort.[23]

It was Mack's humility in the face of an imnipotent nature that brought him the respect of other naturalists. "Thus in nature study is one thing found linked to another and the end nowhere," he wrote in *Bird Rambles in British Columbia.*[24] To Mack, human beings were miserable creatures who only spoiled the wonder and grandeur of nature. A naturalist must never misrepresent nature. Mack would not alter a story to provide it with an ending that had

165

not occurred, nor would he rearrange a sequence of events for dramatic value. Similarly, he refused to keep the meat of specimens collected for the National Museum for food, and if he shot a deer in his nut orchard he would bury the deer without taking any flesh from it. If he needed a deer for food, he would go out and shoot one. Everything had its place, and if "A" had occurred before "B" on a particular goose hunt, then "A" occurred before "B" in the published article describing that goose hunt.[25] Mack's profound realism stemmed from his idealistic refusal to alter what nature had ordained. He owed his considerable success as a nature writer to his tendency to magnify the truth, to reject the dramatic, and to severely limit the imaginative.

Most of Mack's ornithological contemporaries praised the commitment and earnestness of his outdoor articles whenever they appeared in print. In their opinion his integrity contrasted favourably with the self-serving behaviour of several of his more popular contemporaries. As Allan Brooks told him in 1930, "You are doing good work with your sane and practical writing in the magazines and I hope you will keep it up, you are about the only one who is not following the lead of so many of the nature lovers who love only themselves and notoriety."[26] Following a trend established by Seton, both Jack Miner and Grey Owl embarked on lecture circuits to publicize their particular philosophies of natural history. By contrast, Brooks, Taverner and Mack preferred to advance their views in print rather than at the lecture podium, which they saw as a sensationalist means of gaining public attention. As a result, they were somewhat less well known to the public than their high-profile contemporaries Miner and Grey Owl.

In spite of his admirers' frequent urgings Mack never published an anthology of his writings. One such admirer was Allan Brooks, who wrote in 1923, "Several times I have seen some of your newspaper articles, and all are very good, too good for a paper. You must collect them together in book form soon." Dr. Fred Cadham, a classmate at the Winnipeg Collegiate, was another fan who pleaded for such a collection:

As a shrewd and critical observer of all forms of wildlife and their habits with a keen appreciation of the associated factors of habitat and atmosphere, added to the ability to describe what you observe in language few writers on wild life have equalled why then should these literary treasures and sound information of yours remain buried in unseen files of newspapers or forgotten perodicals?[27]

Many of his articles were of a practical or educational nature designed to teach the city dweller and experienced sportsman alike the ways of the wild. Correct sporting behaviour was very important. "What you owe the Game, Mr. Sportsman!" and "Sporting Methods of Hunting" are two articles that teach the sportsman outdoor ethics. Others offer advice on what to eat, what to wear, and where to make the best possible camp in the wilderness. All his articles are educational in the sense that they impart sound outdoor knowledge that he thought the reader should possess. Always the educator, he put together a collection of original nature studies that he hoped would be published for use in Canadian schools. *Canadian Nature Studies*, his tenth book, contains twenty-one lively chapters on common Canadian mammals, birds, trees, shrubs, flowers, molluscs and fish. This book was rejected by Macmillan of Canada in 1937 in spite of the fact that the publisher agreed with Mack that "books of this nature should be in the hands of every Canadian school child."[28]

Between 1927 and 1944 Mack was on the whole too busy farming and museum collecting to write books at his former pace. *Romance of a Stump-Ranch* was completed in the early 1940's. It describes Mack and Ethel's life at Baybrook. Designed as a sequel to *Rural Felicity*, *Romance of a Stump-Ranch* describes married life as "Jack-of-all-trades country living" on a farm where "tabloid crops" such as nuts and fruit were grown.[29] Reflecting Ethel's love of gardening Mack wrote many articles about Baybrook's gardens and flowers, such as "Rock Garden of Cloud Land" and "Western Skunk Cabbage."

Perhaps his most popular stories were his Vancouver Island deer- and cougar-hunting stories. Of these, the cougar stories were the most influential. When Mack moved to Comox in 1922 he met Cecil "Cougar" Smith, a hunting friend of Ronald Stewart's. Smith lived at Campbell River and at Courtenay where he made his living hunting cougars, known locally as "panthers." A bounty of between twenty and forty dollars was offered at the time by the provincial government for each cougar, which posed a threat to livestock and deer. Cougar Smith was one such cougar hunter. Born in England, Smith came to Comox as a ten-year-old in 1887 with his farming parents. At the age of fifteen he shot his first of between 600 to 900 "big cats" on Vancouver Island. His method of catching cougars was to track them through the woods with cougar hounds until the harried cougar sought refuge in a tree, where it was then shot. Smith recalled that "it doesn't require much skill to shoot a cougar, but a lot to find them."[30]

Cougar Smith was not the only "Cougar Man" on Vancouver Island. There was Cougar Lee of Lake Cowichan, Cougar Craig of Craig's Crossing, Annie Rae-Arthur of Hesquiat, and many others. Campbell River naturalist Roderick Haig-Brown even made his living as a cougar hunter to finance his early writing efforts. The contemporary journalist Gwen Cash described the cougar-hunting phenomenon in 1938 in an article called "Cougar Men of Vancouver Island," in her book *I Like British Columbia*:

Ever since I came to B.C. I've always liked listening to cougar stories and talking with cougar men, meaning in western parlance, men who hunt cougars. For just as in pre-white days successful Indian hunters were given picturesque pseudonyms descriptive of their prowess, so men who have hunted and shot numbers of cougars get the word as a sort of accolade. In many parts of B.C. you'll find men called "Cougar Jim" or "Cougar Lem," and you never know any more about them than that they are top-notch cougar hunters.[31]

Mack was intrigued by this phenomenon, prompted by a cougar encounter at Baybrook: one day he was working in his living room when suddenly his dog began to growl. Turning around, he found himself face to face with a cougar that was standing on its hind feet looking in through the picture window. The cougar's interest had been captured by the deer head mounted above the fireplace. The cougar immediately made its escape, but in hopeful anticipation of a similar incident Mack kept a loaded rifle ready in his gun-cupboard for the rest of his life.

He wasted no time in joining the cougar-hunting fraternity of the Comox area. Early in 1924 he wrote to Ethel, "I want to get off with Cougar Smith on a panther hunt. I think he is willing to take me along. I want to get a story out of it." At the same time he wrote to Taverner and elicited a standard, sarcastic response. Taverner felt that cougar hunting was not his idea of true sport.

Luck to you and Cougar Smith. It must be great sport shooting pussy out of a tree — almost as exciting as shooting at a mark, and twice the blood. Better let a little splatter on your gun stock. When dry a little varnish will preserve it and you can thereafter point to it with pride as honest-to-goodness lion blood upon your rusty rifle. It would be more realistic than nicks in the stock.[32]

Mack enjoyed his panther hunts with Cougar Smith in the rain forests of Vancouver Island. Normally he and Smith tracked the panther for several days, with only a little tea and rice to sustain them. Mack remarked that he always took along his big waterproof pack on his panther hunts. "I was wet as a drowned shag," he told Taverner after a January 1925 hunt, "but the contents of my pack were as dry as a Scotchman's throat the day after New Year's."[33] Mack and Smith were kindred spirits of the outdoors and became fast friends. Smith enjoyed hunting with Mack because Mack did all the shooting. This enabled Smith to leave his heavy rifle behind. Mack enjoyed hunting with Smith because he was an entertaining fireside storyteller. From these hunts he got the material for no fewer than eight published cougar stories between 1926 and 1940. The first, introductory story was the journalistic "He Has Killed a Hundred Wild Cats" in *Canadian Magazine* of July 1926. The cougar meat, incidentally, found its way into the kitchens of the Chinese community of Cumberland near Courtenay where it was considered a delicacy. Nevertheless, Mack felt, like Taverner, that shooting treed cougars was not true sport. In 1978 he recalled that "I often hunted with Smith, not because I enjoyed knocking the cat out of a tree after it had been treed by Smith's dogs, but because a cougar story with some pictures was always sure of a market when I was writing professionally."[34]

One of Mack's most successful cougar stories was the simply but elegantly titled "Panthering with Smith," published in *Field and Stream* in 1928. It was based on a rigorous "panther rampage" of early 1925 when he and Smith had chased an "old Tom" through the mountains for a week. He told Taverner what happened during the exhausting hunt.

It was too mild for panthers. . . . Following an old Tom for 3 days and having victory apparently very near, the heavy wind and rain on the 4th day cut away the snow, the old son of a gun came down to lower levels, took to the bare ridges where he couldn't get a toe. . . . We carried bed and board and camped just where night caught us.[35]

Mack and Smith returned to Comox after a week's absence with nothing to show for their efforts. Mack wrote up the story just as it had happened and sent it to *Field and Stream* editor Ray P. Holland (a fellow member of the Brotherhood of Venery) who rejected the story because it lacked a "climax." Holland wrote, "After the long trail you have followed it's disappointing to have nothing happen." For one of a few times in his life Mack compromised. He "faked nature" by rewriting the conclusion of the story for dramatic value so that he and Smith, after losing the trail of old Tom, stumble by chance upon a female cougar, referred to as "Miss Tabby." They take Miss Tabby entirely by surprise and shoot her. This alteration allowed Mack to provide the story with the obligatory hunting climax. "Never," 'Panthering with Smith' concludes, "did I drive a bullet with more spiteful good will."[36]

The "tip-toeing through the big timber," stalking style of "Panthering with Smith" was immensely popular and in the long term helped bring the plight of the cougar to public attention. Mack saw cougars as dangerous vermin, but more recent writers have seen the cougar in light of the modern ecological perspective. Cougars are now a protected species. The west coast "cougar story" genre initiated by Mack in 1926 was developed in 1934 by Roderick Haig-Brown in *Panther*, one of his first books, and perpetuated in 1978 by Lyn Hancock in *Love Affair with a Cougar* and in 1983 by R. D. Lawrence in *The Ghost Walker*.[37]

The short hunting article, such as "Panthering with Smith" was, in fact, Mack's *métier*. At least two of his hunting stories were included in hunting anthologies. These were "A Manitoba Duck Hunt — Indian Style," reprinted in *Wildfowling Tales from the Great Ducking Resorts of the Continent* of 1921; and "Grouse of the Western Skyline," published in *The Field and Stream Game Bag* of 1948. A third article, "Nature's Precocious Babes" was reprinted in *Magazine Article Readings* of 1931.[38]

After Ethel's death Mack wrote another four books. His greatest retrospective work was *Baybrook — Life's Best Adventure* which developed the pioneer homesteading theme of *Rural Felicity* and *Romance of a Stump-Ranch*. *My Neighbours of the Western Shore*, written in the 1950's is a book which describes only those birds, plants and mammals visible along his Comox waterfront. *My Neighbours* is a detailed look at the total environment of his six-acre lot, which by the 1950's was his whole world. In the 1960's Mack and Francis Harper, now in retirement, finally wrote up the report of their 1920 trip to Lake Athabasca, entitled *Birds of Lake Athabasca 1920*. This, his fourteenth book, systematically describes every bird shot, seen or heard on that expedition.

Shortly after Allan Brooks' death in 1946 Mack began to gather material for a biography of his friend, the famous naturalist and bird artist. *Allan Brooks: Artist Naturalist*, despite awards totalling $3,500 from the Humanities Research Council of Canada, was rejected by publishers in Canada, Great Britain and the United States largely on account of its great length. Mack, of course, refused to alter it in any way. In the early 1970's he bitterly wrote: "Since 1910 when I started stringing words together for at least a good part of my living, this biography has presented me with the most frustrating job that ever faced me on my work table."[39] When the British Columbia Provincial Museum published an abbreviated and edited version of *Allan Brooks: Artist Naturalist* in 1979, Mack took the first copy he received in his hands and kissed it. It had been sixty-six years since the appearance of his first and only other published book, *Out With the Birds*. He died a happy man three years later in his hundredth year.

In spite of the fact that most of Mack's books were never published, his writing career is important for several reasons. First, he helped supply a receptive public with wilderness literature on a broad range of subjects from goose hunting, to motorcycle botanizing, and good sporting methods. Characteristic of all his stories is a forthright realism and uncompromising sincerity. The question then arises as to where his writing fits into the general pattern of Canadian outdoor literature. The answer is that his writing fills an intermediate as well as a mediating position between the nineteenth-century amateur naturalists and storytellers such as Burroughs,

XIII

The End of the Trail:
Shakesides, 1944-1982

OH WHAT IS SO RARE AS A DAY IN MAY

WHEN THE MOUNTAINS ARE HIDDEN AND SKIES
    ARE GREY

CAN'T YOU QUITE IMAGINE YOU HEAR ME SAY

AS I GLOWER AT THE WINDOW AND SCAN
    THE BAY,

        DAMN THE WEATHER!

— Hamilton Laing, c. 1960[1]

In July 1944 Mack's world came tumbling down around him. After a brief illness Ethel died of cancer. He wrote: "In 1944 the blow fell; I lost my help-mate. It was the solidest belt on the chin I had ever taken and I was badly staggered but refused to go down."[2] Ethel's death came as a surprise to everyone. Marjorie Brooks wrote from Okanagan Landing:

I simply cannot find the right words to tell you of my intense sorrow and of the shock your letter gave us.... Of all my many friends my dear Ethel is the one I can spare the least. She and I have always been so close — her character was perfect. Allan has always said through the years "Ethel is an angel" and I know all who knew her felt the same. I will not dwell on how my heart goes out to you in your loneliness but I am sure you understand our deep sympathy. I know I am a better woman for her friendship — the blank that is left will never be filled for me.

Allan Brooks was equally shocked.

There is nothing I can say that can express what we feel after we received your letter today. No one seemed further away from death than Ethel always so happy and cheerful.... Now Mack you will be very hard hit but remember the world is still a beautiful place. As I near the completion of my span I realize this more and more and I sit in peaceful contemplation and *feel* its beauty in a way I never used to. May it be the same comforter to you.[3]

Taverner was more pragmatic about Ethel's death. He wrote to Allan Brooks in September 1944: "Sorry to hear of death of Laing's wife. Never met her but greatly admired her. She seemed to have made a perfect wife for Laing. Hope he marries again and raises a family."[4]

Mack's sister Jean Robinson of Dalton, Georgia, lost her husband Harry in November 1944 so she came and stayed with her bereaved brother at Comox until March 1945. Mack wanted her to stay for good but, as he remarked acidly to a friend, "There is too much Yankee in her now to give it up and be a Canadian again — as she was born." Without Ethel, Mack found it difficult to maintain the nut farm, despite the help of Don Corby, an out-of-town teen-ager sent by the local high school principal to board with Mack. "I am enjoying my Man Friday," he wrote Taverner in December 1945:

Dan blew in here one evening last August and said he wanted to live with me — rank indiscretion! — go to high school and work for his grub. He is from Carcross in the Yukon. Quite a lad. He is 6'-3" long, 185 lbs; 17 years; a hunter; very musical; good companion.

I haven't got the guts to play the Brunswick yet; but I surely couldn't keep him out of a couple of hundred records! He doesn't know what it costs me to have to listen to some of them; but he doesn't have to be told twice and now keeps clear of trouble pretty well.[5]

In his retirement Mack continued his activities such as deer-hunting. In 1947 he shot the biggest black-tail deer he had ever killed on Vancouver Island. "The brute was about 140 lbs. field dressed," he told Taverner, "and Brother of the Fire Stick, if you would know how old you *really* are, if you have dwelt lately on these questions of When and How Long, just put a big black-tail on your back and go a roaming in the gloaming!"[6] Mack fought through another two years as a nut farmer before selling the "ranch." His proud letterhead reads:

BAYBROOK NUT ORCHARD
H. M. LAING
WALNUTS AND FILBERTS
FILBERT STOCK A SPECIALTY

Finally in 1949 he sold the farm to James and Elizabeth Stubbs.

Then in 1949 facing an unusually heavy nut crop, I realized that I had bitten off more than I could chew. I advertised Baybrook Nut

Farm — my wife had named it — and sold it to a young English couple who after inheriting a bunch of money were making a start in Canada. Later he reported his crop as 6 tons of filberts and my market were all waiting for him.[7]

In 1950 Mack began to build his second Comox home on the waterfront meadow site to the east of Baybrook where he and Ethel had kept Daisy Mae, their cow. He named his new house "Shakesides" — reminiscent of Seton's Hudson River retreat "Slabsides" and of John Burroughs' upstate New York home, also named "Slabsides."[8] In the 1970's he recalled how he had built this substantial house.

When the unusual snow of '49-'50 had melted I began to build my new home. For the first 6 weeks I did nothing but split cedar shakes, knowing I would need so many of them. I used again the blue print [sic] of my first home — an Aladdin Readicut — but turned the house broadside to the bay instead of end on as before so that with my south-west glance I would see Mt. Arrowsmith's snowy crown and south-west close-up the grand old Glacier and the Queen. The creek-mouth where the birds came to drink is midway. In building I used the new solid, cedar construction: the walls of heavy cedar tongued and grooved vertical planks clamped together, the weather coat of paper and shakes. Every stick of timber that went into housebuilding was nailed by my own hands. I called for professional help only for plumbing and electricity.[9]

Many naturalists and ornithologists came on a pilgrimage to Shakesides. His old students, Charles Guiguet, Allan Sampson, Elgin Hall and Ian McTaggart Cowan, visited regularly. He also established or maintained contact with the postwar generation of naturalists including Clarence Tillenius, David Hatch and Albert Hochbaum in Manitoba, Earl Godfrey and George Holland in Ottawa, and Bristol Foster, Harold Hosford, Yorke Edwards and Fenwick Lansdowne in Victoria. Other visitors included conservationists Tommy and Marion Walker, botanist Erling Porsild, wildlife conservationist David Munro, writer Frank Dufresne and his wife Klondie. The Dufresnes visited in about 1950. Klondie was a celebrated violinist and she brought her violin with her. At the time, Mack was halfway through building his house. Klondie asked him what he would like her to play, and he answered "Humoresque."

To Mack's delight she played it beautifully in the middle of the saw-dust and bare timbers of his new home.

Shakesides also became a mecca for about four generations of the Laing and Mack families. Mack had been a "legend" in his family since as early as 1920. Of all his relations he became especially close to his first cousin David Laing who had stayed on the farm helping Mack's father when Mack went away to the Collegiate in 1898. David was like an older brother to Mack, and because his mother and Mack's mother had been sisters, the connection was indeed very close. The two kept up a fulsome and witty correspondence on moral, religious and philosophical matters. David supplied Mack with gossip about the Mack and Laing families which were rapidly sprawling across the prairies. Regarding their first cousin Mary Simpson, the family historian, David wrote: "She is the only Laing I know that cares about whether they have money in their jeans or not — so long as they have enough to eat and a rag on their back."[10]

Mack had always been a prolific letter writer. For example, his first letter of June 1919 to Taverner — whom he had never met — was six pages long. One of his first letters to Fleming was eight pages long, and begins: "I am afraid to begin this for I am wound up . . . and I haven't the faintest idea when I will stop talking. If I don't quit writing, you will be noting me a public nuisance." His fiancée Ethel cut short one 1923 letter, saying: "Well I better stop this now, or you will be thinking I'm infringing on your rights of long letters." Allan Brooks (who wrote an average of ninety letters a month) considered Mack the "completest" and the "best letter writer I ever knew." Once Mack sent Taverner a postcard written in his "mini-script," which he used only when he had a lot to say in a limited space. Taverner answered: "Judging by the amount of information you have put on one post card you must have had an ancestor who wrote the Lord's Prayer on a dime or was it a nickel, anyway it is good to hear from you again." His letters could be wonderfully descriptive, as his publisher Edward Cave noted in 1926: "Wonderful letter you write. . . . A fellow knows everything, gets everything. I can see that road through the woods, every foot of it. I can see your wild flowers, and you in your working clothes. I can even see Allan Brooks tagging around with you — see you in the house,

176

chinning after supper."[11] In his retirement Mack became even more prolific. When one of his old friends or pupils died, often he would promptly establish contact with the children, and sometimes even with their children. In his nineties he sent Christmas cards to several dozen people, many of whom he had never met. With no radio, telephone or television at Shakesides, the written word remained his sole link with the world outside.

On a local level, Mack gained a possibly exaggerated reputation as a cranky old man who chased children off his beach with a stick and threatened Hydro crews with a shotgun if they touched with their equipment his sole remaining nut tree.[12] And during the first thirty years of his retirement he was a shade withdrawn and misanthropic. Part of the reason for his withdrawal from the world was the death of so many of his friends in so short a time. Fleming had died in 1940, Ethel in 1944, Allan Brooks in 1946, his brother Jim Laing in 1946 and Taverner in 1947. He outlived all his contemporaries and oldest friends, including Haldor Eiriksson, J. A. Munro and Ronald Stewart (all in 1958), R. M. Anderson and Cougar Smith in 1961, his sister Nellie in 1962, and finally Theed Pearse in 1971 and Hoyes Lloyd in 1978. These friends were important not only on a daily basis as neighbours at Comox but also as a link with the outside world and with his past. He later showed unbounded admiration for the attempted cross-country run of cancer victim Terry Fox, because cancer had taken so many of his friends and relatives. He cut out a newspaper photograph of Terry Fox and kept it pinned to his kitchen wall.

His withdrawal was heightened by his inability to sell any of his popular articles or books after 1945. By that time, tastes had changed. As A. L. Fierst, his New York literary agent, told him in 1956, his problem lay not in his competent handling of the material or in his ability to write a fine straightforward piece of natural history. Rather, his problem lay with his illustrations. He continued to submit pre-First World War black and white photographs showing goose hunters in knickerbockers posed with shotguns on the Manitoba prairies to such magazines as *National Geographic*. As Lambert Wilson, another New York literary agent, reminded him in 1956, "As you know, Americans are photograph crazy, and many a sale is made because of the illustrations, not the article!"[13] The gist of the problem, however, lay in a much more radical change in public tastes away from the printed word to television and film. And because most people owned cars in the prosperous post-war years they could drive to the wilderness if they wanted to see it. Or they could watch wildlife documentaries on television. People no longer had the time or concentration to read Mack's intense and comparatively wordy stories.

This is not to say that his writing ability or his interest in natural history declined. In his old age he wrote as fluently as in his prime. His great gift for describing the world exactly as he perceived it never waned. In 1976, aged ninety-two, he wrote to naturalist Dave Hancock:

I wish you could be in my living room at 7.30 A.M. to share with me one of the loveliest mornings I have seen in Comox in 50 odd years. It is routine with me at dawn to roll up on my left elbow and watch the new day aborning. . . .
[At first] I didn't see much sign of life. But when I got up and trained my 10X binoculars on the sun tower from the door with good elbow rests on the door and jamb a speck whiter than white on the Stubbs' tallest spruce turned into a Baldy's head. The top of the tree was flat — Japanesey. And it was clustered with cones now all turned to gold, a mound of maple foliage screamed in all the yellows in tubes — as fine as anything the east ever saw. The sky, the Beauforts, the bay, the grass flat below the window — all were bathed in color. The *air* was full of color. When a flock of siskins took to the air near the Eagle they seemed to be a shower of golden sparks. The show didn't last very long, old Sol went behind a cloud.[14]

At about the same time he went to hospital for a minor operation on his prostate gland. On his return from hospital he wrote: "It is a treat to be alive and to smell the good earth but the sweetest lungful that has primed me yet has been the breath of my patch of blue violets by the woodshed."[15]

In his retirement he continued his relentless assault on predatory animals, concerning which he wrote in 1946: "All here when I came; all here still — and few of them wanted. The coon is public enemy number one. The deer, the squirrel belong in the same class — the rat and muskrat also. Life here is a constant fight against predation. The fall, following the robin war, then the coon war earlier, we shot 57 jays and 23 squirrels, every one of them bent on packing off nuts."[16]

Mack carried his gamekeeping spirit until nearly the end of his life. In 1981 neighbours complained that the ninety-eight-year-old posed a potential threat to their or their children's safety. The Comox suburbs had finally reached Baybrook. R. G. Kew, the Town Administrator, sent Mack the following tactful letter in October 1981 — just five months before his death:

Time brings changes to a community. It has done so in the municipality of Comox. Where once it was a small village, it is now a town with a population in excess of 6,000 people.

The town boundaries have also gone further out, including now within the municipality areas that years ago were rural. It also includes the acreage you have so generously deeded to the municipality and which will be maintained as a nature park....

This past week it has been reported to me that a gun has been heard being fired from the vicinity of your home. Having had this reported to me, it is now my duty to advise you that whoever does this is breaking the [1948] by-law regulations. To continue to do so would necessitate the municipality laying charges against the offender.

We sincerely hope that such action will never be required and that the use of firearms, from your premises, will cease.

You remain a citizen held in high esteem by many and a benefactor to the municipality.[17]

Mack's closeness to the natural history of Comox actually increased rather than diminished in his retirement, as his world gradually grew smaller. He blamed the vastly diminished bird life of Comox bay on industry, oil pollution and overfishing — but he rarely blamed sportsmen, and never collectors, for the state of affairs. In 1973 he described the fifty-year demise of Comox bay from the water bird mecca of Vancouver Island to just another bay.

The first real blow to bird life came with the rape of the herring runs that in the early years came to spawn in the bay. The purse seines were too efficient. There has been only one small herring run in the last 20 years. The herring rake of the old timers is as obsolete today as the model T Ford. With the loss of the herring went all the diving birds that followed the fish: the loons (3 species), the murres and murrelets, guillemots, cormorants (3 species), mergansers (2 species), the grebes (4 species) and gulls in thousands belonging to half a dozen species. Thousands of diving ducks also followed the fish to harvest the spawn — not to eat the fish.

In the spring of one of the late 1920's, one morning during a herring run on a visit to my friend the late Theed Pearse also a naturalist and bird watcher, I stood upon the shore of his Comox village home — (town now) a commanding view — and tried to make a guess-estimate of the number of water birds in the bay because of the herring. "There must be 25,000 birds in the bay" I offered. "There are 50,000" exclaimed Pearse. He could have been more right than I. I can only say that I never saw so many water birds to the square acre as were massed on this herring visit. Gulls of course were more numerous than any other species. Such sights belong to the long past.[18]

Since 1946 Mack had been working on his biography of Allan Brooks, and his inability to find a publisher had depressed him a great deal. At one point he threatened to use the typescript as kindling for his fire. He felt that the work of the pioneer ornithologist had been ignored in the affluent and materialist post-war years. In 1968 he was featured on the Canadian Television Network's Sunday program *W5*, but as the 1970's progressed he felt the world had passed him by and he had not received the recognition he deserved. Alderman Alice Bullen of Comox was the individual responsible for bringing his life, painting and writing to public attention. Bullen was successful in hastening the publication of the Brooks biography and its appearance in 1979 came as the culmination of Mack's later life and work. Alderman Bullen was also responsible for rediscovering his Pratt Institute paintings and drawings and arranging an exhibition which delighted Mack. In 1972 he wrote to his cousin Eileen Robertson:

The only news I have concerns my Art Show. When Mrs. Alice Bullen Alderman discovered from samples in my living room that I was an artist, she was somewhat excited. When I told her I had saved all the best Art School work and that the attic was full of it, nothing could keep her down. She sent for her uncle in Vancouver [Gerald Tyler] who is an Artist, Art Critic, and restorer and cleaner of paintings, professional and he came up and looked my work over. He was a bit excited too. He said I was "hiding my light under a bushel" (Scripture).[19]

The Town of Comox in conjunction with the Public Health Service and the Home Maker service provided valuable assistance, enabling him to remain living independently to the last hours of his life. In 1978 he reported glowingly to Robertson on the town's efforts.

So the town takes good care of me. Provides my wood and coal, splits the wood and lugs the fuel up to my kitchen. Rototills my garden, cuts my grass — big power mower and girls with push mowers. My homemaker Mrs. Johnson comes once a week to take me to town and shopping. The Doctor calls once a week ... last visit the Doc said I was far better than 8 months ago. I dunno, I dunno. I feel pretty good — normal — but as soon as I start anything that resembles real work I get a pain in my ticker. They call me a "heart" case, but I swear it's my circulation ... maybe after I've had a heart like a horse for 90 years I should be thankful.[20]

Bullen's efforts were responsible then, for securing for Mack a place as a senior and respected member of the community. Earlier, Mayor Richard Merrick had fulfilled Mack's wish respecting the disposal of his property, and in 1973 his house and land was willed to the Town of Comox as a nature park.

Not that several parties had not cast covetous eyes on his choice waterfront property. For example one former colleague (who shall remain anonymous and who died before Mack did) wrote to him in 1972:

Mr. Laing, you are a very brilliant man, but I am out and around the world much more than you are. So that I think leaving your property as a park for Comox is a very bad idea. It will become nothing but a bum's roost and a curse to your neighbours. There will be drunken parties — they will destroy the flora, and leave debris around, making it look like a dump. I would suggest that the property be sold on your death, and the money be given to the Comox library or to establish a good ornithological department in the library of the University of Victoria in your name. Of course, [my wife] and I always thought, that we might be living in your place in our old age.[21]

Mack was very proud of his ability to write letters "that will just about make the postage stamps curl up on the corners."[22] Most of his reply to this letter is barely fit for publication. It begins:

After a lot of consideration I feel that we have come to the parting of our ways. If you won't take a hint maybe you'll take a blow. ... For some years you ... have been engaged in a game of stalking me. I should say stalking my 4½ acres of valuable beach front property. Reams of flattery, gifts galore, visits, kindnesses — anything to further the game of persuading me to will this property to you rather than Comox town. All in the name of friendship! I have more respect for a purse-snatcher — who might be hungry — than I have for a man who would work a con game on a professed friend!

I have some good friends and they date back to 1904 of the century. I sent out 75 Christmas cards. Not one of those friends would have written me *such a letter* or questioned my judgment — I never asked you to be my godfather! . . . The nerve of the proverbial canal mule is sheer modesty compared to your brand of gall.

Good honest friendship is one of the few things I view as sacred. It far transcends romantic love — which is only Nature's way of working on our glands to ensure proliferation and salvation of the *species*, about which Mother Nature is so concerned — though she doesn't give a d—— about the individual. Love so often time flies out of the window 6 months after the knot has been tied. No woman loves an impotent old man — or ever did. But — good friendship — without strings to it! — lasts through lifetimes. The oldest friend on my mailing list is a girl who took entrance from my first rural school in 1902. She has sent me an Xmas card or letter every year since, till about 1970 loss of memory and disability prevented writing and now her daughter, herself a grandmother puts her message across for her mother. Do I put my point over? "Not failure but low aim is the crime; hitch your wagon to a star" said Emerson. Yes, but too bad I have to upset such a carefully loaded vehicle! But you have asked for it. From your "dear friend and teacher" with malice aforethought,

Mack Laing

P.S. I know a little about the law of averages. But I know also that the man who has for years carried 50 pounds of viscera in his front elevation to bulge to the girth of a Clydesdale Stallion is not doing anything to further his hold on longevity. I prefer the "lean and hungry look" like Cassius, and there may not be such a difference in our ages as you imagine. You are fighting the Battle of the Bulge in a very dangerous age.[23]

Mack died in February 1982 after a hip operation. It is thought that he had been taking one of his habitual snoozes in the wicker armchair in his kitchen. He stood up and started to walk before the blood had time to circulate properly through his legs. He toppled to the floor breaking his hip on impact. He was found a day or two later where he had fallen and taken to the Comox hospital. Before the operation he cheerfully signed the doctor's copy of his Allan Brooks biography. He survived the delicate operation but while in the post-operative state died of a massive coronary heart attack.

A few weeks later the town held a memorial graveside service at Sandwick Cemetery. About twenty friends turned up for the service and witnessed what Jim Curtis called a "curious, eerie and symbolic episode." Just before the brief service began, Curtis recalled, "four Trumpeter swans flew over us in formation, a sort of benediction and final gesture for a man who would have appreciated it to the full." Equally curious is that sixty years earlier when Mack first entered Comox bay on the *Charmer* he had asked himself, "What bird adventures were to await us among those inlets and sandbars, and on those rural slopes and dark woods ashore? As though to augur well, four blue herons flapped across the inside bay."[24]

To almost the last day of his life Mack recorded in his nature diaries the salient points of his day's observations. He had a remarkable power to sense and record the "total mood," the individuality of one day as opposed to another. He was known to remark that a day might be a "joyful day" or "a day with a promise of growth." His last diaries in places take on a poetic, almost surrealist quality. A few weeks before he died he noted the following qualities of a mid-winter day at Comox:

The lawn pool is vacant. It is a treat to find a semi-doubtful eagle on his tree. Even the air is thick and the big bird is doubtful. There is no wind but I haven't seen a bird stir in the backyard. There is no southern shoreline. The whole world died in the night while I slept. The air is thick soup; there is no far off vision.[25]

XIV
The Character

WELL, AS THE SCOT SAID (WHO SHIVERED OUT
LOUD AND IN CONSEQUENCE WAS HANDED A
BOTTLE) "YE NEVERR KNOW WHEN A RRRANDOM
SHOT WILL HIT THE BULLS-EYE!

— *Hamilton Laing to Percy Taverner*
January 27, 1935[1]

Other than a few old friends such as Theed Pearse and Jim Curtis, no one in Comox knew much about Mack's writing or about his past. As time went by his isolation and loneliness increased, and in his last few years when he began his reminiscences, he grew obsessed with his father's early Manitoba wolf hunts. He told the story of these hunts over and over again in his final days. His last diary entry, of February 18, 1982, records his father's rescue by two Indians and his ill-fated wolf hunt. His last words were: "Within the hour Dad was on his way home 12 miles away suffering from his cold tender hands — and Indians were enjoying their wolf meat at a campfire."[2]

To most Comox people Mack was simply the deaf old man in a perpetual hurry who could be seen jogging along Comox Avenue wearing a pack. But the idea that he was a recluse or a hermit in his old age is not entirely valid. He was known to many Comox people of all ages. His good friends included retired teachers Henry and Zella Spencer, the Stubbses, and the Curtises, who baked cakes and treats for him and invited him around for Christmas dinner. Every year Ethel's old friend Elsie Eiriksson brought him around some jam made from one of Ethel's old recipes, which Mack thought was "very nice" of her. Another friend was his neighbour, logging tycoon Robert J. Filberg of the Comox Logging Company. Filberg presented him with a man-made "hawk tree" after the original fir tree at Shakesides blew down in a storm. Every hawk that perched on the tree was shot. Eventually Mack refused to visit Filberg because, he complained, "Every time I go there Filberg tries to give me a drink. He knows I don't drink." Filberg teased him in return for his abstemious nature. In 1973 for example he sent a postcard reading simply "You should come to Hawaii. Hula girls all love bird men."[3]

Everyone knew Mack as a "character," and a great many people have stories to tell. The first thing that struck people was that Mack was "bird wise." He knew birds extremely well. If any bird in North America did so much as go "tweet," Mack could identify it. In his early days at Baybrook he cut a hole in the front door and fitted it with a sliding cover so that he could shoot pheasants that came to his vegetable garden. Later at Shakesides he fitted a sliding latch to his study window so that without leaving his desk he could blast away at undesirable birds that came to his bird feeder. The deafness that plagued him in his old age did not slow him down because his eyes were almost as sharp as ever. It should be stressed that Mack was not a trigger-happy sadist. His shooting was governed by a strict code that he had learned as a boy. He shot birds only as food, as specimens, as pests or as predators. He did not shoot them for sport. He would shoot every crow, robin or starling within gun range but not the ducks and other water birds on the bay. Sometimes he would walk up to Elsie Eiriksson's and say, "They're just bad birds, robins, they'll eat all your cherries."[4]

What really thrilled the ageing naturalist were the simple, un-expected pleasures of life. Once while staying at his nephew Mack T. and Mary Laing's place in Victoria he showed wonderment at a clip-on tie, which he "couldn't get over." On another occasion he expressed fascination at a guest's electric razor. On the same occasion he marvelled at a camera with a compact wide-angle lens. Once, his cousins Eileen and Clare Robertson came to stay and took home-movies of Mack which they showed him one evening. He sat in his wicker chair watching the movies, tapping his feet on the floor and slapping the arms of the chair in pleasure. The next morning the nurse came around and he told her, "I had a really big night last night I tell you!"[5]

As a boy he had learned his peculiar jog so that he would not be late for school. He maintained this jog until the age of seventy. Yet for most of the next thirty years he still walked very quickly. Armed with his knapsack he used to walk into Comox to do his weekly shopping and pick up his mail, until the Town provided these services. The girls in the Super-Valu helped him to load his pack. He would say to Elsie Eiriksson, "Those are pretty nice girls, they pack my sack and then put it on my back!" On one snowy winter day he was stopped and asked what he was carrying in his knapsack that looked so heavy. He answered, "Rocks to give me traction." Mack would even walk into Courtenay. On one occasion he counted eighty-six cars that passed him. "He couldn't understand what humanity was coming to."[6]

In his old age, food offered Mack a simple but powerful enjoyment. He was an "original health nut." For breakfast he had stewed prunes or porridge with canned milk. For lunch he made salads containing walnuts, onions, turnips and apples which he cut into minute pieces with an ancient and badly worn paring knife. He then poured canned milk over the whole lot. He never drank fresh milk because, he maintained, "The human being is the only animal that drinks milk after it's weaned." He was extremely fond of walnuts. He would not eat very much meat in his old age, but liked fish very much. Brussels sprouts and green vegetables were very high on his list, but he avoided rhubarb because it was so "acid" and potatoes because "They go sour in my stomach." He drank Postum or Ovaltine, tea only sparingly, and avoided coffee altogether.[7] The first time that Jim and Elizabeth Curtis had him over to dinner, in the late 1960's, they started the dinner with grapefruit. This was new to Mack and he complained: "I have grapefruit for breakfast, never for dinner," and "Pink grapefruit's better than white." When they fed him potatoes with the main course, he said "Hate potatoes. Killed a cousin of mine." When they offered him pie for dessert, he asked, "What kind of pie is this?" Elizabeth answered, "Pumpkin." Mack replied, "Don't you know that squash is better than pumpkin?" But he ate it up with lots of whipping cream.[8]

In about 1970 he visited his nephew Mack and Mary Laing in Victoria. Mary gave him a piece of smoked fish which he never let her forget. Later, she served him a can of peas, and he was able to tell her what variety they were. When Mary visited him at the hospital, where he had gone for skin cancer tests, she looked at the chart on his bed and found to her surprise that he had been eating bacon and eggs. She said, "Mack! You've been eating bacon and eggs!" and he smiled and said, "You bet!" Most of the time when refusing luxuries he pleaded poverty, though it transpired that he left $50,000 behind him. Whenever Mack was asked out for meals he was overjoyed, as it meant a temporary respite from a lonely existence and what was essentially a subsistence diet. He would take along a pile of photographs and discuss them at length after dinner. Once, his cousins Eileen and Clare Robertson brought some *Brownies* chicken for his birthday, but it turned out he had cele-brated his birthday the night before. He said, "I'm so lucky!" because he had two birthday parties.[9]

Thrift was an obsession with Mack. He referred to this austerity as his "Scotchness." This obsession with "making do" amounted to almost a religion of thrift, and it may have had as much to do with his Victorian upbringing as his Scottish background — though he did celebrate hogmanay every year. His thriftiness led him to ex-tremes. He would patch the patches on his underwear to avoid buying new ones. He also did his own denture work. His philosophy was "why spend $5.00 on it if I can do it myself?" Once in his last years when he was at the Curtises he complained about his teeth. Jim said, "Mack, why don't you go to a dentist?" Mack answered, "Don't know any." Jim was surprised and said, "Well, Alice's hus-band is a dentist!" And Mack answered, "Who's Alice?" Jim answered, "Alice Bullen!" which jogged his memory. "Oh, she's the mainspring of my life!" he said. And Jim said, "Well, her husband is a dentist." He also made his own furniture, wheelbarrow, road, even his own house. At Shakesides he possessed a well-equipped workshop where in his retirement he tinkered and satisfied his pas-sion for woodwork. Mack had unusually large and powerful hands. In his reminiscences he recalled that as a boy he had been "very early influenced by a sharp knife. That I could cut things opened up a new world. . . . The first thing I ever shaped with a tool was a gun that I whittled from a cedar shake of my dad's kindling." He recalled how his mother had once given him a sound beating after he "decorated" a freshly painted windowsill with a knife. His excuse was: "I was putting my mark on my environment and the knife was lovely and sharp."[10] He made all the furniture from the salt and pepper shakers to his specimen cabinets at Baybrook and Shakesides.

Mack was an unusual man. One friend recalled that he was "not the usual cut at all." Another noted that he was "the kind of person who generated reaction," and "you couldn't just accept him." He was also a "damn self-centred man." He had a singleness of purpose and a perfectionism that made him very impatient with lesser mortals, especially if they were relatives who did not live up to his standards. If he inherited his thrift from his Scottish father, then he acquired his temper from his Irish mother. He was a "terrible damn crank" according to one friend.[11] In 1918, for example, he wrote to a friend: "Say, did I write that last letter without 'a single grouch'? Well it must have been a mistake. I am full of them most of the time. I'll not let it occur again." Once, his nephew brought him some shirts as a present. Mack said, "What are you bringing me these for?" The same nephew once told him he liked his paintings, and Mack snapped back: "What do you know? You don't know anything about art." He was disgusted that he and his nephew were the last of the male Laings in his father's line. He believed that the Laings "weren't a very good breeding stock."[12]

Physically, Mack was a "tough old S.O.B." in superb physical condition. Ian McTaggart Cowan characterizes him as "a dogged, tough, wiry little man with great determination." He was a good boxer, climber, soccer player and was an early advocate of Benarr MacFadden's "Physical Culture," a holistic health cult of the early twentieth century. He even wrote, in 1920, an article called "The Desk Worker's Efficiency Problem — My Solution" for *Physical Culture Magazine.* Part of the doctrine of physical culture was that the initiate have a "cold scrub-down" every morning in the place of a hot bath. He believed that cold water was more bracing. He had a cold scrub-down every morning until the end of his life. As Charles Guiguet recalls, Mack's philosophy was: "If it was rugged it was good for you."[13]

Although Mack was very good with the young men placed under his guidance in his field work, he was highly competitive with men of his own age. For example, Kenneth Racey who worked with

Mack in 1935 warned Charles Guiguet the following year that he was "a very hard man to get along with." It was unwise to get ahead of Mack or find something that he had not yet found. When he worked with Racey and Luscher at Cape Scott, he had a permit to collect a bull elk. For most of the expedition the elk herd managed to elude the collectors, but one day Racey reported that he had located the herd. Without inviting Racey along or even telling him his plans, Mack sneaked out early the next morning while the others were still sleeping and shot the elk. And later, as Guiguet grew more experienced and successful as a collector, Mack accused him of "hogging all the specimens," when Guiguet merely had the good fortune to find the specimens first. Not surprisingly, some of the expeditions turned into competitions to see who could get the best or the most specimens. He was also competitive with his writer-naturalist contemporaries. He "hated Grey Owl's guts" and considered him a "charlatan" and "the biggest fake on the scene," for his preservationist, anti-hunting philosophy, and for the fact that he was the ultimate nature faker — an Englishman posturing as an Indian. Similarly, he tore apart the writings of naturalists such as J. W. Winson, Norman Criddle, and Dan McCowan of Banff, whom he referred to as an "armchair biologist."[14]

Field work brought out Mack's competitive instinct. In the summer of 1922 when he met Taverner and Allan Brooks in the Okanagan, Brooks and Mack while out collecting near Vaseux Lake had to ford a little stream. Mack, who was leading Brooks at the time, hesitated, but Brooks went bounding across the unsafe bridge. Mack described the incident as follows:

But Brooks swept by me, hit the timber two or three times on the run, and was over. "So that's the way!" I said, and joined him. But as we continued up the slope I had a distinct feeling of coolness in the air that had nothing to do with Okanagan sunshine. I felt I had been weighed in the balance and found light — in guts. I had been "chicken" lost caste, face — about everything but my trousers.[15]

His competitiveness was based on the belief that if anyone deserved first prize in anything, it was he. Once he was in Comox post office waiting in line to buy stamps. Everyone in Comox was having trouble growing turnips that summer owing to a plague of flies. The flies could not be eliminated with fly-killer because they would fly away when they sensed an approaching shadow, and return when the shadow had gone. Mack discovered that the anti-fly ingredient had to be applied to the turnips when the sun was directly overhead, and word of his success soon spread around Comox. On this occasion the obstreperous Boer War veteran Captain Guthrie was in the post office. Mack and Guthrie were at opposite ends — "at daggers." Guthrie spotted Mack in the post office and said in a loud voice, "I'd like to see the person who could grow turnips in this country." Mack answered, "Well, there are some people who can. If you want to see them, come down to my place sometime." A week or so later Captain Guthrie came down to Shakesides and said, "Where are these turnips you're talking about, Laing?" Mack answered curtly, "Right over there," and pointed at his garden where the turnips grew in profusion. Jim Curtis, who relates this story, adds: "He wasn't being rude, he was just straightening Guthrie out." Turnips were a main ingredient of Mack's salads. One spring James Stubbs came down to visit Mack and found him in the vegetable garden digging up a turnip that was about a yard long. Stubbs said, "Jeez those are big," and Mack answered, "Yup, if they were any bigger I'd need gunpowder."[16]

Mack had a quiet sense of humour. He rarely told a joke in the normal premeditated sense with a gradual build-up and a punchline. When he did introduce a punchline the joke was often metaphorical. For example, in 1921 he wrote from Oak Lake that: "There is a chipmunk trying to run off with some cotton and it is as funny as a monkey at a prayer-meeting." And in 1926 he wrote to Taverner that Martukoo and Allan Brooks had set a trap on the Comox Spit. "But last time I visited it," he wrote, "I found it was so rusty and tight that nothing less than a hippo doing the Charleston on the pinnacle could spring it." He did not appreciate puns like the one from Taverner in 1922: "Dear Mack — By the way 'Mack Laing' sounds something like a fire gong doesn't it?" Most of his jokes were not so much jokes as anecdotes with wry or ironic undertones. In *Bird Rambles in British Columbia* he records how he and Allan Brooks set up a camp in rattlesnake country at the foot of a sage-brush slope in the Okanagan: "It was thought best to make night camp in an open short-grassed spot here; for no matter how callous one may be towards snakes by day, he is apt to have a horror of such company at night. Not that snakes roam about at night, but then —."[17] He used to tell of the two great tea drinkers he had known, his hunting partners Martukoo and Cougar Smith. Both were Englishmen, and both drank tea while out hunting. To Mack this fact alone was very funny. Both Martukoo and Smith died of "prostate gland" — perhaps, he thought, as a result of drinking tea. In a taped interview with Alice Bullen in 1981 Mack told how he had visited Martukoo at Masset, Queen Charlotte Islands.

He was having tea seven times a day. He had a tea and a cigarette first thing in the morning when he got up. He had tea for breakfast. He had tea about 10 or 11 o'clock ... he had tea with his lunch. Four o'clock he had tea. And he had tea before he went to bed at night. And he died on his way to Vancouver. He died on the boat going down for his fourth operation on his prostate gland.[18]

Another story that illustrates that Mack's sense of humour could also be spontaneous, dates from a hunting trip to the Cariboo made with Neville Mayers in 1936. They were wading through a swamp carrying guns, decoys, packs and cameras when an enormous bull moose appeared out of nowhere. "Is that a bull or a boxcar coming across the lake?" asked Mack. "We'd better get out of here!" The hunters escaped without incident.[19]

Mack wanted to be buried at Sandwick Cemetery with a good view of the Comox Valley, next to his good fishing pal Haldor Eiriksson. (Ethel's ashes had been sent to Portland in 1944.) He selected the site before his death. "In my own family," he wrote in 1978, "I am the last autumn leaf on the tree." He planned to stay at Shakesides until he came to the end of his life, which he termed wistfully "That long bridge that runs from here to there and the traffic is all *one way*." He wanted to be buried six feet under, not cremated which he referred to as being "buried inside someone else's urn." He did, however, expect that his private papers would be burned. He was fond of saying regarding his giant collection of manuscripts and letters, "Someone will sure have a big bonfire when I turn up my toes!"[20]

Appendices

Newspaper and Magazine Articles

NUMBER OF KNOWN PUBLISHED ARTICLES AT RIGHT

American Boy		
American Forests and Forest Life	1930-31	2
American Rifleman		1
Auk	1935-47	2
Bird Lore	1926	1
Blue Jay	1980	1
Boys' Life	1931	1
Boys' World	1918	1
Canadian Alpine Journal	1925	1
Canadian Field Naturalist	1920-56	12
Canadian Forestry Association	1929-30	8
Canadian Geographic Journal	1934-41	4
Canadian Homes and Gardens	1928-33	7
Canadian Magazine	1916-26	13
Condor	1942	1
Country Life		
Country Life in America	1914-20	2
Explosives Engineer (photographs)	1937	1
Field	1932-33	2
Field and Stream	1912-42	29
The Flower Grower	1926	1
Illustrated Canadian Forest and Outdoors	1927-41	36
Forest and Stream	1923-29	10
Comox *Free Press*	1923	1
Manitoba *Free Press*	1921-30	427
Game and Gun	1933-43	15
Garden and Home Beautful	1927	1
Garden and Home Builder	1927	1
Toronto *Globe*	1919-24	c. 150
Harper's	1917	1
House Beautiful	1921	1
The New York *Independent*	1917	1

Leslie's	1917	1
Maclean's Magazine	1934	2
Montague Fish Tales	1932	1
National Geographc (photographs)	1936	1
Nature Magazine	1930-37	9
Outers' — Recreation	c. 1920	4
Outdoor Life	1929-39	14
Outdoor Life — Outdoor Recreation		8
Outing	1912-15	13
Physical Culture Magazine	1920	1
Popular Science	c. 1927	1
Vancouver *Province*	1922-33	c. 50
Reader's Digest	1934	1
Recreation	1911-26	20
Rod and Gun	1931	1
St. Nicholas	1917-18	4
Scientific American	1916-20	2
Sports Afield	1934-44	7
Toronto *Star*	1933	3
Sunset	1916-23	17
Tall Timber	1915	1
Travel	1932-35	5
New York *Tribune*	1907	1

Abbreviations

B.C.P.M.	British Columbia Provincial Museum
M.M.M.N.	Manitoba Museum of Man and Nature
N.M.N.S.	National Museum of Natural Sciences
P.A.B.C.	Provincial Archives of British Columbia
P.A.C.	Public Archives of Canada
P.A.M.	Provincial Archives of Manitoba
R.O.M.	Royal Ontario Museum

Notes

Foreword

1 Hamilton Laing to Percy Taverner, April 24, 1923, N.M.N.S.

2 See, e.g., "Collecting Equipment for H. M. Laing. Shipped to Oliver, B.C., by Express, April 25, 1929." N.M.N.S.

3 H. M. Laing, Nature Diary, June 28, 1922, B.C.P.M.

Chapter I

1 H. M. Laing, *Bird Rambles in British Columbia*, Ch. II, p. 103, ts., P.A.B.C.

2 H. M. Laing, "The William Laings, Clearspring Pioneers," p. 1, ms., P.A.B.C.; Ed and Alice Laing to Richard Mackie, September 1983; David Laing to H. M. Laing, September 23, 1958, P.A.B.C.

3 W. A. Oswald to Laing, February 1932, P.A.B.C.; additional Mack and Laing family data supplied to author by Eileen and Clare Robertson of Victoria, B.C.; Ed and Alice Laing of Steinbach, Manitoba; Lloyd Mack of Langford, B.C., and Mack Tripney and Mary Laing of Victoria, B.C.

4 Laing, "The William Laings," p. 1.

5 David Laing to Laing, February 28, 1951; Laing to John Mack, April 10, 1981, P.A.B.C.

6 David Laing to Laing, March 9, 1946, P.A.B.C.

7 David Laing to Laing, February 28, 1951, P.A.B.C.; Laing, "The William Laings," p. 2; David Laing to Laing, February 28, 1951, P.A.B.C.; Laing to John Mack, April 10, 1981, P.A.B.C.

8 Laing, "The William Laings," p. 2.

9 W. O. Laing to James and Mary Mack, October 15, 1872, P.A.B.C.

10 David Laing to Laing, February 28, 1951, P.A.B.C.

11 W. O. Laing to James and Mary Mack, October 7, 1873, P.A.B.C.

12 [H. M. Laing] "William Oswald Laing," p. 2, ts., P.A.M.; Mrs. W. O. Laing to H. M. Laing, March 16, 1924, P.A.B.C.; *The Manitoba Directory for 1877-78* (Winnipeg: Manitoba Directory Publishing Co., 1877).

13 H. M. Laing, "Early Memories," p. 6, ts., P.A.B.C.; ibid., p. 9; H. M. Laing, "Authorship," p. 3, Ms., P.A.B.C.

14 H. M. Laing, untitled biographical data prepared for Bernard Boivin, n.d., P.A.B.C. (hereafter referred to as Laing, Boivin ms.); Laing, "The William Laings," p. 3; Laing, "Authorship," p. 1.

15 Laing, "Early Memories," pp. 1-3.

16 Ibid., p. 7.

17 Ibid., pp. 4-6.

[18] Ibid., pp. 10-11.

[19] Laing, "Authorship," p. 3; "Early Memories," p. 13.

[20] Laing, "Early Public School Years," p. 10.

[21] Laing, "Early Memories," p. 7.

[22] James and Elizabeth Curtis, interview, June 1983. Interviews with Laing's friends and relatives were carried out in Victoria, Duncan, Qualicum and Comox, B.C. Interviews are identified by the name of the informant and the date the interview took place.

Chapter II

[1] Laing, "Early Public School Years," p. 5.

[2] Ridgewood School Register, 1888, P.A.M.

[3] Laing, "Early Public School Years," p. 1; Laing, "The William Laings," p. 3.

[4] Laing, "The William Laings," p. 3.

[5] Laing, "Authorship," p. 2.

[6] H. M. Laing, "Early Days of Public School," p. 1, ts., P.A.B.C.

[7] Ibid., pp. 1-2.

[8] Laing, "Early Public School Years," pp. 4-5.

[9] Laing, "Early Days of Public School," p. 3.

[10] Laing, "Early Public School Years," p. 2; "Early Days of Public School," p. 3.

[11] Laing to Eileen Robertson, November 22, 1972, P.A.B.C.

[12] Laing, "Early Public School Years," p. 7; "Early Days of Public School," p. 2.

[13] Laing, "Early Public School Years," pp. 7-8.

[14] Laing, "Early Days of Public School," p. 2; "Early Public School Years," p. 8.

[15] Laing, "Early Public School Years," p. 8.

[16] Ibid., pp. 8-9.

[17] Laing, "Early Days of Public School," p. 4.

[18] Ibid., p. 5.

[19] Laing, "Early Public School Years," p. 10.

[20] Ibid., p. 9.

[21] E.g., Laing, *Bird Rambles*.

[22] Ibid., p. 10. See also Hamilton M. Laing, *Allan Brooks: Artist Naturalist* (Victoria: British Columbia Provincial Museum, 1979).

[23] Laing, "Authorship," p. 1; Laing, "The High School Years Form I," p. 3, ms., P.A.B.C.

[24] Ibid., p. 2, and James and Elizabeth Curtis, interview, June 1983.

[25] Dr. Fred Cadham to H. M. Laing, January 10, 1958, P.A.B.C.

[26] F. H. Schofield, *The Story of Manitoba*, 3 vols. (Winnipeg: The S. J. Clark Publishing Co., 1913).

[27] David Merritt Duncan, *A History of Manitoba and the Northwest Territories* (Toronto: W. J. Gage and Co. Ltd., 1903).

[28] Dr. Fred Cadham to H. M. Laing, January 10, 1958, P.A.B.C.

[29] Laing to J. H. Fleming, February 8, 1926, R.O.M.

[30] Laing, "Authorship," p. 1.

[31] Ibid., pp. 1-3.

[32] Ibid., p. 3.

[33] Ibid., p. 1. George Atkinson was a skilful taxidermist and author of *Manitoba Birds of Prey and the Small Mammals Destroyed by Them* (Winnipeg: Stovel Co., 1899).

[34] Laing to Eileen Robertson, November 22, 1972, P.A.B.C.

Chapter III

[1] Laing to P. A. Taverner, June 5, 1919, N.M.N.S.

[2] Gregor Fraser, testimonial to H. M. Laing, August 6, 1908, P.A.B.C.

[3] H. M. Laing, "A Canuck Out of Doors," ts., P.A.B.C.

[4] Laing, "Authorship," p. 4.

[5] Laing to Arlie Hogg, March 24, 1968, P.A.B.C.

[6] Mrs. Hogg, quoted in Lyman A. Smith to Richard Mackie, June 17, 1983.

[7] League of American Sportsmen, member's ticket issued to H. Laing, Boissevain, Manitoba, expires November 21, 1904, P.A.B.C.

[8] Laing, "Authorship," p. 4; and James and Elizabeth Curtis, interview, June 1983.

[9] Laing to Taverner, June 5, 1919, N.M.N.S.

[10] Beverly Sharman to Laing, July 27, 1947, P.A.B.C.

[11] Laing, "Authorship," p. 4.

[12] Laing to Fleming, n.d., R.O.M.

[13] D. Barry Dickson to Richard Mackie, December 26, 1984.

[14] H. M. Laing, "Caranton School Days," ms., P.A.B.C.

[15] A. Earl Henderson to Richard Mackie, July 8, 1983.

[16] National Press Association, Diploma, January 19, 1905, Town of Comox.

[17] Laing, "Authorship," p. 4.

[18] Ibid., p. 7.

[19] See Teacher certificates and letters of reference, 1900-1913, P.A.B.C.

[20] Alex McIntyre to Laing, June 24, 1913, P.A.B.C.

[21] Francis Mayers to Laing, May 21, 1913, P.A.B.C.

[22] Laing, "Authorship," p. 5.

[23] Bill Alford to Laing, May 27, 1950, P.A.B.C.

[24] Laing to Taverner, June 5, 1919, N.M.N.S.

25 R. L. Stevenson from "Royal Sport Nautique," notes by H. M. Laing, P.A.B.C.

26 Laing, "Authorship," p. 1.

27 Laing, *Bird Rambles*, Ch. III, p. 72.

28 Laing, "Authorship," pp. 5-6.

Chapter IV

1 Laing, *Allan Brooks*, p. 242.

2 Laing to Fleming, February 3, 1923, R.O.M.

3 Betty Keller, *Black Wolf: The Life of Ernest Thompson Seton* (Vancouver: Douglas and McIntyre, 1984).

4 Ernest Thompson Seton, *Trail of an Artist-Naturalist* (New York: Scribner's, 1940), p. 349.

5 W. J. Keith, *Charles G. D. Roberts* (Toronto: The Copp Clark Publishing Company, 1969), p. 15.

6 Ibid., p. 86.

7 Quoted in Keller, *Black Wolf*, p. 157.

8 Laing, *Allan Brooks*, p. 229.

9 H. M. Laing, portfolio of early bird drawings, P.A.B.C.

10 Laing, *Allan Brooks*, p. 238.

11 Laing to Fleming, February 2, 1921, R.O.M.

12 Laing, *Allan Brooks*, p. 226.

13 Laing, "Early Memories," pp. 8-9.

14 H. M. Laing, "The End of the Trail," New York *Tribune*, March 24, 1907.

15 Laign to Taverner, February 6, 1923, P.A.B.C.; Laing, "Authorship," p. 7.

16 Laing, "Authorship," p. 3.

17 Edward Cave to Laing, November 29, 1933, P.A.B.C.; Laing to Ethel Hart, March 18, 1926, P.A.B.C.; Laing to Eileen Robertson, September 29, 1978, P.A.B.C.

18 Laing, *Allan Brooks*, p. 238.

19 Laing to Elizabeth Lloyd, October 11, 1978.

20 Laing to Robertson, September 29, 1978, P.A.B.C.

21 Keith, *Charles G. D. Roberts*, p.p. 110-11.

22 (Reviewer unknown), New York *Nation*, July 11, 1913.

23 H. M. Laing, "Wild Goose ms." Chapter entitled "Canadas," P.A.B.C.

24 Laing to Fleming, February 21, 1920, R.O.M.

Chapter V

1 Smith M. Johnson to Laing, May 26, 1930, P.A.B.C.

2 Laing to Arlie Hogg, March 24, 1968, P.A.B.C.

[3] Laing, "Authorship," p. 1.

[4] Laing, Boivin ms.

[5] Ada Dillon to Laing, April 21, 1970, P.A.B.C.; see also Beverly Sharman to Laing, July 27, 1947, P.A.B.C.

[6] Laing, "Authorship," p. 6.

[7] Ibid., pp. 6-7.

[8] Pratt Institute yearbook description, 1915, included in Deborah Bassinger (Alumni Resources, Pratt Institute) to Richard Mackie, June 27, 1983.

[9] Deborah Bassinger to Richard Mackie, June 27, 1983.

[10] Laing, "Authorship," p. 8.

[11] Laing to Ada Dillon, January 12, 1914, P.A.B.C.

[12] Ibid.

[13] Alice Bullen, interview, July 14, 1983.

[14] See Association of American Painters and Sculptors, *The Armory Show: International Exhibition of Modern Art, 1913* (New York: Arno Press, 1972).

[15] Laing, *Allan Brooks*, p. 230.

[16] Ibid., p. 229.

[17] H. M. Laing, Miscellaneous natural history clippings, P.A.B.C.

[18] Laing to Taverner, November 29, 1924, N.M.N.S.

[19] Fanny A. Sharman to Laing, December 11, 1941, P.A.B.C.

[20] James and Elizabeth Curtis, interview, June 1983.

[21] Laing, "Authorship," p. 7.

[22] Ibid., p. 8.

[23] Ibid., see also Laing, Boivin ms., and Laing to Elizabeth Lloyd, October 11, 1978.

[24] Laing, "Authorship," p. 8.

[25] Ibid.

[26] Ibid., pp. 8-9.

[27] Conversation compiled from varying accounts in Laing, "Authorship," pp. 7-8, and James and Elizabeth Curtis, interview, June 1983.

[28] Laing to John E. Witney, June 3, 1915, P.A.B.C.; Laing to Catherine Capes, September 8, 1978, P.A.B.C.; Laing to Elizabeth Lloyd, October 1978; Mack Tripney and Mary Laing, interview, June 9, 1983.

[29] Laing to Elizabeth Lloyd, October 11, 1978.

[30] Laing to Hoyes Lloyd, [n.d.], P.A.C.

[31] Laing to Elizabeth Lloyd, October 11, 1978.

[32] Laing to Eileen Robertson, November 22, 1972, P.A.B.C.

[33] Laing to Taverner, June 17, 1923, N.M.N.S.

[34] H. M. Laing, taped interview entitled "Laing's Life with Alice Bullen, September 1981"; John Robinson to H. M. Laing, March 16, 1963, P.A.B.C.

[35] Pratt Institute, *Alumni Directory,* 1916 (P.A.B.C.), p. 39.

[36] Laing, "Authorship," p. 9.

[37] Ibid.

Chapter VI

[1] Laing to Taverner, May 6, 1936, N.M.N.S.

[2] H. M. Laing, Nature Diary, November 13, 1917, B.C.P.M.

[3] Laing to [?], July 25 and 26, 1918, P.A.B.C.

[4] Laing, Nature Diary, November 13, 1917.

[5] Ibid.

[6] Ibid., December 5, 1917.

[7] Ibid., November 19, 1917.

[8] Ibid., November 23, 1917.

[9] Ibid., November 21, 1917.

[10] See Alan Sullivan, *Aviation in Canada* (Toronto: Rous and Mann, c. 1919), p. 251; S. F. Wise, *Canadian Airmen and the First World War* (Toronto: University of Toronto Press, 1980), p. 98.

[11] Laing, Nature Diary, February 1, 1918; March 13, 1918.

[12] Wise, *Canadian Airmen,* pp. 87-88.

[13] Laing, Nature Diary, November 13, 1917.

[14] Ibid., June 7, 1918.

[15] Wise, *Canadian Airmen,* p. 103.

[16] Laing to Mrs. Henry Stevens, July 25, 1918, B.C.P.M.

[17] Laing to Lloyd, October 12, 1918, P.A.C.

[18] Elna Tifford to Laing, November 10, 1935, P.A.B.C.

[19] Laing to Lloyd, July 13, 1918, P.A.C.

[20] Laing, Nature Diary, July 17-18, 1918.

[21] Ibid., November 29, 1917.

[22] Lloyd to Laing, June 1918, P.A.B.C.

[23] The *Auk,* Vol. XXV (April 1918), p. 268.

[24] See Janet Foster, *Working for Wildlife: The Beginning of Preservation in Canada* (Toronto: University of Toronto Press, 1978), p. 159.

[25] Lloyd to Laing, May 3, 1918, P.A.B.C.; Laing to Lloyd, May 13, 1918, P.A.C.

[26] Laing to Elizabeth Lloyd, October 11, 1978.

[27] Fleming to Laing, June 3, 1918, P.A.B.C.; Laing to Lloyd, October 12, 1918, P.A.C.

[28] Lloyd to Laing, March 21, 1919, P.A.B.C.

[29] Laing to Fleming, February 21, 1920, R.O.M.

[30] Lloyd to Laing, July 26, 1918, P.A.B.C.

31 Laing to Lloyd, August 24, 1918, P.A.C.

32 H. M. Laing, "Lakeshore Bird Migration at Beamsville, Ontario," *The Canadian Field Naturalist*, Vol. XXXIV (February 1920), pp. 21-26.

33 Fleming to Laing, July 1, 1920, P.A.B.C.

34 Harper to Taverner, August 22, 1915, N.M.N.S.

35 Laing, Nature Diary, December 14, 1918; Laing to Lloyd, December 26, 1918, P.A.C.; H. M. Laing, Royal Air Force Record, provided by Ruth Masters, Courtenay, B.C., 1983.

36 P. A. Taverner, "Hamilton M. Laing," *The Canadian Field Naturalist*, Vol. XXXII (November 1919), pp. 99-100.

37 Laing, *Allan Brooks*, p. 112.

38 Laing to Fleming, May 18, 1919, R.O.M.

39 Laing to Eileen Robertson, September 8, 1978, P.A.B.C.

40 Laing to Taverner, June 5, 1919, N.M.N.S.

41 Ibid.

42 Laing to Fleming, May 18, July 24 and August 29, 1919, R.O.M.; Laing to Taverner, August 18, 1919, N.M.N.S.

43 H. M. Laing, "List of Birds Obesrved in Princeton Region, B.C. . . . July 4th-August 8th 1919"; "List of Mammals observed Princeton Region, B.C., July 4th-August 8th 1919," United States Fish and Wildlife Service, Field Reports, Smithsonian Institution Archives, Washington, D.C., U.S.A

44 Laing to Lloyd, June 8, 1919, P.A.C.

45 Harper to Laing, August 19, 1919, P.A.B.C.

46 Foster, *Working for Wildlife*, p. 161.

47 Lloyd to Laing, November 8, 1919, P.A.B.C.

48 Harper to Laing, December 21, 1919; Lloyd to Laing, November 29, 1919, and December 19, 1919, P.A.B.C.

49 Taverner to Laing, January 22, 1920, P.A.B.C.

50 Fleming to Laing, February 3, 1920, P.A.B.C.

51 Laing to Fleming, August 16, 1919; Harper to Laing, December 21, 1919, P.A.B.C.

52 Laing to Fleming, August 29, 1919, R.O.M.

Chapter VII

1 Laing, *Bird Rambles*, Ch. IV, p. 4.

2 Laing to Fleming, January 23, 1914, R.O.M.

3 E. W. Wilson to Hon. Benjamin Lawton, February 18, 1920, E. A. Preble Papers, Smithsonian Archives.

4 Harper to E. A. Preble, August 11, 1918, E. A. Preble Papers, Smithsonian Archives; Francis Harper, Memorandum to Mr. Nelson in regard to personnel of Athabasca party, March 18, 1920, E. A. Preble Papers, Smithsonian Archives; Warburton Mayer Pike, *The Barren Grounds of Northern Canada* (London: Macmillan, 1892); Angus Buchanan, *Wild Life in Canada* (Toronto: McClelland, Goodchild and Stewart Limited, 1920).

5 Edward Preble, *A Biological Investigation of the Athabasca-Mackenzie Region* (Washington, D.C., United States Biological Survey, 1908); Ernest Thompson Seton, *The Arctic Prairies* (New York: Charles Scribner's Sons, 1912).

6 Harper to Laing, December 2, 1919, P.A.B.C.; Laing to Fleming, March 22, 1920, R.O.M.

7 Harper to Laing, March 14, 1920, P.A.B.C.

8 Laing, "Authorship," p. 8.

9 J. Alden Loring to Laing, May 10, 1927, P.A.B.C.; Laing to Lloyd, June 9, 1918, P.A.C.

10 Laing, "Authorship," p. 10; Laing to Taverner, November 25, 1921, N.M.N.S.

11 Ibid.; Laing, Boivin ms.

12 Laing to Fleming, April 4, 1920, R.O.M.

13 Laing to Fleming, August 29, 1926, R.O.M.

14 Harper to Laing, March 27, 1921, P.A.B.C.; Mack later concluded that Harper "has absolutely no tact in getting on with other folks and I think he had a row with Nelson or Goldman." H. M. Laing to J. H. Fleming, November 30, 1920, R.O.M.

15 Rafton-Canning obtained this information from Father Laforet: A. Rafton-Canning to Laing, December 22, 1921, P.A.B.C.

16 Laing, "Authorship," p. 10.

17 Laing to Taverner, March 13, 1921, N.M.N.S.

18 Laing, "Authorship," pp. 10-11.

19 Taverner to Laing, May 12, 1928, P.A.B.C.; Taverner to Fleming, June 5, 1921, R.O.M.

20 Laing to Taverner, October 21, 1921, N.M.N.S.; Laing, "Authorship," pp. 11-12.

21 Laing to Taverner, November 25, 1921, N.M.N.S.

22 Edna [Burns] to Laing, February 10, 1959, P.A.B.C.

23 Laing to Fleming, April 8, 1922, R.O.M.

24 Taverner to Laing, October 22, 1921, N.M.N.S.

25 Laing to Taverner, November 25, 1921, N.M.N.S.

26 See Laing, *Allan Brooks.*

27 Fleming to Laing, May 9, 1921, P.A.B.C.; Laing to Ethel Hart, November 8, 1925, P.A.B.C.; Laing to Fleming, March 21, 1919, R.O.M.

28 Laing, *Allan Brooks*, p. 2. With the publication of *Birds of Western Canada* in 1926, Taverner's stammer seemed to improve: "Taverner must be getting over his stuttering. He actually spoke several times in public — something I had never dreamed of his attempting." Harper to Laing, October 17, 1926, P.A.B.C.

29 Brooks to Taverner, quoted in Taverner to Laing, February 26, 1923, P.A.B.C.; Laing to Fleming, [1922?,] R.O.M.

30 Laing to Fleming, [1922,] R.O.M.

[31] Laing, "Authorship," p. 12.

[32] Laing, *Bird Rambles*, Ch. I, pp. 29-30. See also K. Lacey, "Valentine Carmichael Haynes," *Okanagan Historical Society*, Twenty-Seventh Report (1963), pp. 117-18.

[33] Taverner to Fleming, June 17, 1922, R.O.M. See also Laing, *Allan Brooks*, p. 4, and H. J. Parham, *A Nature Lover in British Columbia* (London: H. F. and G. Witherby Ltd., 1937), p. 67.

[34] Taverner to Laing, December 28, 1922, N.M.N.S.; Laing to Fleming, February 3, 1923, R.O.M.

[35] Laing to Taverner, May 30, 1929, N.M.N.S.

[36] Parham, *A Nature Lover*, pp. 233-42.

[37] D. Alan Sampson to Alice Bullen, March 23, 1982, P.A.B.C.; Laing, *Bird Rambles*, Ch. III, p. 125.

[38] Brooks to Laing, July 26, 1922, P.A.B.C.

[39] H. M. Laing, "Laing's Life with Alice Bullen, September, 1981," taped interview.

[40] Laing, *Bird Rambles*, Ch. IV, p. 1.

[41] Ibid., Ch. IV, p. 3.

[42] Laing to Fleming, October 24, 1922, R.O.M.

[43] Laing to Lloyd, May 25, 1923, P.A.C.

[44] Laing to Fleming, April 21, 1923, R.O.M.

[45] See Brooks to Laing, November 19, 1923; Taverner to Laing, September 20, 1923, P.A.B.C.

[46] Laing, Boivin ms.

[47] Laing to Hart, March 1, 1924, P.A.B.C.

[48] Hart to Laing, May 18, 1924, P.A.B.C.

[49] Brooks to Laing, July 3, 1924, P.A.B.C.; Taverner to Laing, April 2, 1924, P.A.B.C.; Laing to Taverner, April 17, 1924, N.M.N.S.; Laing to Hart, March 1, 1924, P.A.B.C.

[50] Laing to Taverner, June 11, 1924, N.M.N.S.

[51] Laing to Taverner, May 2, 1924, N.M.N.S.

[52] Neville and Myrtle Mayers, interview, July 12, 1983.

[53] Laing to Taverner, June 13, 1924, N.M.N.S.

[54] Laing to Fleming, October 25, 1924; Taverner to Fleming, August 25, 1924, R.O.M.

[55] Taverner to Laing, August 27, 1924, P.A.B.C.

[56] Taverner to Francis Kermode, November 13, 1922, British Columbia Provincial Museum, Correspondence, P.A.B.C.

[57] Laing to Taverner, February 13, 1924, N.M.N.S.

[58] R. M. Anderson to H. M. Laing, March 30, 1925; Taverner to Laing, December 18, 1924, P.A.B.C.

[59] Anderson to Asabel Curtis, March 28, 1925, N.M.N.S. See also Paddy Sherman, *Cloud Walkers: Six Climbs on Major Canadian Peaks* (Toronto: Macmillan of Canada, 1965).

60 Anderson to Laing, April 15, 1925, N.M.N.S.; Laing to Fleming, August 31, 1925, R.O.M.; see also Sherman, *Cloud Walkers*, pp. 1-38.

61 Laing to Hart, May 31, 1925, P.A.B.C.

62 Charles and Muriel Guiguet, interview, July 18, 1983.

63 Sherman, *Cloud Walkers*, p. 12.

64 Laing to Fleming, August 31, 1925, R.O.M.

65 Laing, Boivin ms.

66 A. E. Porsild, "Contributions to the Flora of Alaska," *Rhodora*, Vol. 41, May 1939.

67 H. M. Laing, P. A. Taverner, and R. M. Anderson, *Birds and Mammals of the Mount Logan Expedition, 1925* (Ottawa: National Museum of Canada, 1929).

68 Anderson to Laing, November 4, 1925; Allen Carpe to Laing, February 15, 1926, P.A.B.C.

69 Laing to Fleming, February 8, 1926, and August 31, 1925, R.O.M.

70 H. M. Laing, "Mack Laing at Filberg House, September 2, 1981," taped interview with Alice Bullen and Helen Curtis.

71 Laing to Hart, May 21, 1926; Taverner to Laing, February 5, 1929, P.A.B.C.

72 Taverner to Laing, February 26, 1923, P.A.B.C.

73 See Jack Cranmer-Byng, "The Great Lakes Ornithological Club: The Origin and Early Years, 1905-1911," *Ontario Birds*, Vol. 2, No. 1 (April 1984), pp. 4-12.

74 See Marianne Ainley, "The Contribution of the Amateur to North American Ornithology — A Historical Perspective," *Living Bird*, Vol. 18 (1979-80).

75 For example, the residents of Duncan, a small town on Vancouver Island, ordered between three and four hundred copies of *Birds of Western Canada*.

76 Taverner to Laing, April 30, 1936; Anderson to Laing, November 2, 1935, N.M.N.S.

77 Laing to Taverner, May 6, 1936; Taverner to Laing, April 3, 1936, N.M.N.S.

78 Taverner to Laing, March 31, 1927, P.A.B.C.

Chapter VIII

1 Laing to Taverner, September 24, 1922, N.M.N.S.

2 Laing, *Bird Rambles*, Ch. I, p. 23.

3 Laing, *Allan Brooks*, p. 167; Brooks to Laing, April 3, 1926, and November 13, 1923, P.A.B.C.; Laing to Taverner, October 5, 1922, N.M.N.S.

4 Laing to Taverner, October 21, 1922, N.M.N.S.

5 Laing to Taverner, December 4, 1923, N.M.N.S.

6 Laing to Taverner, April 11, 1923, N.M.N.S. Mack later recommended that Curtis be hired as a student assistant: he was "bugs on birds" and "would be rearing to go," Laing to Taverner, March 6, 1925, N.M.N.S.

7 Laing to Taverner, April 13, 1933, N.M.N.S.; Elsie Eiriksson, interview, June 1983.

8 Hart to Laing, April 9, 1923; Taverner to Laing, February 26, 1923, P.A.B.C.

9 Laing to Taverner, November 25, 1922; Taverner to Laing, April 16, 1923; Laing to Taverner, April 24, 1923, N.M.N.S.

10 Taverner to Laing, April 16, 1923; Laing to Taverner, April 24, 1923; Laing to Taverner, November 25, 1922, N.M.N.S.

11 Taverner to Laing, December 14, 1923, P.A.B.C.

12 Interview, Alan and Suzanne Stewart, June 1983; interview, Charles and Muriel Guiguet, July 18, 1983; Brooks to Laing, August 18, 1922, P.A.B.C.; Laing to Taverner, December 28, 1945, and January 27, 1946, N.M.N.S. See also Hamilton M. Laing, "In Memoriam Ronald M. Stewart, 1881-1958," *The Murrelet*, Vol. 39 (May-August 1958).

13 Laing, *Allan Brooks*, p. 168.

14 Laing, Nature Diary, June 18, 1918, B.C.P.M.

15 Laing to Fleming, January 23, 1919, R.O.M.; Laing to Taverner, November 10, 1922, N.M.N.S.; Laing to Taverner, September 11, 1924, N.M.N.S.; Laing to Fleming, October 17, 1919, R.O.M.

16 Fleming to Laing, May 17, 1923, P.A.B.C.; Laing, taped interview with Alice Bullen, "Laing's Life with Alice Bullen, September 1981."

17 Hart to Laing, May 3, 1920; Laing to Hart, December 1, 1922, P.A.B.C.

18 Hart to Laing, September 11, 1923, P.A.B.C.

19 Hart to Laing, September 11, 1923, and June 26, 1922, P.A.B.C.

20 Hart to Laing, September 29, 1921, P.A.B.C.

21 Hart to Laing, June 1, 1922, and March 28, 1923, P.A.B.C.

22 Hart to Laing, May 11, 1922, and October 6, 1922, P.A.B.C.

23 Hart to Laing, June 28, 1923, P.A.B.C.

24 Hart to Laing, October 16, 1923, P.A.B.C.; Laing to Taverner, August 26, 1923, N.M.N.S.; Laing to Hart, January 29, 1924, P.A.B.C.; Laing to Taverner, May 25, 1924, N.M.N.S.

25 Laing to Hart, September 7, 1925, P.A.B.C.

26 Hart to Laing, September 17, 1926, P.A.B.C.

27 Laing to Fleming, February 6, 1927, R.O.M.; Winson to Laing, November 24, 1927, P.A.B.C.

28 Fleming to Laing, January 28, 1919; Taverner to Laing, April 28, 1926; Taverner to Laing, November 16, 1926; Taverner to Laing, February 8, 1927; Taverner to Laing, July 29, 1927, P.A.B.C.

29 Taverner to Laing, May 12, 1928, P.A.B.C.

30 Taverner to Laing, May 12, 1928, P.A.B.C.; Anderson to Laing, April 1, 1930, P.A.B.C.; Laing to Taverner, April 4, 1930, N.M.N.S.

31 Taverner to Laing, April 16, 1930, N.M.N.S.

32 Hart to Laing, October 21, 1922; Laing to Ethel Laing, December 7, 1928, P.A.B.C.

33 Ethel Laing to Laing, May 10, 1927, and August 28, 1927, P.A.B.C.

Chapter IX

1 Laing to Lloyd, February 26, 1928, P.A.C.

2 Taverner to Laing, April 21, 1927, P.A.B.C.

3 Laing to Taverner, April 7, 1927, N.M.N.S.

4 Taverner to Laing, April 21, 1927, P.A.B.C.; Anderson to Laing, April 15, 1925, N.M.N.S.

5 Anderson to Laing, 1928, P.A.B.C.; see also W. H. Collins to Laing, [Memorandum for orders for field work by Hamilton M. Laing, 1928,] N.M.N.S.

6 John Keast Lord, *The Naturalist in Vancouver Island and British Columbia* (London: R. Bentley, 1866); Viscount Milton and W. B. Cheadle, *The North-west Passage by Land* (London: Cassell, Peter and Galpin, 1867).

7 Laing to Anderson, July 23, 1927, N.M.N.S.; Laing to Taverner, June 21, 1927, N.M.N.S.; Laing to Elizabeth Lloyd, October 11, 1978.

8 Laing to Anderson, July 23, 1927, N.M.N.S.; on Chief Billy Sepass and Ed Wells, see Ralph Maud, *A Guide to B.C. Indian Myth and Legend* (Vancouver: Talonbooks, 1982), pp. 152-59; the description of Winson is by Ian McTaggart Cowan, telephone interview, July 1983. See also J. W. Winson, *Wildwood Trails* (Vancouver: Chapman and Warwick, 1942).

9 Laing to Anderson, February 17, 1932, N.M.N.S.; see also Margaret Ormsby, *A Pioneer Gentlewoman in British Columbia* (Vancouver: University of British Columbia Press, 1976), p. 182.

10 Laing to Taverner, November 1, 1927, N.M.N.S.

11 Taverner to Laing, May 12, 1928, P.A.B.C.; Laing to Lloyd, October 31, 1928, P.A.C.; Laing, *Allan Brooks*, p. 138.

12 Anderson to Laing, January 10 and June 28, 1929; Anderson to Laing, September 10, 1928, P.A.B.C.

13 Ian McTaggart Cowan, telephone interview, July 1983; Laing to Lloyd, February 12, 1927, P.A.C. On Lloyd's earlier efforts to hire Mack see Lloyd to Laing, December 19, 1919, P.A.B.C.; Taverner to Laing, July 4, 1923, P.A.B.C.; Lloyd to Laing, March 23, 1927, P.A.B.C., and Lloyd to Laing, December 30, 1926, P.A.C.

14 Newspaper clipping dated August 16, 1930, entitled "Nature Guide for National Parks," unknown source, N.M.N.S.; J. W. Winson to Laing, July 1, 1931, P.A.B.C.

15 J. B. Harkin to Laing, January 9, 1930, P.A.B.C.; see also Foster, *Working for Wildlife.*

16 Taverner to Laing, September 8, 1930, P.A.B.C.

17 Anderson to Laing, December 26, 1929, P.A.B.C.

18 Laing to Arlie Hogg, July 7, 1972, P.A.B.C.; Laing to Anderson, November 18, 1930, N.M.N.S.; Anderson to Laing, March 8, 1930, P.A.B.C.; see Dan McCowan, *Tidewater to Timberline* (Toronto: Macmillan, 1951).

19 See Mrs. W. O. Laing to Laing, October 12, c. November 15 and November 20, 1930, and January 11, 1931, P.A.B.C.

20 Jean Robinson to Laing, December 26, 1930, P.A.B.C.

21 Jean Robertson to Laing, January 18, 1931, P.A.B.C.

[22] Laing to John M. Robinson, March 10, 1963, P.A.B.C.

[23] Laing to Fleming, June 21, 1931, R.O.M.

[24] Laing to Fleming, June 28, 1932, R.O.M.; Brooks to Laing, July 5, 1931, P.A.B.C.

[25] Laing to Taverner, April 22, 1935, and April 13, 1933, N.M.N.S.

[26] Baybrook Nut Records, 1942-1948, P.A.B.C.; Laing to Taverner, March 30, 1943, N.M.N.S.; Taverner to Laing, November 6, 1935, N.M.N.S.

[27] Laing to Taverner, October 19, 1936, N.M.N.S.; Baybrook Farm Records, 1937-1943, P.A.B.C.; Laing to Eileen Robertson, November 25, 1972, P.A.B.C.

[28] Laing to Fleming, July 10, 1932, R.O.M.; Anderson to Laing, September 12, 1932, P.A.B.C.; Laing to Fleming, April 28, 1933, R.O.M.; Brooks to Laing, November 22, 1938, P.A.B.C.

[29] Laing to Fleming, April 28, 1933, R.O.M.; Anderson to Laing, September 12, 1932, P.A.B.C.; Laing to Taverner, February 19, 1933, N.M.N.S.; Laing, *Allan Brooks*, p. 208; G. Burrard to Laing, September 12, 1932, P.A.B.C.

[30] H. M. Laing, "The Arm of Erikson," ts., P.A.B.C.

[31] E.g., A. L. Fierst to Laing, April 20, 1926, and April 20, 1956, P.A.B.C.

[32] Taverner to Laing, March 26, 1934, P.A.B.C.; Laing to Taverner, June 26, 1934, N.M.N.S.

[33] Anderson to Laing, April 5, 1935, and March 17, 1930, P.A.B.C.

[34] Laing to Taverner, June 22, 1934, N.M.N.S.; Brooks to Laing, November 3, 1924, P.A.B.C.

[35] Anderson to Laing, October 19, 1935, P.A.B.C.

[36] G. P. Holland to Laing, December 29, 1945, P.A.B.C.

[37] Anderson to Laing, May 9, 1936, P.A.B.C.

[38] Laing to Ethel Laing, June 18, 1938, and September 11, 1938, P.A.B.C.; Anderson to Laing, June 9, 1937, P.A.B.C.; Laing to Fleming, December 31, 1937, R.O.M.

[39] Hammer to Laing, November 13, 1939, and July 7, 1940, P.A.B.C.

[40] Laing to Ethel Laing, July 9, 1938, P.A.B.C.

[41] James and Elizabeth Curtis, interview, June 1983 and January 1984; Charles and Muriel Guiguet, interview, July 18, 1983.

[42] Charles and Muriel Guiguet, interview, July 18, 1983; Anderson to Laing, May 29, 1940, P.A.B.C.; Laing to Taverner, November 13, 1940, N.M.N.S.

[43] Anderson to Laing, December 28, 1940, P.A.B.C.

[44] Charles and Muriel Guiguet, interview, July 18, 1983; Laing to E. H. Laing, September 7, 1939, P.A.B.C.

[45] Laing to Arlie Hogg, October 24, 1980, P.A.B.C.

[46] Boivin ms.

[47] Laing to Ethel Laing, August 10, 1940, P.A.B.C.

[48] Laing to Taverner, May 4, 1927, N.M.N.S.

[49] Mack Tripney and Mary Laing, interview, June 9, 1983; Kay Pollock, interview, June 4, 1983.

[50] Laing to Fleming, November 6, 1938, R.O.M.; James and Elizabeth Curtis, interview, June 1983; Elsie Eiriksson, interview, June 1983.

[51] Taverner to Laing, April 22, 1932, N.M.N.S.

[52] Laing to Taverner, April 30, 1933, N.M.N.S.

[53] Laing to Taverner, January 31, 1934, N.M.N.S.; Ethel Laing to Laing, June 20, 1927, P.A.B.C.

[54] Laing to Taverner, April 22, 1935, N.M.N.S.

[55] Anderson to Laing, May 28, 1943, P.A.B.C.; Laing to Taverner, August 20, 1943, N.M.N.S.

[56] Laing to Taverner, August 6, 1944, N.M.N.S.

Chapter X

[1] Laing to Taverner, July 26, 1921, N.M.N.S.

[2] Bonnycastle Dale to Taverner, [1935,] N.M.N.S.

[3] Laing to Gary Leib, November 14, 1978, P.A.B.C.

[4] Laing, "Early Memories."

[5] Laing to Taverner, November 25, 1922, N.M.N.S.

[6] Minutes to the 43rd Annual Meeting of the Brotherhood of Venery, New York, March 23, 1970, Laing Papers, P.A.B.C.

[7] Laing to Lloyd, December 3, 1926, P.A.C.

[8] Brotherhood of Venery Annual Reports, Laing Papers, P.A.B.C.

[9] Laing, *Bird Rambles*, Ch. II, p. 45.

[10] Laing to Fleming, February 12, 1919, R.O.M.; James and Elizabeth Curtis, interview, June 1983.

[11] A. C. Bent to Laing, February 19, 1924, P.A.B.C.; see also A. C. Bent, *Life Histories of North American Marsh Birds* (Washington, D.C.: Smithsonian Institution, 1926), pp. 247-49.

[12] Harper to Taverner, August 22, 1915, N.M.N.S.

[13] Witmer Stone, "Laing's 'Out with the Birds,'" *Auk*, vol. XXXII, 1915, p. 510; Hamilton M. Laing, "On the Trail of the Wavies," *Outing*, Vol. LXIV (September 1914), p. 705; Laing, *Bird Rambles*, Ch. II, pp. 82, 89, 110; Ch. IV, pp. 17, 22, 29, 30, 31, 47; Ch. VI, p. 7.

[14] Laing, *Bird Rambles*, Ch. IV, pp. 30-31.

[15] Laing to Lloyd, July 13, 1918, P.A.C.

[16] James and Elizabeth Curtis, interview, June 1983.

[17] Laing to Taverner, December 28, 1920, N.M.N.S.; Taverner to Laing, January 12, 1926, P.A.B.C.

[18] Anderson to Laing, September 12, 1932, P.A.B.C.

[19] Laing, *Allan Brooks*, p. 200; Laing, *Bird Rambles*, Ch. I, p. 15; Laing, *Allan Brooks*, p. 229.

[20] See James Fisher, *The Shell Bird Book* (London: Ebury Press and M. Joseph, 1966).

21 Keller, *Black Wolf*, p. 133; Laing, *Allan Brooks*, p. 200; Fisher, *The Shell Bird Book*, p. 72.

22 Laing, *Bird Rambles*, Ch. VI, p. 7, and Ch. II, p. 73; Parham, *A Nature Lover*, p. 237.

23 Laing, *Bird Rambles*, ch. IV, p. 9, and Ch. I, p. 16.

24 These passages are taken from Ronald Stewart's Migratory Bird Permit, dated 1920, in the possession of his son Alan Stewart, Ambleside, Duncan, British Columbia.

25 Some of the collections are those of Ronald Stewart and Mack Laing (Comox), S. J. Darkus (Kelowna), A. C. Mackie (Coldstream, Vernon), Allan Brooks (Okanagan Landing), and Walter McGuire (New Westminster).

26 Fisher, *The Shell Bird Book*, p. 94.

27 Theed Pearse, *Birds of the Early Explorers in the Northern Pacific* (Comox: T. Pearse, "The Close," 1968); Laing to Taverner, April 22, 1935, N.M.N.S.; Taverner to Pearse, February 24, 1924, N.M.N.S.; Laing, *Bird Rambles*, Ch. II, p. 74.

28 Parham, *A Nature Lover*, pp. 234, 236-37, 204, 239; see also the illuminating Taverner-Parham correspondence, N.M.N.S.

29 Laing to Anderson, January 20, 1926; Laing to Taverner, March 6, 1923, N.M.N.S.

30 Charles and Muriel Guiguet, interview, July 18, 1983.

31 A. E. Porsild to Laing, January 24, 1939, P.A.B.C.; Francis Harper, "A New Marsh Wren From Alberta," *Boston Society of Natural History*, Vol. 5 (1926), pp. 221-22; Taverner to Laing, April 22, 1932, P.A.B.C.; Laing to Fleming, February 6, 1927, R.O.M.

32 John Tayliss, personal communication, January 1984; Anderson to Laing, July 27, 1932, P.A.B.C.; Laing to Fleming, April 28, 1933, R.O.M.

33 James and Elizabeth Curtis, interview, June 1983 and January 15, 1984.

34 Hamilton M. Laing, "Feathered Pioneers of Canadian Northwest," *Canadian Geographical Journal*, Vol. XIII (May 1936), p. 47.

35 James and Elizabeth Curtis, interview, June 1983 and January 15, 1984.

Chapter XI

1 Laing, Nature Diary, November 20, 1917, B.C.P.M.

2 On the early conservation movement see Foster, *Working for Wildlife*, pp. 1-33; John F. Reiger, *American Sportsmen and the Origins of Conservation* (New York: Winchester Press, 1975); Gordon C. Hewitt, *The Conservation of Wildlife in Canada* (New York: Scribner, 1921); Laing, *Allan Brooks*, pp. 24, 229.

3 H. M. Laing, "Little Folks Along the Shore," *Outing*, Vol. LXIV (May 1914), pp. 227-34.

4 See Foster, *Working for Wildlife*.

5 Laing to Lloyd, December 3, 1926, P.A.C.; Foster, *Working for Wildlife*, p. 33.

6 Taverner, *Birds of Western Canada*, p. 12.

7 On Brooks the gamekeeper see Laing, *Allan Brooks*, pp. 138, 171. The game-keeping theme is discussed also in the review article by Barry Leach, "Living with Wildlife," *B.C. Outdoors*, Vol. 37, No. 3 (March 1981), pp. 29-37.

8 Seton, *Wild Animals I Have Known* (New York, Scribner's, 1898), p. 83.

9 Laing, *Bird Rambles*, Ch. I, p. 14; Ch. II, pp. 73, 75, 76; Laing to Lloyd, March 9, 1925, P.A.C.

10 Laing, "Early Public School Years," p. 10; Laing, *Bird Rambles*, Ch. II, pp. 75-76; Ch. III, p. 131; Laing to Lloyd, April 15, 1919, P.A.C.

11 Laing to Taverner, February 11, 1929, and February 20, 1937, N.M.N.S.

12 Laing to Fleming, June 21, 1931, R.O.M.

13 F. R. Butler to Laing, February 1924, P.A.B.C.; Laing, *Bird Rambles*, Ch. I, p. 17; James and Elizabeth Curtis, interview, June 1983.

14 Seton, *Wild Animals I Have Known*, p. 12; see also Margaret Atwood, *Survival: A Thematic Guide to Canadian Literature* (Toronto: Anansi, 1972), pp. 75-79.

15 Keith, *Charles G. D. Roberts*, pp. 102, 112; Alec Lucas, "Nature Writers and the Animal Story," in Carl F. Klinck, ed., *Literary History of Canada* (Toronto: University of Toronto Press, 1965), pp. 364-88.

16 Laing, *Bird Rambles*, Ch. V, pp. 15-16.

17 Laing to Taverner, July 26, 1921, N.M.N.S.

18 Richard H. Pough to Laing, December 13, 1939, P.A.B.C.

19 Foster, *Working for Wildlife*.

20 See Lovat Dickson, *Wilderness Man* (Toronto: Macmillan of Canada, 1973).

21 On the creation of bird sanctuaries see Lloyd to Laing, January 22, 1921, P.A.B.C.

22 Brooks to Laing, July 7, 1932; Munro to Laing, December 19, 1923, P.A.B.C.

23 Brooks to Laing, June 15, 1936, P.A.B.C. The baking powder story is from Charles and Muriel Guiguet, interview, July 18, 1983, and Yorke Edwards, interview, July 1983.

24 Brooks to Laing, July 9, 1930, P.A.B.C.

25 Brooks to Laing, May 21, 1937, P.A.B.C.

26 Brooks to Laing, March 12, 1923; December 12, 1933; July 4, 1923; January 7, 1939; June 5, 1939; August 16, 1931; July 9, 1930; January 9, 1932; and February 14, 1930, P.A.B.C.

27 Laing to Fleming, June 21, 1931, R.O.M.; Laing to Taverner, November 21, 1946, N.M.N.S.; Joseph Grinnell, "Conserve the Collector," *Science*, Vol. 1 (February 1917), pp. 115-28.

28 This quotation is from the original typescript of H. M. Laing, *Allan Brooks: Artist-Naturalist*, P.A.B.C. The editors of the version of this typescript published by the British Columbia Provincial Museum in 1979 deleted this and several other phrases.

29 Laing, *Bird Rambles*, Ch. II, p. 42; Laing to Taverner, November 28, 1914, N.M.N.S.

30 Laing, *Bird Rambles*, Ch. VI, p. 1.

31 Laing to Taverner, February 26, 1928, N.M.N.S.

32 Brooks to Laing, April 15, 1940; Brooks to Laing, November 16, 1930, P.A.B.C. On Jack Miner's views on predation see James M. Linton and Calvin W. Moore, *The Story of Wild Goose Jack* (Toronto: C.B.C. Enterprises, 1984), pp. 162-72.

33 Ray P. Holland to Laing, April 4, 1938, P.A.B.C.; Brooks to Laing, November 16, 1930, P.A.B.C. [Re: Jack Miner]; Yorke Edwards, interview, July 1983.

34 Laing to Taverner, January 4, 1940, N.M.N.S.; Laing to Fleming, July 12, 1931, R.O.M.

35 Taverner to Laing, April 22, 1932, P.A.B.C.; Hamilton M. Laing, "Page Mr. Bubo: How You Can Eliminate This Killer," *Field and Stream*, Vol. XLI (December 1936), pp. 24-25.

36 Brooks to Laing, July 7, 1932, P.A.B.C.; Ray P. Holland to Laing, April 4, 1938, P.A.B.C.; Hamilton M. Laing, "Befuddled Conservation: A Sportsman-Conservationist has Something to Say About Hawks," *Field and Stream*, Vol. XLI (April 1937); Hamilton M. Laing, "Predation in the Backyard," *Field and Stream*, Vol. XLII (December 1939).

37 Hampton L. Carson, Jr., to Laing, March 24, 1937, P.A.B.C.

38 Laing to Taverner, February 11, 1940, N.M.N.S; Laing, "Predation in the Backyard," p. 66.

39 Pough to Laing, January 28, 1938, and December 13, 1939; Taverner to Laing, September 20, 1923, P.A.B.C.

40 Taverner to Laing, April 22, 1932, P.A.B.C.

41 Taverner to Laing, December 20, 1939, P.A.B.C.; for Taverner's views on predation see also Foster, *Working for Wildlife*, p. 185.

42 Laing to Taverner, February 11, 1940, N.M.N.S.

Chapter XII

1 Edward Cave to Laing, May 23, 1941, P.A.B.C.

2 George Altmeyer, "Three Ideas of Nature in Canada, 1893-1914," *Journal of Canadian Studies*, Vol. II, No. 3 (August 1976), pp. 21-35; p. 22. On the origins of the wilderness movement see also John Henry Wadland, *Ernest Thompson Seton: Man in Nature and the Progressive Era 1880-1915* (New York: Arno Press, 1978), and Robert H. MacDonald, "The Revolt Against Instinct," *Canadian Literature*, Vol. 84 (Spring 1980), pp. 18-28.

3 Douglas Cole, "Artists, Patrons and Public: An Enquiry into the Success of the Group of Seven," *Journal of Canadian Studies*, Vol. 13, No. 2 (Summer 1978), pp. 69-78, 74-75.

4 See J. D. Logan, "The Literary Group of 6," *The Canadian Magazine*, Vol. XXXVII (October 1911), pp. 555-63.

5 Laing to Kay Berry, [1978,] P.A.B.C.

6 Laing, *Allan Brooks*, p. 171; Laing, *Rural Felicity*, Ch. I, P.A.B.C.

7 Altmeyer, "Three Ideas," p. 20. See also Alfred O. Gross, "History and Progress of Bird Photography in America," in F. M. Chapman and T. S. Palmer, *Fifty Years' Progress of American Ornithology 1883-1933* (Lancaster, Pa.: American Ornithologists' Union, 1933).

8 [Review of *Out With the Birds*,] *Christian World*, New York, September 6, 1913.

9 F. F. Appleton of Musson Book Company to Laing, May 28, 1920; William Briggs to Laing, February 26, 1917, P.A.B.C.

10 Houghton Mifflin and Company to Laing, October 17, 1916, P.A.B.C.

11 Laing, *The Transcontinentalist, or The Joys of the Road*, Ch. I, P.A.B.C.

12 Fleming to Laing, January 28, 1919, P.A.B.C.; Laing to Fleming, March 21, 1919, R.O.M.

13 Laing to Fleming, January 23, 1919, R.O.M.; Laing to Taverner, February 15, 1921, N.M.N.S.; Laing to Fleming, March 26, 1919, R.O.M.; Laing to Taverner, November 25, 1921, N.M.N.S.; Laing to Taverner, October 21, 1922, N.M.N.S.

14 Keller, *Black Wolf*, p. 157; Fleming to Laing, May 11, 1919; Lloyd to Laing, May 21, 1919; C. P. L. Fowler to Laing, February 9, 1925; Taverner to Laing, February 25, 1919, P.A.B.C.

15 Laing to Fleming, November 25, 1926, R.O.M.

16 Laing to Fleming, December 1923, R.O.M.; Fleming to Laing, November 6, 1924, P.A.B.C.; Laing to Taverner, February 16, 1923, N.M.N.S.

17 Laing to Fleming, December 29, 1918, and March 21, 1919, R.O.M.; Harper to Laing, April 3, 1922, P.A.B.C.

18 Laing to Taverner, February 16, 1923, N.M.N.S.; J. Vernon McKenzie to Laing, March 3, 1923, P.A.B.C.; Laing to Taverner, March 10, 1923, N.M.N.S.

19 Laing to Taverner, October 21, 1922, N.M.N.S.

20 Albert Durrant Watson and Lorne Albert Pierce, eds., *Our Canadian Literature: Representative Prose and Verse* (Toronto: The Ryerson Press, 1923), pp. 317-18.

21 Laing to Taverner, 1924, N.M.N.S.

22 Taverner to Harper, January 27, 1925; Laing to Taverner, March 13, 1921, N.M.N.S.

23 Donald L. Clark and Dr. Ernest Brennecke, *Magazine Article Readings* (New York: Macmillan Co., 1931), p. 656.

24 Laing, *Bird Rambles*, Ch. 11, p. 94.

25 Harold Hosford, interview, July 1983.

26 Brooks to Laing, November 16, 1930, P.A.B.C.

27 Brooks to Laing, November 19, 1923; Dr. Fred Cadham to Laing, January 10, 1958, P.A.B.C.

28 Macmillan Company of Canada to Laing, October 3, 1937, P.A.B.C.

29 Laing, *Romance of a Stump-Ranch*, Ch. I, P.A.B.C.

30 P.A.B.C., Vertical File, "Cougar Smith."

31 Gwen Cash, *I Like British Columbia* (Toronto: Macmillan, 1938), p. 126.

32 Laing to Ethel Hart, January 29, 1924; Taverner to Laing, February 12, 1924, P.A.B.C.

33 Laing to Taverner, April 24, 1925, N.M.N.S.

[34] Laing to Lloyd, January 21, 1947, P.A.C.; Laing to Earl Henderson, November 28, 1978, P.A.B.C.

[35] Laing to Taverner, February 5, 1925, N.M.N.S.

[36] Ray P. Holland to Laing, December 3, 1926; Laing, "Panthering with Smith," *Field and Stream* (December 1928).

[37] Roderick Haig-Brown, *Panther* (London: J. Cape, 1934); Lyn Hancock, *Love Affair with a Cougar* (Toronto: Doubleday Canada Limited, 1978); R. D. Lawrence, *The Ghost Walker* (Toronto: McClelland & Stewart, 1983).

[38] Laing, "A Manitoba Duck Hunt — Indian Style," in *Wildfowling, Tales from the Great Ducking Resorts of the Continent* (Chicago: William C. Hazelton, 1921), pp. 1-17; Laing, "Grouse of the Western Skyline," in Robeson Bailey, ed., *The Field and Stream Game Bag* (New York: Doubleday and Company, 1948), pp. 89-95; Laing, "Nature's Precocious Babes," in Donald L. Clark and Dr. Ernest Brennecke, *Magazine Article Readings* (New York: Macmillan Co., 1931), pp. 41-48.

[39] Bernard Ostry to Laing, February 2, 1961: Laing to [?], n.d., P.A.B.C.

Chapter XIII

[1] Laing, envelope jotting, P.A.B.C.

[2] Laing, Boivin ms.

[3] Marjorie Brooks to Laing, July 27, 1944; Allan Brooks to Laing, July 26, 1944, P.A.B.C.

[4] Taverner to Brooks, September 12, 1944, N.M.N.S.

[5] Laing to Taverner, December 28, 1945, N.M.N.S.

[6] Laing to Taverner, December 7, 1947, N.M.N.S.

[7] Laing, Boivin ms.

[8] Keller, *Black Wolf*, p. 154; Farida A. Wiley, ed., *John Burrough's America* (New York: Doubleday and Company, Inc., 1961), p. xv.

[9] Laing, Boivin ms.

[10] James and Elizabeth Curtis, interview, June 1983; Eileen and Clare Robertson, interview, June 9, 1983; David Laing to Laing, February 22, 1950, P.A.B.C.

[11] Laing to Fleming, February 12, 1919, R.O.M.; Ethel Hart to Laing, June 28, 1923; Brooks to Laing, September 23, 1925, and June 27, 1926; Taverner to Laing, July 1, 1920; Edward Cave to Laing, April 5, 1926, P.A.B.C.

[12] Mack Tripney and Mary Laing, interview, June 9, 1983; Laing to Mayor Richard Merrick, January 6, 1977.

[13] A. L. Fierst to Laing, April 20, 1956; Lambert Wilson to Laing, March 9, 1956, P.A.B.C.

[14] Laing to Dave Hancock, November 6, 1975, P.A.B.C.

[15] Laing, envelope jotting, P.A.B.C.

[16] Laing to Taverner, November 21, 1946, N.M.N.S.

[17] R. G. Kew to Laing, October 27, 1981, P.A.B.C.

[18] Laing to Dr. Hatter, July 19, 1973, P.A.B.C.

[19] Laing to Robertson, December 31, 1972, P.A.B.C.

[20] Laing to Robertson, September 18, 1978, P.A.B.C.

21 [?] to Laing, November 8, 1972, P.A.B.C.

22 Laing to Ethel Hart, [1925,] P.A.B.C.

23 Laing to [?], [1973,] P.A.B.C.

24 James and Elizabeth Curtis to Richard Mackie, October 1983; Laing, *Bird Rambles*, Ch. IV, p. 2.

25 Alice Bullen, interview, July 14, 1983; Laing, Nature Diary, January 20, 1982, B.C.P.M.

Chapter XIV

1 Laing to Taverner, January 27, 1935, N.M.N.S.

2 Laing, Nature Diary, February 18, 1982, B.C.P.M.

3 Elsie Eiriksson, interview, June 1983; Alan and Suzanne Stewart, June 1983; Robert J. Filberg to Laing, [1973,] P.A.B.C.

4 Ian McTaggart Cowan, telephone interview, July 1983; Charles and Muriel Guiguet, July 18, 1983; Alan and Suzanne Stewart, June 1983; Elsie Eiriksson, June 1983.

5 Mack T. and Mary Laing, interview, June 9, 1983; Eileen and Clare Robertson, June 9, 1983.

6 Elsie Eiriksson, interview, June 1983; Kate Munson, July 1983; James and Elizabeth Curtis, June 1983.

7 Alan and Suzanne Stewart, interview, June 1983; Alice Bullen, July 14, 1983; James and Elizabeth Stubbs, June 1983; Mack T. and Mary Laing, June 1983; Neville and Myrtle Mayers, July 12, 1983.

8 James and Elizabeth Curtis, interview, June 1983.

9 Mack T. and Mary Laing, interview, June 9, 1983; Alice Bullen, July 14, 1983; Eileen and Clare Robertson, June 9, 1983.

10 James and Elizabeth Curtis, interview, June 1983; Mack T. and Mary Laing, June 9, 1983; Laing, "Authorship," p. 2.

11 Ian McTaggart Cowan, telephone interview, July 1983; Harold Hosford, July 1983; Alan and Suzanne Stewart, June 1983.

12 Laing to [?], c. 1918, P.A.B.C.; Mack T. and Mary Laing, interview, June 9, 1983; Alice Bullen, July 14, 1983.

13 Charles and Muriel Guiguet, interview, July 18, 1983; Ian McTaggart Cowan, telephone interview, July 1983; Jessie L. Thompson to Laing, July 15, 1920, P.A.B.C.; Alice Bullen, interview, July 14, 1983.

14 Charles and Muriel Guiguet, interview, July 18, 1983; James and Elizabeth Curtis, January 15, 1984; Neville and Myrtle Mayers, July 12, 1983.

15 Laing, *Allan Brooks*, p. 224.

16 James and Elizabeth Curtis, interview, June 1983; James and Elizabeth Stubbs, June 1983.

17 Laing to Taverner, July 21, 1921, and February 26, 1926, N.M.N.S.; Taverner to Laing, April 11, 1922, N.M.N.S.; Laing, *Bird Rambles*, Ch. II, p. 77.

18 Laing, taped interview with Alice and Dennis Bullen, n.d.

19 Neville and Myrtle Mayers, interview, July 12, 1983.

20 Laing to Elizabeth Lloyd, October 11, 1978; Alice Bullen, interview, July 14, 1983; Mack T. and Mary Laing, June 9, 1983.

Bibliography

PRIMARY SOURCES

Allan, Hazel, "Hamilton Laing: Dynamo at 92," *Comox District Free Press*, June 18, 1975.

Anderson, R. M., *Catalogue of Canadian Recent Mammals* (Ottawa: Department of Mines and Resources, 1946).

————, Correspondence, Vertebrate Zoology Division, N.M.N.S.

Atkinson, George, *Manitoba Birds of Prey and the Small Mammals Destroyed by Them* (Winnipeg: Stovel Co., 1899).

Belton, Brian, "Hamilton Laing — Author, Nut Farmer, Bird Watcher," *Comox District Free Press*, February 10, 1978.

Bent, A. C., *Life Histories of North American Birds*, 17 Vols. (Washington: Smithsonian Institution, 1922-1953).

British Columbia Provincial Museum, Correspondence, P.A.B.C.

Buchanan, Angus, *Wild Life in Canada* (Toronto: McClelland, Goodchild and Stewart Limited, 1920).

Bullen, Alice, Interview, Comox, British Columbia, July 14, 1983.

Burroughs, John, "Real and Sham Natural History," *Atlantic Monthly*, Vol. 91 (March 1903).

Cash, Gwen, *I Like British Columbia* (Toronto: Macmillan, 1938).

Chapman, F. M., *Color Key to North American Birds* (New York: Doubleday, Page, 1903).

Town of Comox, Miscellaneous documents and correspondence.

Cowan, Ian McTaggart, Telephone interview, Victoria, British Columbia, July 1983.

Curtis, James and Elizabeth, Interviews, Comox, British Columbia, June 1983, January 1984, January 1985.

Duncan, David Merritt, *A History of Manitoba and the Northwest Territories* (Toronto: W. J. Gage and Co. Ltd., 1903).

Edwards, Yorke, Interview, Victoria, British Columbia, July 1983.

Eiriksson, Elsie, Interview, Comox, British Columbia, June 1983.

Fleming, J. H., Correspondance, Library Archives, R.O.M.

————, Correspondence, Ornithology Division, R.O.M.

Grinnell, Joseph, "Conserve the Collector," *Science*, Vol. 1 (February 1917).

Guiguet, Charles and Muriel, Interview, Victoria, British Columbia, July 18, 1983.

Haig-Brown, Roderick, *Panther* (London: J. Cape, 1934).

Hancock, Lyn, *Love Affair with a Cougar* (Toronto: Doubleday Canada Limited, 1978).

Harper, Francis, "A New Marsh Wren from Alberta," *Boston Society of Natural History*, Vol. 5 (1926).

Hewitt, C. Gordon, *The Conservation of Wild Life in Canada* (New York: Scribner, 1921).

Hosford, Harold, Interview, Victoria, British Columbia, July 1983.

Jorden, Terry, "Honors for Naturalist," *Comox District Free Press*, August 19, 1981.

———, "The Legacy of Laing: A Young Historian Examines a Lifetime's Work," *Comox District Free Press*, March 12, 1982.

Keller, Keith, "Valley Loses a Remarkable Man," *Comox District Free Press*, February 19, 1982.

Laing, H. M., *Allan Brooks: Artist-Naturalist*, original ts., P.A.B.C.

———, *Allan Brooks: Artist-Naturalist* (Victoria: British Columbia Provincial Museum, 1979).

———, "The Arm of Erikson," ts., P.A.B.C.

———, "Authorship," ms., P.A.B.C.

———, *Baybrook: Life's Best Adventure*, ts., P.A.B.C.

———, "Befuddled Conservation," *Field and Stream*, Vol. XLI (April 1937).

———, *Bird Rambles in British Columbia*, ts., P.A.B.C.

———, Taverner, P.A., Anderson, R. M., *Birds and Mammals of the Mt. Logan Expedition* (Ottawa: National Museum of Canada, 1929).

———, *Birds Collected and Observed During the Cruise of the Thiepval in the North Pacific, 1924* (Ottawa: Department of Mines, 1925).

———, *The Birds of Heart's Desire or The Diary of a Bird Man*, ts., P.A.B.C.

———, and Harper, Francis, *The Birds of Lake Athabasca, 1920*, ts., P.A.B.C.

————, "Boivin ms," P.A.B.C.

————, *Canadian Nature Studies*, ts., P.A.B.C.

————, *A Canuck Out of Doors*, ts., P.A.B.C.

————, "Caranton School Days," ms., P.A.B.C.

[————, and Carpe, Allen,] "The Conquest of Mt. Logan," [1925,] National Film, Television and Sound Archives, Ottawa.

————, Correspondence, P.A.B.C.

————, "Early Days of Public School," ts., P.A.B.C.

————, "Early Memories," ts., P.A.B.C.

————, "Early Public School Years," ts., P.A.B.C.

————, "The End of the Trail," New York *Tribune*, March 24, 1907.

————, "Feathered Pioneers of Canadian Northwest," *Canadian Geographical Journal*, Vol. XIII (May 1936).

————. *The Goose Trail*, ts., P.A.B.C.

————, "Grouse of the Western Skyline," in Robeson Bailey, ed., *The Field and Stream Game Bag* (New York: Doubleday and Company, 1948).

————, "The High School Years," ms., P.A.B.C.

————, "In Memoriam Ronald M. Stewart, 1881-1958," *The Murrelet*, Vol. 39 (May-August 1958).

————, Taped interview with Alice and Dennis Bullen, n.d.

————, Taped interview with Alice Bullen, September 1981.

————, Taped interview with Alice Bullen and Helen Curtis, September 2, 1981.

————, "Lakeshore Bird Migration at Beamsville, Ontario," *The Canadian Field Naturalist*, Vol. XXXII (November 1919).

————, "List of Birds and Mammals Observed in Princeton Region, B.C., July 4th-August 8th 1919," United States Fish and Wildlife Service, Field Reports, Smithsonian Institution Archives, Washington, D.C., U.S.A.

————, "Little Folks Along the Shore," *Outing*, Vol. LXIV (May 1914).

————, "A Manitoba Duck Hunt — Indian Style," in *Wildfowling Tales from the Great Ducking Resorts of the Continent* (Chicago: William C. Hazelton, 1921).

————, *My Neighbours of the Western Shore*, ts., P.A.B.C.

————, Nature Diaries, 1901-1910, M.M.M.N.

————, Nature Diaries, 1910-1982, Ornithology Division, B.C.P.M.

————, "Nature's Precocious Babes," in Donald L. Clark and Dr. Ernest Brennecke, *Magazine Article Readings* (New York: Macmillan Co., 1931).

————, "On the Trail of the Wavies," *Outing*, Vol. LXIV (September 1914).

————, *Out with the Birds* (New York: Outing Publishing Company, 1913).

————, "Page Mr. Bubo," *Field and Stream*, Vol. XLI (December 1936).

————, "Panthering with Smith," *Field and Stream* (December 1928).

————, Photographs, 1906-1960, Visual Records Division, P.A.B.C.

————, Portfolio of early bird drawings, P.A.B.C.

————, "Predation in the Backyard," *Field and Stream*, Vol. XLII (December 1939).

————, *Romance of a Stump-Ranch*, ts., P.A.B.C.

————, *Rural Felicity*, ts., P.A.B.C.

————, *Three Moniases Down North*, ts., P.A.B.C.

————, *The Transcontinentalist or The Joys of the Road*, ts., P.A.B.C.

————, *Wild Goose ms.*, ts., P.A.B.C.

————, "The William Laings, Clearsprings Pioneers," October 23, 1951, ms., P.A.B.C.

————, "William Oswald Laing," ts., P.A.B.C.

Laing, Mack Tripney and Mary, Interview, Victoria, British Columbia, June 9, 1983.

Lawrence, R. D., *The Ghost Walker* (Toronto: McClelland & Stewart, 1983).

Lloyd, Hoyes, Correspondence, P.A.C.

Manitoba Directory for 1877-78 (Winnipeg: Manitoba Directory Publishing Co., 1877).

Mayers, Neville and Myrtle, Interview, Qualicum Beach, British Columbia, July 12, 1983.

McCowan, Dan, *Tidewater to Timberline* (Toronto: Macmillan, 1951.

MacDonnell, Duncan, "Dream Come True. At 96, Hamilton Laing Lives to see his Extensive Biography in Printed Form," *Comox District Free Press*, November 14, 1979.

Milton, Viscount, and Cheadle, W. B., *The North-West Passage by Land* (London: Cassell, Peter and Galpin, 1867).

Munro, J. A., and Cowan, Ian McTaggart, *A Review of the Bird Fauna of British Columbia* (Victoria: British Columbia Provincial Museum, 1947).

Parham, H. J., *A Nature Lover in British Columbia* (London: H. F. and G. Witherby Ltd., 1937).

Pike, Warburton Mayer, *The Barren Grounds of Northern Canada* (London: Macmillan, 1892).

Pollock, Kay, Interview, Comox, British Columbia, June 4, 1983.

Porsild, A. E., "Contributions to the Flora of Alaska," *Rhodora*, Vol. 41 (May 1939).

Pratt Institute, Brooklyn, N.Y., *Alumni Directory*, 1916.

Preble, Edward, *A Biological Investigation of the Athabasca-Mackenzie Region* (Washington, D.C.: U.S. Biological Survey, 1908).

———, Papers, Smithsonian Institution Archives, Washington, D.C.

Provincial Archives of British Columbia, Vertical Files of Newspaper Clippings.

Register of Ridgewood School, Manitoba, 1888, P.A.M.

Robertson, Eileen and Clare, Interview, Victoria, British Columbia, June 9, 1983.

Schofield, F. H., *The Story of Manitoba*, 3 Vols. (Winnipeg: The S. J. Clarke Publishing Co., 1913).

Seton, Ernest Thompson, *The Arctic Prairies* (New York: Charles Scribner's Sons, 1912).

———, *Trail of an Artist-Naturalist* (New York: Scribner's, 1940).

———, *Wild Animals I Have Known* (New York: Scribner's, 1898).

Stewart, Alan and Suzanne, Interview, Duncan, British Columbia, June 1983.

Stone, Wilmer, "Laing's 'Out With the Birds,'" *Auk*, Vol. XXXII (1915).

Stubbs, James and Elizabeth, Interview, Comox, British Columbia, June 1983.

Sullivan, Alan, *Aviation in Canada* (Toronto: Rous and Mann, 1919).

Tappan, E. M., and Saul, John D., *England's Story: A History for Public Schools* (Toronto: George N. Morang and Company, Limited, 1903).

Taverner, P. A., *Birds of Western Canada* (Ottawa: Department of Mines, 1926).

———, Correspondence, Vertebrate Zoology Division, N.M.N.S.

———, "Hamilton M. Laing," *The Canadian Field Naturalist*, Vol. XXXII (November 1919).

———, "Ornithologists One Should Know," [1925,] National Film, Television and Sound Archives, Ottawa.

Tonkin, Doris May, "Bird Man of Comox," Victoria *Daily Colonist*, May 13, 1973.

Watson, Albert Durrant, and Pierce, Lorne Albert, eds., *Our Canadian Literature: Representative Prose and Verse* (Toronto: The Ryerson Press, 1923).

Winson, J. W., *Wildwood Trails* (Vancouver: Chapman and Warwick, 1942).

SECONDARY SOURCES

Ainley, Marianne, "The Contribution of the Amateur to North American Ornithology — A Historical Perspective," *Living Bird*, Vol. 18 (1979-80).

Altmeyer, George, "Three Ideas of Nature in Canada, 1893-1914," *Journal of Canadian Studies*, Vol. II, No. 3 (August 1976).

Association of American Painters and Sculptors, *The Armory Show: International Exhibition of Modern Art, 1913* (New York: Arno Press, 1972).

Atwood, Margaret, *Survival: A Thematic Guide to Canadian Literature* (Toronto: Anansi, 1972).

Berger, Carl, *Science, God and Nature in Victorian Canada* (Toronto: University of Toronto Press, 1983).

Burnham, John B., "Conservation's Debt to Sportsmen," *The North American Review*, Vol. CCXXVI (September 1928).

Cole, Douglas, "Artists, Patrons and Public: An Enquiry into the Success of the Group of Seven," *Journal of Canadian Studies*, Vol. 13, No. 2 (Summer 1978).

Cranmer-Byng, Jack, "The Great Lakes Ornithological Club: The Origin and Early Years, 1905-1911," *Ontario Birds*, Vol. 2, No. 1 (April 1984).

Dickson, Lovat, *Wilderness Man* (Toronto: Macmillan of Canada, 1973).

Fisher, James, *The Shell Bird Book* (London: Ebury Press and M. Joseph, 1966).

Foster, Janet, *Working for Wildlife: The Beginning of Conservation in Canada* (Toronto: University of Toronto Press, 1978).

Gould, Ed., *Ralph Edwards of Lonesome Lake* (North Vancouver: Hancock House Publishing Ltd., 1981).

Gross, Alfred O., "History and Progress of Bird Photography in America," in F. M. Chapman and T. S. Palmer, eds., *Fifty Years' Progress of American Ornithology* (Lancaster, Pa.: American Ornithologists' Union, 1933).

Keith, W. J., *Charles G. D. Roberts* (Toronto: The Copp Clark Publishing Company, 1969).

————, "Roderick Haig-Brown," *Canadian Literature*, Vol. 71 (Winter 1976).

Keller, Betty, *Black Wolf: The Life of Ernest Thompson Seton* (Vancouver: Douglas and McIntyre, 1984).

Lacey, K., "Valentine Carmichael Haynes," *Okanagan Historical Society*, Twenty-seventh Report (1963).

Leach, Barry, "Living with Wildlife," *B.C. Outdoors*, Vol. 37, No. 3 (March 1981).

Linton, James M., and Moore, Calvin W., *The Story of Wild Goose Jack* (Toronto: C.B.C. Enterprises, 1984).

Logan, J. D., "The Literary Group of 6," *The Canadian Magazine*, Vol. XXXVII (October 1911).

Lucas, "Nature Writers and the Animal Story," in Carl F. Klinck, ed., *Literary History of Canada* (Toronto: University of Toronto Press, 1965).

Maud, Ralph, *A Guide to B.C. Indian Myth and Legend* (Vancouver: Talonbooks, 1982).

MacDonald, Robert H., "The Revolt Against Instinct: The Animal Stories of Seton and Roberts," *Canadian Literature*, Vol. 84 (Spring 1980).

Ormsby, Margaret, *A Pioneer Gentlewoman in British Columbia* (Vancouver: University of British Columbia Press, 1976).

Pearse, Theed, *Birds of the Early Explorers of the Northern Pacific* (Comox: T. Pearse, "The Close," 1968).

Polk, James, "Lives of the Hunted," *Canadian Literature*, Vol. 53 (Summer 1972).

S.S. *Charmer*, 9, 86, 183
St. Anne des Chênes, Manitoba, 15, 17
Steinbach, Manitoba, 22, 28
Stewart, Miss B. F., 30, 32, 41, 53
Stewart, Ellen (née Holmes), 101, 108
Stewart, Ronald Macdonald ("Martukoo"), 10, 86, 99, 100, 102, 105, 108, 167, 177, 191, plate 43
  background, 101
  and hunting, 98, 101, 130
  collector, 10, 119
  as tea-drinker, 192
Stevens, Henry, 81, plate 11
Stevenson, Robert Louis, 40
St. Nicholas, 62
Strait of Georgia, British Columbia, 120, 121
Stubbs, Elizabeth, 174, 175, 178
Stubbs, James, 174, 175, 178, 191
Stuie, British Columbia, plate 36, plate 37
Summerland, British Columbia, 85
Sunset: The Pacific Monthly, 62, 72
Sutton, George Miksch, 121
Swarth, Harry, 88

Tall Timber, 62
Taverner, Martha H. (née Weist), 107, 126
Taverner, Percy Algernon, 9, 40, 70, 84, 85, 86, 88, 91, 92, 93, 97, 98, 102, 111, 112, 113, 119, 121, 131, 139, 144, 146, 149, 150, 160, 163, 169, 174, 177, 185, 191, plate 24, plate 25, plate 34, plate 35
  appearance, 80, 95
  architectural suggestions, 99-100
  background, 59, 72, 95, 100
  and Canadian ornithology, 72, 75, 94, 95, 107, 110
  as collector, 85-86, 95, 137
  feud with Anderson, 77, 81, 92, 94-96, 107, 109
  and Mack's character, 89, 100, 113, 134-35, 176
  meets Mack, 80-81, 83, 132, 190
  and music, 126-27
  opinion of Mack, 162
  outdoor philosophy, 142-43, 147, 151, 153-55
  and stutter, 83, 202 n. 28

and women and marriage, 105, 106, 107-08
Telegraph Creek, British Columbia, 139
Thacker, Lindsay, 111
H.M.C.S. *Thiepval*, 88-90, 138
Thomson, Tom, 158
Thoreau, Henry David, 158
Tifford, Philip, 69
Tillenius, Clarence, 175
Toronto, Ontario, 65, 66, 69, 70, 131, 134
Toronto *Globe*, 70, 71, 72, 73, 84, 161, 162, 163, 164
Toronto *Star*, 163
Trail, British Columbia, 150
Trees
  broad-leaved maple, 87, 178
  nut, 118-19, 125, 167, 174, 177, plate 77
  ponderosa pine, 149
  Sitka spruce, plate 31, plate 40
  western red cedars, plate 23
  yellow pines, 84
Tufts, Robie, 76, 131
Tweedsmuir Lodge, 124
Tweedsmuir Park, 122, 123
Tyler, Gerald, 55, 180

Union Bay, Vancouver Island, 150
United States Biological Survey, 74, 78, 80
University of British Columbia, 114, 137
University of Manitoba, 31
University of Pennsylvania, 152
University of Regina, 81
University of Toronto, 66
University of Victoria, 181
Urseth family, 123

Van B., Mr. 117
Vancouver *Province*, 106, 111, 163
Vancouver Island Militia Rangers, 127
Vaseux Lake, British Columbia, 84, 85, 104, 137, 190, plate 25
Vernon, British Columbia, 112

Waddell, Rachel (née Laing), 18, 28, 57, 177, plate 3
Walker, Marion, 123, 175
Walker, T. A. (Tommy), 124, 138, 175, plate 33, plate 37
Weist, Martha, *see* Martha Taverner